The ABC of Contract Bridge has proved so popular with people learning to play bridge that it has become known as 'the beginner's bible'. It takes the reader from being a complete beginner, through to being a learner-player, concentrating on the basic facts. Included in the book are sections on the mechanics of the game and scoring, the auction and how to bid, and the play of the cards both in defence and attack.

The sections on bidding are based purely on the Acol System. This down-to-earth, commonsense system with, fundamentally, few complications was put on the map and popularised by the late Ben Cohen and Terence Reese.

There are also quizzes and answers for each chapter, a table of standard leads, a scoring table and a glossary of bridge terms. *The ABC of Contract Bridge* is a book no would-be player can afford to miss.

Other books on Bridge:

ACOL-ITE'S QUIZ by Rhoda Lederer
ALL ABOUT ACOL by Ben Cohen and Rhoda Lederer
BASIC ACOL by Ben Cohen and Rhoda Lederer
MASTER BRIDGE BY QUESTION AND ANSWER by Alan Truscott
WHY YOU LOSE AT BRIDGE by S. J. Simon
YOUR LEAD PARTNER by Ben Cohen and Rhoda Lederer

The ABC of Contract Bridge

Being a Complete Outline of the Acol Bidding System and the Card Play of Contract Bridge Especially Prepared for Beginners

BEN COHEN and RHODA LEDERER

Revised by Rhoda Lederer

London
UNWIN PAPERBACKS
Boston Sydney

First published in Great Britain by George Allen & Unwin 1964
Third edition 1977
First published in Unwin Paperbacks (Fourth edition) 1979

UNWIN® PAPERBACKS
40 Museum Street, London WC1A 1LU

British Library Cataloguing in Publication Data

Cohen, Ben
The ABC of contract bridge. - 4th ed.
1. Contract bridge
I. Title II. Lederer, Rhoda
795.4'15 GV1282.3 79-40278

ISBN 0-04-793040-3

Printed in Great Britain by
Hazell Watson & Viney Ltd,
Aylesbury, Bucks

CONTENTS

♠♡♣◇♠♡♣◇♠♡♣◇♠♡♣◇♠♡♣◇♠♡♣◇♠♡♣◇♠♡♣

INTRODUCTION

♠♡♣◇♠♡♣◇♠♡♣◇♠♡♣◇♠♡♣◇♠♡♣◇♠♡♣◇

SO you want to learn to play Contract Bridge. Well, you will find it a most rewarding occupation. Look around you at the thousands of people who play Contract Bridge today, and not only play it but play it superbly well. They were all complete beginners once, they went through the initial stages and came safely out the other side as learner-players and thence to being Contract Bridge players. So for you too suddenly the penny will drop, and even if you don't yet play the game expertly, you will find that you are playing, understanding, and enjoying it.

When embarking on something new it is always better to develop the correct habits and methods right from the start. Careless or slipshod ways may take months to eliminate later, and may even dog your footsteps for life. In this book, therefore, you will be taken right from the very earliest stages when you are a complete beginner, through to being a learner-player. If you are already a learner-player, at least read over Section I to make sure that you are not unwittingly committing some crime such as, for instance, saying "Pass" when you mean "No bid"!

One of the troubles of being a complete beginner at any game more complicated than Snap is that there is a lot to be learned before things fall into place in your mind and make sense. Imagine yourself being led for the first time onto a tennis court when you had never seen or heard of a ball game such as tennis before. You would have a racquet pushed into your hand and you wouldn't know what to do with it or how you were supposed to do it. You wouldn't know what the lines on the court were for or what you were trying to achieve, how to score, or even how to toss up for ends and partners. Someone would babble such words as "service", "30-15", "game and set", and would show you how to hold the racquet. Would all this stay in your memory? Of course it wouldn't. You would be so busy trying to hit the balls, let alone get them back across the net, that it would be days before the mechanics of the game became clear to you. In the same way, you will find that there is a great deal to learn before Contract Bridge becomes really clear to you.

You must not be discouraged by this preamble. Indeed, it is intended to encourage you because any experienced bridge teacher knows that nothing you have read or been told will seem to make sense to you at first. But only at first—once you have got over your initial muddle and have grasped the idea of what it is really all about, you will find that you are understanding and learning the game and, very soon, getting from it all that it has to give to you.

Like every game Contract Bridge should, ideally, be learned from a qualified teacher, and not from "just another bridge player" who, like Topsy, grow'd without being efficiently taught. Thousands of would-be players, however, have neither the time nor the money to attend a bridge school or pay for lessons, and if you are one of these, try to supplement what your friends may tell you by study from books and guided practice. Do the exercises at the end of the chapters too, and don't let yourself be depressed at the number of errors you will make because they are inevitable. You will find them an excellent way of helping the facts to sink into your mind and, if you come back to them another day, you will suddenly realise that light has dawned and that previous enigmas hold no problems for you at all.

The sections on bidding in this book are based purely on the Acol System. This is a down-to-earth, commonsense system with, fundamentally, few complications. It is easily learned, easily assimilated, and highly efficient. Apart from these merits it might well be termed the Esperanto of the bridge world except that it has accomplished what Esperanto never really did—it has become world-wide in popularity.

You will not, in these pages, be taught more than the basic bids and responses. There are many refinements and "frills" which have no place in a book for beginners but which you will probably want to learn eventually: For these you should go on to one of the main text books on the system such as "All About Acol", which begins where this leaves off, assuming that you know, as you will by then, the basic workings of what is called "approach-forcing" bidding.

Actual card play is even more universal than bidding methods. Different players may develop different techniques in lead sequences or discards, neither of which need give you a moment's concern. If you learn to handle your card soundly you will be equipped to play anywhere on earth.

Please remember, dear readers, that THE ABC OF CONTRACT BRIDGE is what it says it is, the ABC. There is a vast mass more to learn, but don't let it concern you that much of it is not included in these pages. If some would-be know-it-all picks up your book and says "but there's nothing about 'Stayman', nothing about 'Flint', nothing about 'Swiss'..." Remember that you can't learn to run before you can walk, and if you get your basic facts right there's nothing to prevent you – and I hope you will – from going on to fuller and more advanced books or more advanced classes.

Here's one last word of advice before you start out on your studies. Don't give up in despair because at first it all seems so difficult. It *will* fall into place. It *will* make sense. It *will* become an enthralling and intriguing pastime, and for some of you it may even become a dedication and a life's work.

SECTION I

An Outline of the Game of Contract Bridge

CHAPTER I

The Preliminaries

CONTRACT Bridge is a game for four players. It is also, as in "doubles" at tennis, a partnership game, though unlike tennis in which the partners play side by side, in bridge they face each other across the table.

At your first session you will not expect to progress very far. You will be concentrating on the preliminaries of the game and if this seems rather dull, remember that in your first year in Kindergarten you had to learn your alphabet before you could apply it to the interesting task of reading.

Requirements for Contract Bridge: A card table and chairs, two packs of cards, score cards and pencils and, of course, four eager players.

Object: The object of the game is to win what is called the **rubber.** This is the best of three games and goes to the pair who first win two games. Thus a Rubber may consist of two games won by one pair in succession, or three games, when each pair win one to begin with.

Cutting for Partners: There is a definite procedure laid down for arranging the two partnerships. First, one of the two packs is spread face downwards across the table and each of the four players draws a card. Note that these cards must not be from either the first or last four cards of the spread pack, or adjoining a card drawn by another player. The two who have drawn the highest cards play as partners, so the remaining two play as the other partnership.

The player with the highest card of all has all the privileges. He may choose his seat—and his partner, of course, sits opposite—he may select which of the two packs will belong to his side for this Rubber, and he also becomes the first to deal.

The Pack: A word here about the pack of cards· No Jokers are used and Aces count "high", followed by the King, Queen, Knave and so on down to the lowest in each suit, the Two. When writing about cards abbreviations are always used. An Ace is A., a King is K., a Queen is Q., and a Knave is J., (for Jack as it is often called). The remaining cards are either shown as numbers or, if they are unimportant to the explanation being given, indicated as "x".

The four suits, which rank in this order in importance are **Spades** then **Hearts,** the two major suits, then **Diamonds** and lastly **Clubs,** the two minor suits. For writing purposes these also have their abbreviations, ♠ for Spades, ♡ for Hearts, ◇ for Diamonds and ♣ for Clubs. Remember this ranking order as it is vital to the whole game.

In the light of the previous paragraph, if the four cards in the cut for partners were the ♡A, the ◇7, the ♠7 and the ♣3, the ♠7 ranks above the ◇7 so the partnerships would be the ♡A with the ♠7 for one and the ◇7 with the ♣3 for the other. Substitute the ◇8 for the ◇7 and now the ♡A and ◇8 would play together against the ♠7 and ♣3.

The Deal: After these preliminaries and with the partners seated opposite to each other, comes the deal, the player who cuts the highest of the four cards being the first dealer. After him the deal passes round the table in clockwise rotation. The player on the dealer's left shuffles the pack chosen by the dealer (who, by the way, has the right to shuffle again if he wishes but seldom does so). The shuffled pack is passed across to the dealer's right and his right-hand opponent then "cuts" it by dividing it into two portions. The "cut" should be made towards the *dealer* and the bottom portion of the pack left untouched by the cutter. The dealer himself then "closes the cut" by taking the bottom portion of the pack and putting it on top of the other portion. He then deals the pack, one card at a time, clockwise, starting with the player on his left and ending with himself. Each player will then have a "hand" of thirteen cards and when the whole deal has been completed, picks them up and sorts them into suits.

Meanwhile the dealer's *partner* should have shuffled the second pack and placed it face downwards on his right, where it is ready for the next dealer to pick up and pass to his right-hand opponent to cut in exactly the same way as before.

Thus the pack not actually in use will always be found ready on the left of the dealer-to-be, a handy way of remebering if, in the heat of battle, you have forgotten whose turn it is to deal!

If these preliminaries sound confusing, practice them a few times, step by step, round the table. You will soon find that they become second-nature to you and that you don't have to think about them at all.

QUIZ ON CHAPTER 1

1. Which suit or suits, if any, rank above the following?
   (a) Hearts.
   (b) Clubs.
   (c) Spades.
   (d) Diamonds.

2. Which suits are known as the major suits and which as the minor suits?

3. Which pairs of players would play together as partners if the four cards cut were the following?
   (a) ♠ 2: ♠ 9: ♣ K: ♢ Q:
   (b) ♡ A: ♠ J: ♣ K: ♢ 4:
   (c) ♡Q: ♣ 5: ♢ Q: ♠ Q:
   (d) ♠ 7: ♡ 10: ♣ 10: ♢ J:

4. Which of the four players in each case in Question 3 above would become the first to deal?

5. If, in terms of bridge symbols, your hand contained the following, what cards would you actually hold? (Pick them out of a pack if you feel that would be easier.)
   (a) ♠ A: ♡ K J x x x x: ♢ A Q x x: ♣ x x:
   (b) ♠ Q J 10 x: ♡ —: ♢ A J x x x: ♣ Q 10 x x:
   (c) ♠ x x: ♡ Q x x x: ♢ A K J x x: ♣ A x:
   (d) ♠ J 10 x x: ♡ K Q J: ♢ x x: ♣ A K Q J:

QUIZ ON CHAPTER 1—ANSWERS

1. (a) Spades rank above hearts.
   (b) All three suits rank above clubs.
   (c) The highest ranking suit.
   (d) Spades and hearts.

2. Spades and hearts are the major suits, diamonds and clubs the minor suits.

3. (a) The ♠ **K** and ♢ **Q** would play together and the ♠ **9** and ♠ **2**.
   (b) The ♡ **A** and ♣ **K**: the ♠ **J** and ♢ **4**.
   (c) The ♠ **Q** and ♡ **Q**: the ♢ **Q** and ♣ **5**.
   (d) The ♢ **J** and ♡ **10**: the ♣ **10** and ♠ **7**.

4. The dealer in each case would be:
   (a) ♠ **K**.
   (b) ♡ **A**.
   (c) ♠ **Q**.
   (d) ♢ **J**.

5. (a) The Spade Ace, six hearts to the King-Knave, the Ace-Queen to four diamonds and two small clubs.
   (b) Four spades to the Queen-Knave-ten, a void in hearts, five diamonds to the Ace-Knave, and four clubs to the Queen-10.
   (c) Two small spades, four hearts to the Queen, the Ace-King-Knave to five diamonds and the Ace and a small club.
   (d) Four spades to the Knave-ten, the King-Queen-Knave of hearts, two small diamonds and the Ace-King-Queen-Knave of clubs.

CHAPTER 2

The Second Stage

♠♡♣♢♠♡♣♢♠♡♣♢♠♡♣♢♠♡♣♢♠♡♣♢♠♡♣♢

THE deal completed we come to the game itself, which falls into two distinct parts, the Auction and the play of the cards.

The Auction: If you have played Whist you will know that the denomination in which any given hand will be played is pre-determined, and will know the exasperation of picking up a wonderful collection of spades when diamonds are named as trumps. In Contract Bridge the two partnerships compete against each other for the right to determine trumps.

The dealer, privileged again, is entitled to the first bid in the auction which then proceeds clockwise round the table. Each player tries to show his values to his partner and, with none worth mentioning, he *passes*. The correct way to do this is to say "No bid". The auction continues until three players in rotation have said "No bid" thus, as in all self-respecting auctions, the last and highest bidder wins.

Trumps: Each hand is played either at a Trump or No Trump contract, the last bid in the auction becoming *the contract* for that hand. The object of the auction is to discover which suit would be mutually most agreeable for you and your partner to use as trumps or whether a No Trump contract would be best. Meanwhile your opponents are also at the table and may be bidding against you.

When one suit has finally been agreed as trumps any card of that suit, even the lowly 2, ranks higher than any card of any other suit for trick-taking purposes, and can only be beaten by a higher trump. Thus the trump suit becomes, as one might say, the teeth of the hand, able to bite off the winning cards held by your opponents in the other suits. At a No Trump contract all suits are equal, none having a higher trick-taking ability than any other.

The Bidding: Generally one of the four players has enough values to open the bidding, the most usual opening bid being either one of a suit, (as One Heart) or One No Trump. No Trump bids rank first of all in order of precedence, out-ranking any of the four suits.

When a player bids a suit in the auction he tells his partner that this suit would be his first choice as trumps. The player on his left then gets a turn to bid and, if he wishes to do so, must make a bid which out-ranks the first. Thus if the first bid were 1♡ it could be out-ranked by either a bid of 1♠ or 1 N.T., but in diamonds or clubs, which rank *below* hearts, the bid would have to be 2♣ or 2♢. Going clockwise round the table each player in turn may bid, either "supporting" his partner in the suit he has chosen, showing a suit of his own or bidding No Trumps, each bid made *out-ranking* the previous one.

At the end of the auction, that is, when three players in rotation have passed by saying "No bid", one pair will have contracted (hence the name Contract Bridge) to make a specified number of tricks. This number, or contract, **does not include the first six tricks won by that pair.** If, therefore, you contract to make 2♡, you are aiming at making eight tricks with hearts as trumps, first six, generally known as "the book", and then two for your contract.

After the auction we get to the second part of the game, the play of the hand, for which one of the four players will be "Declarer".

Declarer: Declarer is the player who, in the course of the auction, has declared his intention of trying to make a particular contract. He is, however, the *first* player of the partnership to have named that denomination, not necessarily the final bidder. As this is frequently a stumbling block for beginners, we will examine a couple of examples.

You	*1st Opponent*	*Your Partner*	*2nd Opponent*
1♡	1♠	2♣	2♠
3♣	No	3♡	No
No	No		

In this first example your opening of 1♡ was over-called by 1♠ and your partner bid 2♣ to show you he had these. Next opponent raised his partner's spade bid and you out-ranked this by supporting your partner's clubs. He then bid 3♡ and all passed. He was the last to bid hearts, but you were the first, so you become Declarer at a contract of 3♡ (nine tricks to make).

You	*1st Opponent*	*Your Partner*	*2nd Opponent*
1♡	1♠	2♣	2♠
3♣	No	No	No

Here, after the same start, the auction stops short at your 3♣ bid. You are the last to bid clubs, but your partner was the first, so he becomes Declarer at 3♣.

Declarer is the important member of the partnership for this hand, as he plays both his own and his partner's cards. His partner becomes:—

Dummy: When the auction is over the player on

declarer's *left* plays his first card, which is called the opening lead. Declarer's partner then, after the lead, spreads his hand face upwards on the table arranged in suits, with the trumps, if any, on his right. He has now become Dummy and, thereafter, may take no part in the game except to draw attention to any irregularities committed by the opponents, and to keep an eye on his partner and try to check him before he breaks any of the Laws.

The Defenders: The defenders, alias opponents or opposition, are the other two players, sitting one on either side of declarer. Declarer will be trying to make his contract and the defenders will be trying to break, or defeat him. All three players can see dummy's cards, but declarer has the advantage of being able to see his own and dummy's together as a whole and to plan the two hands as one unit.

Tricks: Each player *strictly in turn* plays a card to the one led, the trick being won by the pair playing the highest card in the suit led. If, however, one player plays a trump, this will win the trick unless capped by a higher trump.

Each player is under an **absolute obligation** to play a card of the suit led, that is, to follow suit if he can. If he fails to follow suit when he could he is said to "revoke", for which there is a costly penalty when his error is discovered.

If a player *cannot* follow suit he may either "discard", that is, throw away a card of a different suit which, perhaps, he does not want or, if he has one, he may play a trump. It is excellent if you can trump your opponents' Aces, but you'll need a good alibi if the Ace happens to belong to your partner!

When four cards, one from each hand in rotation,

have been played, the trick is complete. If either declarer or dummy has won it, declarer gathers the cards together and places them face downwards on the table in front of him. If a defender's card has won it, it is gathered by the defence, and it is customary for the *partner* of the winner of the first defence trick to gather all the tricks won by his side during that hand.

The player who has won the trick makes the lead to the next trick, and this applies equally to declarer and dummy. If a card from dummy's hand won the trick, the next lead card *must* come from dummy's hand and vice versa if declarer won it. Expensive penalties may loom if this Law is broken.

At the end of the hand each side counts its tricks, the important ones being declarer's. He may have won precisely enough to fulfil his contract, that is, six tricks plus the contracted number or, if he has won more, he will have made *overtricks*. Alas, all too frequently, he will have "gone down" by not making enough tricks, of which you will see the significance in Chapter 3.

In all bridge literature the four players are designated by the four compass points. Hands are set out, as it might be, round a table top, with the thirteen cards for each hand at the appropriate compass point. Bidding sequences are also arranged under these headings, abbreviated to N. E. S. W., and in that order. A pass or "No bid" is indicated by a dash or the word "No". Thus in this bidding sequence you can see that South dealt and passed, West

	N	
W		E
	S	

N.	*E.*	*S.*	*W.*
		No	No
1♠	No	2♠	No
No	No		

passed, and North opened with 1♠. East passed, South raised to 2♠ and all three players passed. So North, the first to bid spades, became declarer at 2♠, having been the first to bid this suit. North and South are, of course, partners against East and West.

QUIZ ON CHAPTER 2

	N.	*E.*	*S.*	*W.*	
1.	?		1♡	No	What is North's correct bid if he wishes to show that he holds a suit of (a) Spades (b) Clubs ?
2.	?		1◇	No	What is North's correct bid if he wishes to show that he holds a suit of (a) Hearts (b) Clubs (c) Spades ?
3.	?		1◇	1♡	What is North's correct bid if he wishes (a) to support his partner's opening bid (b) to show that he holds a suit of spades (c) to show that he holds a suit of clubs ?
4.	?		1♠	2♡	What is North's correct bid if he wishes (a) to support his partner's opening bid (b) to show that he holds a suit of clubs (c) to show that he holds a suit of diamonds ?

	N.	*E.*	*S.*	*W.*
5.			1♠	2♣
	2♠	3♣	4♠	No
	No	No		

(a) Which pair has won the Auction ?
(b) How many tricks have they contracted to make ?
(c) Which player will be Declarer ?
(d) Which player will make the opening lead ?
(e) Which player will be Dummy ?
(f) When will Dummy put his hand on the table ?
(g) Which suit will Dummy put at the right hand side ?

	N.	*E.*	*S.*	*W.*
6.			1♠	2♣
	2♠	3♣	4♠	Dbl.

(a) Is the Auction over yet ?
(b) If not, which players may still bid ?
(c) If no one else bids, what is the final contract and who will be declarer ?
(d) If Declarer makes his contract, how many tricks will he have won ?

	N.	*E.*	*S.*	*W.*
7.	1♠	2♣	2♡	3♣
	4♡	No	No	No

(a) What is the final contract ?
(b) How many tricks has declarer contracted to make ?
(c) Which player will be Declarer ?
(d) Which player will make the opening lead ?
(e) Which player will be Dummy ?

	N.	*E.*	*S.*	*W.*
8.	2♣	No	2♡	No
	3♠	No	4♠	No
	7♡	No	?	

(a) There are two other possible bids South could make. What are they ?
(b) Can East or West still make a bid and if so what, if South passes ?
(c) If East, South and West all say No Bid, what is the final contract ?
(d) How many tricks will declarer have contracted to make ?

	N.	*E.*	*S.*	*W.*

(e) Which player will become Declarer ?

(f) Which player will make the opening lead ?

9.	**1♠**	**2♢**	**2NT**	—
	3NT			

(a) Which other players following North may still make a bid ?

(b) If the other players all say No Bid, who will be Declarer ?

(c) What will the contract be ?

(d) How many tricks will declarer have contracted to make ?

10.	**1♡**		**1♠**	**2♢**
	2NT	—	**4♡**	—
	—	**Dbl.**		

(a) If South, West and North now all say No Bid, what is the final contract ?

(b) Could South bid again if he wished ?

(c) Who will become declarer if no one else bids ?

(d) If three passes follow East's double, which player will make the opening lead?

QUIZ ON CHAPTER 2—ANSWERS

1. (a) 1♠, a higher-ranking suit than hearts.
   (b) 2♣, lower ranking suit than hearts, so you have to bid 2♣ over 1♡.

2. (a) 1♡, as this ranks higher than 1◇.
   (b) 2♣, clubs ranking below diamonds.
   (c) 1♠, again a higher-ranking suit than diamonds.

3. (a) 2◇, which beats West's 1♡.
   (b) 1♠, which beats West's 1♡ again.
   (c) 2♣, as 1♣ would not beat 1♡, the higher ranking suit.

4. (a) 2♠ which, of course, outranks West's 2♡. Later you will learn that North could support by jumping to 3♠ or even 4♠.
   (b) 3♣, the lowest call he can make in clubs to beat 2♡.
   (c) 3◇, as in the case of clubs, diamonds also rank below hearts.

5. (a) North and South have won the Auction.
   (b) They have contracted to make ten tricks.
   (c) South, because he was the *first* of the pair to bid in spades.
   (d) West will make the opening lead as he will be the player on Declarer's left.
   (e) North will be Dummy.
   (f) North will put his hand down as soon as West has made his lead.
   (g) Spades, trumps for this hand, must be put on the right.

6. (a) No, there must always be three "no bid's" to end the Auction.
   (b) North, East and South have yet a turn to bid.
   (c) If no one else bids, South will be Declarer in 4♠ doubled.
   (d) He will have won 10 tricks, the "book" of 6 plus the contract of 4.

7. (a) The final contract is 4♡.
   (b) Declarer has contracted to make ten tricks.
   (c) South, who first mentioned hearts, will be Declarer.
   (d) West, the defender on South's left, will make the opening lead.
   (e) North, Declarer's partner, will be Dummy.

8. (a) South could bid 7♠ or 7 N.T., either of which ranks above 7♡.
   (b) Yes, unlikely though it may seem, if South passes West could still bid 7♠ or 7 N.T. but he could also double—much more likely!
   (c) If no one else bids the final contract will be 7♡.
   (d) Declarer will have contracted to make all thirteen tricks.
   (e) South, who first bid the hearts, will be Declarer.
   (f) West, on Declarer's left, will make the opening lead.

9. (a) East, South, and West may still make bids and, indeed, must do so, even if only to pass, before the Auction is closed.
   (b) South will be Declarer.
   (c) The contract will be 3 N.T. by South.
   (d) South will have contracted to make nine tricks in No Trumps.

10. (a) The final contract will be 4♡ doubled.
    (b) Yes, South can bid again as there have not yet been three passes.
    (c) North will be Declarer.
    (d) East, on declarer's left, will make the opening lead.

CHAPTER 3

The Score

YOUR ultimate aim is to win the Rubber, the best of three games, and it is essential for you to learn to score properly because you must, at any given moment, know how many more points either you or your opponents need, the bonus points you could gain, or the penalties to which you may be liable. Printed score cards may be purchased very cheaply, and look like this. Note the vitally important horizontal line across the middle of the card. Only points which can be scored *below* this line count towards a game, of which you need two to win the rubber, and penalty and bonus points are scored *above* the line. The "We" column is for points gained by you and your partner while "They" are your opponents.

We	They

The defenders are never permitted to score points below the line towards a game—**only declarer and his partner can do this.** Hence the importance of winning the auction, so that you or your partner become declarer with a chance of scoring a game. Declarer and his partner may score contract points *below* the line, either going towards a game or completing one.

You need 100 *points below the line* to complete a game, and these are the trick values which may be scored below the line for successful contracts:—

The first trick in a No Trump Contract .. 40 points
Each subsequent trick in a No Trump contract 30 points
(Thus 3 N.T. bid and made yields 40 + 30 + 30 = 100, a complete game.)
Each trick in Spades or Hearts, the major suits .. .. 30 points
(Thus 4♠ or 4♡ bid and made yields 4 × 30 = 120, a complete game.)
Each trick in Diamonds or Clubs, the minor suits .. .. 20 points
(Thus 5◇ or 5♣ bid and made yields 5 × 20 = 100, a complete game.)

You may only score below the line towards a game the actual number of tricks you contracted to make, hence the importance of learning to bid to the full value of your hand. If your final contract is 2♡ (8 tricks) and you make ten tricks, you may only score the 2♡ of your contract (2 × 30 = 60) below the line. The additional 60 points for the two overtricks is scored above the line. If you had bid the 4♡ to cover the ten tricks you actually made you would have scored the full 120 points below the line, thus completing a game.

You are allowed to build up gradually to your 100 game points by bidding and making several part-score contracts but—and this is the big **but** which matters so much—if during the course of building up your score in this way your opponents sweep in and bid and make a game, a line is drawn right across the two columns and your little part-scores are ruled off. They no longer count towards your game score.

This is why the auction is so often competitive between the two sides. Both would clearly like to win it so that any score they make may count below the line for a game. Even if they can't score below the line they may prefer to bid until they win the auction, though they risk contracting to make more tricks than they can and incurring a penalty, as this will prevent the opposition from scoring or completing a game.

Penalty Points: There are penalty points for failing to make your contract, and these differ according to whether or not you have yet won a game. A pair who has *not* won a game is "Not vulnerable", and each trick by which their contract fails will cost them 50 points, scored *above* the line to their opponents. Thus if you, not vulnerable, bid 4♡ (10 tricks) and make only 8 tricks, you will be "two down", or 100 points above the line to "they".

A pair who has already won a game is "vulnerable" and each trick by which their contract fails will cost them 100 points instead of 50.

Sometimes, particularly in the competitive sort of auction mentioned above, a player may become certain that his opponents' contract will fail, in which case he may **double** the last bid made. (The correct way to do this is to say "Double", never "I double", or "double 4♡"). A declarer who contrives to make his contract after being doubled gets extra points but the penalties are much greater if he fails. Not vulnerable, the first trick "down" costs 100 points, and each subsequent trick 200 points. If the doubled declarer is vulnerable, the penalties are even more horrifying, the first trick down costing 200 points and each subsequent trick 300 points.

If a player is doubled but still feels confident of making his contract he may redouble. This makes the penalties for failure twice as much again though, if successful, there will again be compensations. A double or redouble may be "taken out" by a subsequent suit bid, or a No Trump bid, though both the double and redouble count as bids which must be followed by three passes before the auction is closed.

Bonus Points: Tricks won in excess of declarer's contract are known as overtricks, and are scored at their trick value *above* the line. For example, if the contract is 3♡ (nine tricks) and declarer makes eleven tricks, he scores $3 \times 30 = 90$ points below the line towards game, and the tenth and eleventh tricks are two overtricks, $30 \times 2 = 60$ points *above* the line for overtricks.

If the contract has been doubled and is then made, the trick score below the line is doubled; thus 90 points for 3♡ bid and made would, if doubled, become 180 points. In this case overtricks are *not* scored at the normal trick value above the line, but at 100 points each if not vulnerable and 200 points each if vulnerable. In addition to this, any declarer who makes a doubled contract scores an extra bonus of 50 points above the line "for the insult".

A redoubled contract, if made, redoubles, that is, multiplies by four, the trick points scored below the line. Overtricks score 200 points each if not vulnerable and 400 points each if vulnerable, and there is again the 50 point "insult" bonus.

There are three other classes of bonus points scored above the line, honours, slams, and the rubber.

The top five cards in each suit, that is, the Ace, King, Queen, Knave and Ten, are the five honours. At a trump contract, any hand containing all five trump honours scores a bonus of 150 points. For any four of the five in one hand the bonus is 100 points. At No Trump contracts only the four Aces count as honours, and all four in one hand scores a bonus of 150 points.

The slam bonus points are inducements to bid up to the skies as there are splendid rewards if successful. There are two categories of slams, Little Slam which means contracting to make twelve of the thirteen tricks, and Grand Slam, which means contracting to make all thirteen tricks. Here are the bonus points available:—

Little Slam bid and made, not vulnerable..	500 points
Little Slam bid and made, vulnerable ..	750 points
Grand Slam bid and made, not vulnerable	1,000 points
Grand Slam bid and made, vulnerable ..	1,500 points

Lastly, there are bonus points for being the first pair to win two games, thus completing the rubber. In a straight two-game rubber the bonus is 700 points to the winning pair, and in a three-game rubber, 500 points to the winners. If a rubber has to be abandoned unfinished the pair, if any, who has scored one game gets a bonus of 300 points or, if one side only has a part score towards a game, their bonus is 50 points.

When a rubber is finally over, both columns of the score card are added up and the smaller total deducted from the larger, which gives the net number of points by which the rubber has been won. Scores of or below the 50-mark count to the nearest lower hundred, and scores above the 50-mark count to the next higher hundred.

In Rubber Bridge it is usual to play for money stakes and this, normally, is so-much-per-hundred. If, as beginners, you are playing for the modest amount of 1d. per 100, you and your partner would each be able to claim 8d. from your opponents if you won the rubber by 800 points. It all adds to the spice of life!

A full table of the scores is given for your convenience on p. 275-6.

A Score Card in Detail: Now let's examine a score card in detail, noting how each amount is made up, where it is scored, and how the final result is achieved. Don't let it worry you if you find it difficult at first—it will all fall into place and become almost second-nature to you when you have had a bit of practice.

We	They
500[10]	100[6]
750[9]	50[5]
30[9]	400[5]
100[8]	100[4]
500[6]	60[4]
60[1]	50[2]
60[1]	
30[3]	120[4]
100[7]	80[5]
190[9]	
2,320[11]	960[11]
960	
1,360	

1. We bid 2♠ and make ten tricks, scoring 60 below towards a game and 60 above. A wasted opportunity as if we had bid 4♠ we could have scored the full 120 below the line and completed a game.
2. We bid 1 N.T. which would have given us our 40 points for game but our opponents would not let it go so quietly and bid 2♢. Over this we tried 2 N.T. but only made seven tricks, one down, 50 above to "they".
3. We bid 1♡ and just make it, scoring 30 points below. Still only 90 below and not yet a game.
4. Opponents sweep in and bid 4♡, actually making twelve tricks. They score 120 below the line completing a game, 60 above the line for the two overtricks, and 100 point bonus because declarer had four heart honours in his hand. Note how your 90 points towards game has vanished.
5. Your opponents bid up to 2♣ which unwisely you doubled and they made ten tricks in all. The normal 40 points below becomes 80, the two overtricks, doubled and vulnerable are 200 each, and there is a 50 point "insult bonus".

6. You got a little of your own back here. Your opponents bid 6♠ which you doubled and they went two down, making ten tricks instead of twelve. This gives you 200 + 300 = 500 above the line and all they scored was 100 above as they again had four honours in one hand.
7. Now we bid 3 N.T. and make it, scoring 100 below for our first game. The line across is drawn again, ruling off their part-score of 80.
8. We bid up to 4♡ which, if we had been allowed to make it, would have given us game and Rubber. Our opponents, however, overcalled us with 4♠ which we didn't even double. They made nine tricks, one down, 100 above the line to us.
9. We bid 6 N.T. and made all thirteen tricks. This is 190 below, 30 above for the overtrick, and 750 for the vulnerable Little Slam bonus. This is rather hard luck on our opponents who could have won the Rubber themselves if they had not over-ambitiously tried for a Little Slam earlier. They would also have got off more cheaply as it happens if they had let us play and make our 4♡ at No:8 as now we've gone on to score the Little Slam bonus as well as the Rubber.
10. For the "Game All" rubber bonus, we score 500 points.
11. We add up both columns, deduct the smaller "they" score from the larger "we" score, which leaves us a net win of 1,360 points. This counts to the next higher hundred, 1,400, or 1/2d. at 1d. per hundred!

QUIZ ON CHAPTER 3

Get yourself a few score cards. If you haven't got printed ones, draw them as shown on p. 32 and then make out the scores for the Rubbers from the data given below. You will have to be very careful as you are told only the result on each individual hand. You yourself will have to notice as the card progresses when you ("We" on the score card) or your opponents ("They" on the score card) become vulnerable by winning a game.

1. (1) You bid 3♣ and make eight tricks.
   (2) You bid 3 N.T. and make seven tricks.
   (3) They bid 2 N.T. and make ten tricks.
   (4) They bid 1 N.T. and make six tricks.
   (5) You bid 3 N.T. and make ten tricks.
   (6) You bid 5♣ which they double, and you make ten tricks.
   (7) You bid 4♡ and make nine tricks. Your heart holding was ♡ **KQ J 10 x x.**
   (8) You bid 1 N.T. and make eight tricks.
   (9) They bid 3♢ and make nine tricks.
   (10) They bid 2♠ and make seven tricks.
   (11) You bid 2♢ and make eight tricks.
   (12) In a highly competitive Auction, each side trying to outbid the others, they bid 5♡, you double, and they make eight tricks.
   (13) They bid 1 N.T. and make eleven tricks.
   (14) You bid 6♡ and make twelve tricks.
   (15) What is the exact score at this point?

* * *

2. (1) They bid 1 N.T. and make ten tricks.
   (2) They bid 2♣ and make eight tricks.
   (3) You bid 4♠ and make nine tricks.
   (4) They bid 1 N.T. and make six tricks.
   (5) You bid 5♢, are doubled, and make twelve tricks.
   (6) They bid 2 N.T. and make eight tricks.
   (7) They bid 2♡ and make seven tricks.
   (8) They bid 1 N.T., are doubled, and make four tricks.
   (9) They bid 6♢ and make thirteen tricks. Declarer's diamond holding was ♢ **A K J 10 x.**
   (10) You bid 4♠, they double, and you make eight tricks.
   (11) You bid 3♡ and make ten tricks.
   (12) They bid 2 N.T. and make eight tricks.
   (13) You bid 1 N.T. and make seven tricks. In your hand you had the ♠A, ♡A, ♢A and ♣A.
   (14) What is the exact score at this point?

3. Here's one more scoring exercise, very different from the previous two.

(1) You bid 4♠ and make eleven tricks. Your spade holding was ♠ **A K Q J 10 5.**

(2) You bid 7♡ and make thirteen tricks.

(3) What is the score at this point ?

QUIZ ON CHAPTER 3—ANSWERS

1.

We	They
500[14]	
750[14]	
500[12]	120[13]
50[10]	100[7]
30[8]	200[6]
100[7]	60[3]
30[5]	100[2]
50[4]	50[1]
100[5]	70[3]
40[8]	60[9]
40[11]	40[13]
180[14]	
2,370	800
800	
1,570[15]	

1. 50 above to "they" for going down one trick not vulnerable.
2. 100 above to "they" for going down two not vulnerable.
3. "They" score 70 below (40 and 30) and 60 above for the two overtricks.
4. 50 above to you because they went one down.
5. You score 100 below for your 3 N.T. and 30 above for the overtrick. This gives you game, makes you vulnerable, and wipes off their 70-below.
6. One down doubled and vulnerable, 200 above to "they".
7. One down vulnerable is 100 above to "they" and you score a bonus of 100 above for the four honours.
8. You score 40 below towards your next game and 30 above for the overtrick.
9. They score 60 below, 3 × 20, for making 3♢.
10. They go one down but are not yet vulnerable, so only 50 to you above the line.
11. You score 2 × 20 = 40 below for your contract.
12. As they contracted to make eleven tricks they are three down, not vulnerable, 100 + 200 + 200 = 500 above to you.
13. They score 40 below (enough to give them game) and 120 above for the four overtricks at 30 points each.
14. You score 180 below, 6 × 30, which, being vulnerable, gives you game and Rubber. You also score 750 above for the Little Slam bonus and 500 for winning the Rubber in three games.

15. Your total is 2,370 and their's is 800. Deducting 800 from 2,370 we get 1,570 which means that you win by 1600.

* * *

2.

We	They
500[13]	
150[13]	
30[11]	500[10]
500[8]	100[9]
50[7]	500[9]
50[5]	20[9]
100[5]	50[3]
50[4]	90[1]
200[5]	40[1]
	40[2]
	70[6]
	120[9]
90[11]	70[12]
40[13]	
1,760	1,600
1,600	
160[14]	

1. 40 below for 1 N.T. and 90 above for three overtricks—a wasted chance to score game—to "they".
2. 2 × 20 = 40 for 2♣ bid and made, below to "they".
3. You went one down not vulnerable, 50 above to "they".
4. They went one down not vulnerable, 50 above to you.
5. Your 100 for 5♢ is doubled, becoming 200 below for game. You also score 100 above for the overtrick and 50 "insult bonus". Their 80 is ruled off.
6. They score 70 below for making 2 N.T.
7. They go one down, 50 above to you as they are not vulnerable.
8. They are three down but, luckily for them, not vulnerable. 100 + 200 + 200 = 500 above to you.
9. They complete their game by scoring 6 × 20 = 120 below. Above they get 20 for the overtrick and 500 for the non-vulnerable Little Slam bonus, and 100 for honours.
10. You are two down doubled and vulnerable, 200 + 300 = 500 above to "they".
11. You score 90 below towards your next game and 30 above for the overtrick.
12. They score 70 below towards their next game.

13. You complete your game and Rubber with 40 below and score 150 above for the four Aces, plus 500 for the Rubber.
14. Your total, 1,760, less their total, 1,600, leaves you winning by 160, or two points after all that work!

* * *

3.

We	They
700[2] 1,500[2] 150[1] 30[1]	
120[1]	
210[2]	
2,710[3]	

1. You score your game with 120 below, 30 above for the overtrick, and 150 bonus for five honours in one hand.
2. For the vulnerable Grand Slam bid and made you score 7 × 30 = 210 below and the Grand Slam bonus of 1,500 above. You also score 700 for the "Love Rubber".
3. Your total, with nothing to deduct, is 2,710, or a win by 27 points.

SECTION II
The Auction

CHAPTER 4

To Bid or Not to Bid

NOW comes the time to learn to calculate the value of your hand so that you know whether or not to make an opening bid and this, at any rate during the early stages of learning the game, is done on a very easy-to-remember point count.

The Point Count: The Acol system employs Milton Work's count, named after its originator, but to help learners it also uses an extension of this count. Applying it, your hand must add up to a minimum of 13 points to qualify as an opening bid, calculated as follows:—

Ace = 4 points: King = 3 points: Queen = 2 points: Knave = 1 point.

As there are an Ace, King, Queen and Knave in each of the four suits, there are 40 honour points in the pack, so an average hand would contain ten. Most frequently, however, one hand will have enough extra to bring it up to the requirements for an opening bid.

In addition to these points for honour cards, as a prospective opening bidder you may add one point for each card over four in any one suit.

The Count at Work:

♠ **A K Q x x** ♡ **x x x** ◇ **A Q x x** ♣ **x**	9 points for the ♠ **A K Q**, one for the fifth spade, and 6 for the ◇ **A Q**, a total of 16, well over the minimum of 13 and worth an opening bid of 1♠, the suit you would clearly like to suggest as trumps.

♠ x x ♡ A Q x x x x ◇ x ♣ A K J x	6 points for the ♡ **A Q**, two for the fifth and sixth hearts, and 8 for the ♣ **A K J**, again 16 points and a good opening bid of your favourite suit, hearts.

The Choice of Bid: If a hand contains two suits with attractive prospects as trumps there are easy-to-learn rules which give the best chance of showing them both. *Please* remember though, that as your skill progresses you will learn to modify them, but as a beginner you must have very precise guidance to help you.

It may take one or more rounds of bidding to discover the best contract for the combined hands held by you and your partner, but clearly if you have two suits, you want your partner to be able to take his choice. The suits, you will remember, rank Spades, Hearts, Diamonds and then Clubs. Spades and Hearts are *adjacent* suits, as are Hearts and Diamonds, and also Diamonds and Clubs. The *divided* suits are Spades and Diamonds, Spades and Clubs, and Hearts and Clubs.

1. Always bid your *longest* suit first.
2. With two suits of equal length, bid the higher ranking of adjacent suits first, and the lower ranking of divided suits.

♠ Q 10 x x x ♡ x x ◇ A K Q x ♣ A x	♠ **Q** = 2 pts. and 1 for the fifth spade. The ◇ **A K Q** = 9 points and the ♣**A**=4, total 16. Open 1♠, the longest suit, not 1◇ because it is headed by so many pretty pictures.
♠ J 10 x x x ♡ A K x x x ◇ A x ♣ x	♠**J** = 1 point and 1 for the fifth spade. ♡ **A K** = 7 points and 1 for the fifth heart. Add 4 for the ◇**A** and the total is 14. Open 1♠, the higher ranking of two equal lengthed and adjacent suits.

♠ J 10 x x x ♡ x ◇ A x ♣ A K x x x	Compare this with the previous hand. It is identical except that the hearts and clubs have changed places. Open 1♣ with two suits of equal length which are *divided*.
♠ K Q J x x ♡ x x ◇ K Q x x x x ♣ —	♠K Q J = 6 points and 1 for the fifth spade. ◇ K Q = 5 points and 2 for the fifth and sixth diamonds. Open 1◇, not because it is the lower of divided suits, but because it is your longest suit.
♠ x x ♡ A K J x ◇ A Q J x ♣ x x x	These last three hands all total 15 points with none added for " long " cards, and are identical except that the suits change places. With two equal and adjacent red suits, open 1♡, the higher ranking.
♠ x x ♡ A K J x ◇ x x x ♣ A Q J x	Now you have two equal but divided suits, so open the lower ranking, 1♣.
♠ A K J x ♡ x x ◇ x x x ♣ A Q J x	This again is a 1♣ opening bid on equal and divided suits. If they were spades and diamonds instead, you would open 1◇, not 1♠.

* * *

You require a minimum of 13 points to open the bidding, but this does not mean that all hands of 13 points or more are opened as one-bids in a suit. An opening one-bid normally varies from 13 points upwards to about 20 points, and later you will learn other opening bids which show evenly balanced hands, exceptionally strong ones, or unusual distribution. Don't worry about them until we get to them.

As dealer or second hand when you open the bidding, in addition to 13 points *you also promise your partner that you can bid again*. You promise, in fact, what is known as a "rebid". The reason for this is that you are trying to discover what denomination will suit the combined partnership hands best and it is very possible that your partner will want to hear your rebid before he can take his rightful share in the decision. If he *knows* you will bid again he need not rush things but can explore gradually.

You will notice, however, that this promise to rebid is given only by first or second hand. This is because, at this point, partner has not yet had a turn to bid, his strength is completely unknown and may be even greater than opener's. Conversely, if first and second hands have passed and the auction is opened by third or fourth hand, both these players, already having heard a pass from partner, know the hand opposite contains less than 13 points, so a third or fourth hand opening bidder may please himself as to whether he rebids or not. This brings us to a fundamental point, what a "biddable suit" is and what makes it "rebiddable".

Any four-card suit is biddable, though as learners you will be well advised to ignore those not headed by an Ace or King or at least two of the other three honours. Four-card suits, however, are *not rebiddable*. Five-card suits are rebiddable unless they are very weak, and six-card suits are always rebiddable. Three-card suits are never biddable at all, except when you progress to the use of "prepared minors".

If a four-card suit is not rebiddable and yet, on the second round, you rebid your suit, it follows that you promise that your suit is at least a five-card one. Do you see how the exchange of information gradually takes shape ? You are trying to assess not only the best denomination, but the number of points you have between you because, roughly speaking, 26 points between the combined hands should produce a game.

Here is a table of the combined counts required to fulfil various contracts. They are somewhat arbitrary as, in the final analysis, both "fit" and "distribution" can more than make up for a low count, but by and large, if you work to these figures until your experience develops further, you won't go far wrong.

You need:

To open with a bid of one of a suit	A minimum of 13 points.
To make the ten tricks required for a major suit game	26 points between the two combined hands.
To make the 11 tricks required for a minor suit game	A little more—say 28 or 29 points,
To make the nine tricks required for a No Trump game	24 or 25 points with a 5-card suit and 26 on evenly balanced hands.
To make the twelve tricks required for a Little Slam contract	31-33 points in a suit contract. 34-35 points in No Trumps.
To make the 13 tricks required for a Grand Slam contract	37 points.

QUIZ ON CHAPTER 4

On each of the hands below count the number of points, both high card and distributional, and say what opening bid you would make, if any, as dealer.

1. ♠ x x
   ♡ Q J x x x
   ◇ A K Q x x
   ♣ x

2. ♠ A K J x x
   ♡ K x x
   ◇ —
   ♣ K J 10 x x

3. ♠ A K J x x
   ♡ K x x
   ◇ x
   ♣ K J x x

4. ♠ x x x
   ♡ Q J x x
   ◇ A K Q x
   ♣ x x

5. ♠ Q J x x
   ♡ x x x
   ◇ A K Q x
   ♣ A x

6. ♠ x x x x
   ♡ K J x x
   ◇ A K J x
   ♣ A

7. ♠ Q x x
   ♡ A K J
   ◇ A Q 10
   ♣ J 10 x x

8. ♠ K Q J x x
   ♡ K Q J x x x
   ◇ x
   ♣ x

9. ♠ A Q x x
   ♡ A K x x
   ◇ x x x
   ♣ x x

10. ♠ K x x
    ♡ x x
    ◇ A Q J x x x
    ♣ Q x

11. ♠ A K Q J
    ♡ x x
    ◇ 10 9 x x x x
    ♣ A

12. ♠ A K x x
    ♡ A K x
    ◇ 10 9 8 x x x
    ♣ —

QUIZ ON CHAPTER 4—ANSWERS

1. ♡ **Q J** = 3, fifth heart = 1, ◇ **A K Q** = 9 and fifth diamond = 1, total 14 points. Open 1♡, the higher ranking of two adjacent and equal suits.
2. ♠ **A K J** = 8 and fifth spade = 1, ♡ **K** = 3 and ♣ **K J** = 4 + 1 for fifth club, total 17 points. Open 1♣, the lower of two equal and divided suits.
3. ♠ **A K J** = 8 + 1 for fifth spade, ♡ **K** = 3 and ♣ **K J** = 4, total 16 points. Open 1♠, your longest suit.
4. ♡ **Q J** = 3 and ◇ **A K Q** = 9, total 12 points, worth only an original pass.
5. ♠ **Q J** = 3, ◇ **A K Q** = 9 and ♣ **A** = 4, total 16 points. Open 1◇, the lower of two equal and divided suits.
6. ♡ **K J** = 4, ◇ **A K J** = 8 and ♣ **A** = 4, total 16 points. Your spades not qualifying as "biddable", open 1♡, the higher ranking of equal and adjacent suits.
7. ♠ **Q** = 2, ♡ **A K J** = 8, ◇ **A Q** = 6 and ♣ **J** = 1, total 17 points. Open 1♣, your only 4-card suit.
8. ♠ **K Q J** = 6, ♡ **K Q J** = 6. Add 1 for the fifth spade and two for the fifth and sixth hearts, total 15 points. Open 1♡, your longest suit.
9. ♠ **A Q** = 6, ♡ **A K** = 7, total 13 points. Open 1♠, the higher ranking of two equal and adjacent suits.
10. ♠ **K** = 3, ♡ **A Q J** = 7 + 2 for fifth and sixth diamonds, and ♣ **Q** = 2, total 14 points. Open 1◇, your 6-card long suit.
11. ♠ **A K Q J** = 10, the fifth and sixth diamonds = 2 and the ♣ **A** = 4, total 16 points. Open 1◇, the long suit, **not** 1♠ because of the pretty pictures!
12. ♠ **A K** = 7, ♡ **A K** = 7 and 2 for the fifth and sixth diamonds. Open 1◇, the long suit again.

CHAPTER 5

Responder Takes the Field

♠♡♣◇♠♡♣◇♠♡♣◇♠♡♣◇♠♡♣◇♠♡♣◇♠♡♣◇

FOR the whole of this lesson you are going to be *responding* to your partner who has opened the bidding. You could, obviously, like the suit he bid. You could, perhaps, not definitely dislike it without having a very specific suit of your own, or you could have one or more suits which you in turn would like to suggest as trumps. You could have a weak hand, a moderate hand, or a good hand. All this information you must learn to convey to your partner, and already you are in the advantageous position of knowing that he holds a minimum of 13 points. He may have more, which he will convey to you in his *rebid* but *you* already know the combined minimum of the two hands.

In this chapter we shall be dealing exclusively with the Acol Responder's Limit Bids which cover the first two situations mentioned, when you like the suit your partner has bid, or when you are not actively allergic to it whilst having no specific suit of your own. First we shall consider only the two major suits, spades and hearts, as dealing with the minor suits is somewhat different. Eleven tricks are needed to make a club or diamond game but only ten in spades or hearts and, best of all, only nine in No Trumps. It is frequently easier to make nine tricks in No Trumps than it is to make eleven in a minor suit, for which reason, if a major suit fit cannot be found, it is wise to explore towards a No Trump contract when the opening bid is in a minor.

Responder's Limit Bids:

(*a*) *When Agreeing Partner's Suit.*

If your partner opens 1♡ or 1♠ and you have *primary trump support*, that is, a 4-card fit for his suit, no further search for the right denomination is necessary, and the only thing to be decided is at what level you will play. Bear in mind that you need to bid 4♡ or 4♠ to score a game and that 26 points between your combined hands, of which you know partner has at least 13, should achieve this. He may, however, have anything up to 20 points and you must at this stage give him the benefit of the doubt, even with as little as 6 points. Most beginners are horrified at the idea of having to bid on 6 points, but remember this is *not* an opening bid. It is a *responding* bid made in the knowledge that partner has reasonable strength and may have a great deal more.

Here are the point counts required to make a responder's Limit Bid in the major suit opened by partner which apply when, and *only* when, responder holds at least four cards in the suit bid:—

Raise 1♡ or 1♠ to two of that suit on 6–9 points.
Raise 1♡ or 1♠ to three of that suit on 10–12 points.
Raise 1♡ or 1♠ to four of that suit on 13–15 points.

Thus if you raise 1♠ to 2♠, you are telling your partner that you have a minimum of four spades and a count of between 6 and 9 points. Adding this information to his own strength, he can tell whether your combined hands will approximate to the necessary 26 points. If they do he will bid 4♠, and if not, he'll pass. Similarly, if you raise 1♠ to 3♠ you are promising at least four spades but with 10–12 supporting points. In the third case, when you hold 13–15 points, *you* know that the combined count is at least 26 points, so you don't risk any contract lower than game.

There is one little complication here which is that, as responder, you have to learn a slightly different way of valuing your hand, but be of good cheer—it's not very difficult!

With 4-card trump support for your partner's major suit you count your honour card points exactly as you did as opener, but this time you add points for *short* side-suits, not for long suits. The reason is that, with ample trumps and, say, no clubs at all, the club "void" is nearly as good as holding the ♣A because your partner will be able to trump his little clubs in your hand. If you have a club "singleton", then even if your partner hasn't got the ♣A himself, he will only have to lose one club trick before he is able to start trumping the suit.

With a minimum of 4-card trump support add:—

3 points for a void (no card at all in a side-suit).
2 points for a singleton (one card in a side-suit).
1 point for a doubleton (two cards in a side-suit).

Don't confuse this count of *short suits* as responder with your count as opener, when you add points for *long suits*. You can't count all this and heaven too, and if as opener you have added 2 points for a fifth and sixth spade you can't add points for singletons and voids as well. It is because you already expect to be able to use the "long" cards to advantage that you have counted them as extra values.

These responses are called Limit Bids because they announce both the upper and lower limits of the strength of the hand in one bid. Furthermore Limit

Bids are **never forcing,** that is, they do not compel your partner to bid again. He is released from his obligation to produce a rebid and instead, having been told the close limits of the value of your hand, he is expected to assess their combined strength and, in the light of this, make the final decision.

♠ Q 10 x x
♡ K 10 x x
◇ J x x
♣ x x

If partner opens 1♡ or 1♠, raise him to two of that suit. He may have a much stronger hand than his guaranteed minimum of 13 points and be able to bid to game once he knows you have four trumps and at least 6 points.

♠ K x x x
♡ K J x x
◇ A x x
♣ x x

If partner bids 1♡ or 1♠ your hand counts 11 points + 1 for the doubleton club, justifying a raise to three of either of these suits.

♠ K Q x x
♡ A x x x
◇ x
♣ Q 10 x x

If partner opens 1♡ or 1♠ you have 13 points with the two for the singleton diamond, so should raise either suit direct to four. You know the combined strength cannot be less than 26 points

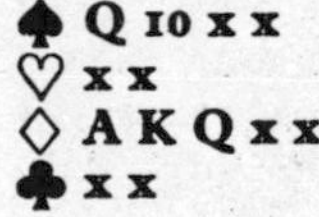

♠ Q 10 x x
♡ x x
◇ A K Q x x
♣ x x

If partner opens 1♠ you have 13 points, a direct raise to 4♠. If he opens 1♡ you cannot **raise** hearts and would, in fact, have to respond in diamonds, about which you will learn in a later chapter.

Now we must turn to the use of these Limit Bids when partner has opened in one of the minor suits and when, you may remember, your best final contract may well be in No Trumps.

You may raise 1♣ or 1◇ to either the *two* or *three* level exactly as you would do in the major suits *provided you have nothing more constructive to say.* Bidding a 4-card major suit in preference to making a minor suit Limit Bid is more likely to lead to a better final contract.

If your partner were dealer he would have opened 1◇, not 1♠. As responder you can keep the bidding at the one-level with a bid of either 1♡ or 1♠. Thus if you respond 1♠ when your partner has this hand, he will know that a fit has been found.

You will learn about these change-of-suit responses in Chapter 7, but it is necessary to point out the distinction here, as it affects the Limit Bids in the minor suits.

Here you would certainly make a Limit Bid of 2◇ in response to an opening 1◇ from your partner. You are too good to pass and have nothing more constructive to offer.

This hand counts 11 points in support of an opening 1◇ bid, so you would raise to 3◇.

Although you count 12 points in support of a 1◇ bid this is a typical hand for **not** making a 3◇ Limit Bid. Instead you would bid 1♡ which may well pave the way for a final No Trump contract.

The direct raise from one to four on 13–15 points which you have learned for use with the major suits is altogether non-existent in the minor suits, because it cuts out what may well be the far easier level of 3 N.T. If you can't bid a direct 3 N.T. yourself, which you will be learning about in the next section of this chapter, you will have to think of some other bid because, with opener's known minimum of 13, you know you have enough for game once you find the best spot for the combined operation of the two hands. This is one of the main reasons for the rule that an opening bid promises a rebid. *If you make a change-of-suit response* and not a Limit Bid, opener is forced to bid again. In this way you can give yourself time to explore for the best contract.

(*b*) *Limit Bids in No Trumps:*

The second type of responder's Limit Bid is in No Trumps, and operates on a wide selection of hands where you have not got a 4-card fit for your partner's suit, and you have no major suit to show over his opening bid.

With a more or less evenly balanced hand, that is, one with something in everything—which means that you have at least two or three small ones of the suit your partner has bid, you can make a Limit Bid in No Trumps, but you cannot, of course, if proposing to play without a trump suit, count extra points for short suits to make up your values. Here is a table of the counts required for the No Trump Limit Bids:—

Holding 6– 9 points	..	bid 1 N.T., except over 1♣.
Holding 10–12 points	..	bid 2 N.T.
Holding 13–15 points	..	bid 3 N.T.

Remember the exception—that over one of a minor it is more constructive to bid one of a major if you can. The other exception, except over 1♣, is because 1♣ is the lowest possible opening bid over which a response of one of any other suit can be made on as little as 6 points. In practice, therefore, it has been found a great advantage if 1 N.T. over 1♣ is used as a positive rather than a negative bid for which 8–10 points are required. Don't worry about this, but just try to remember it.

As with the suit Limit Bids, these No Trump Limit Bids give opener a very accurate picture of your hand. The first promises 6-9 points, less than four of his bid suit, but enough strength to warrant "keeping the bidding open" in case he wants to show a second suit or has a near "rock-crusher" which, plus your minimum of 6 points, will give a play for game.

The 2 N.T. Limit Bid guarantees 10-12 points, leaving opener in a good position to judge his next bid, if any.

On 13-15 points and a balanced hand you may bid 3 N.T. direct. It is generally better to explore your way first if possible, but hands do crop up on which you would be in real difficulties without this bid. However you do it, though, remember that *you* know the combined hands total at least 26 points, so it is up to you to see that a game contract is reached.

You will have noticed that the table of counts for trump or no-trump limit bids is exactly the same. All that is required of you is a little judgement and not to go as high as three of a major or 2 N.T. if you hold a thoroughly bad 10 points, i.e., isolated honours and only small "pip cards".

♠ x x x ♡ Q x ◇ K J x x ♣ Q x x x	Opposite 1♡ or 1♠ bid 1 N.T. Opposite either 1♣ or 1◇ it is better to raise to two of the suit than to bid 1 N.T. with so little in the majors.
♠ K x x x ♡ Q x ◇ K J x x ♣ Q x x	Opposite 1♠ raise to 3♠. Opposite 1♡ you have no trump support, and should bid 1♠. Opposite either 1♣ or 1◇ make the more constructive bid of 1♠ too.
♠ K x x ♡ Q x x ◇ K x x x ♣ J 10 x	An evenly-balanced 9 points. Opposite any opening 1-bid respond 1 N.T. Add one point, say the ◇J, and you have 10 points. Bid 1 N.T. over 1♣ but 2◇ over either 1◇, 1♡ or 1♠.
♠ K x x x ♡ Q x ◇ K J x x ♣ Q x x	Opposite 1♣, 1◇ or 1♡ bid 1♠, the most constructive thing you can do. Opposite 1♠, however, the hand is worth an immediate raise to 3♠.

♠ A Q x ♡ J x x ◇ Q J x x ♣ Q J x	Opposite any opening 1-bid you have no valid bid except a direct 3 N.T. If you bid 3◇ over 1◇ partner may pass while *you* know you have 26 points between you. Neither do you really want to try for 11 tricks in diamonds.
♠ Q J x ♡ Q x ◇ 10 x x x ♣ J x x x	Opposite 1♡ or 1♠ bid 1 N.T., but raise 1♣ or 1◇ to two of that suit.

You may have noticed that these responder's Limit Bids all stop short at 15 points, and wondered what you do if you find you have 16 points or more. These very strong hands come into quite a different category for which you will learn "forcing responses" in due course.

QUIZ ON CHAPTER 5

What is the point value, as responder, of each of the following hands, if partner opens the bidding with:—

(a) 1♣: (b) 1◇ : (c) 1♡ : (d) 1♠ ?

1.	♠ K J x x ♡ x ◇ K J x x ♣ x x x x	What is the correct response if partner opens 1♠ ?
2.	♠ x x x x ♡ Q 10 x x ◇ K J x ♣ x x	What is the correct response if partner opens 1♡ ? And what if he opens 1♠ ?
3.	♠ A x ♡ Q 10 x ◇ K J x x ♣ Q 10 x x	What is the correct response if partner opens 1♡ ? And what if he opens 1♠ ?
4.	♠ x x ♡ K J x x ◇ J 10 x ♣ K J x x	What is the correct response if partner opens 1♡ ? And what if he opens 1♠ ?

5.	♠ K x x ♡ A x x ♢ J 10 x x ♣ A x x	What is the correct response if partner opens 1♣? And what if he opens 1♢, 1♡ or 1♠?
6.	♠ x x ♡ A x x ♢ K x x ♣ K J x x x	What is the correct response if partner opens 1♣?
7.	♠ Q J x ♡ Q x x ♢ 10 x x x ♣ A x x	What is the correct response if partner opens 1♣?
8.	♠ A Q J x x x ♡ J x x x ♢ x ♣ K x	What is the correct response if partner opens 1♡? And what if he opens 1♠?
9.	♠ K x x ♡ K Q x ♢ Q 10 x x ♣ Q x x	What is the correct response if partner opens 1♢? And what if he opens 1♡ or 1♠?
10.	♣ J 10 ♡ K J x x ♢ K J x ♣ Q J x x	What is the correct response if partner opens 1♡? And what if he opens 1♠?

QUIZ ON CHAPTER 5—ANSWERS

	Opening Bid	*Responder's Point Value*	*Responses*
1.	1♣	10	to 1♠ . . . 3♠
	1♢	10	
	1♡	8	
	1♠	10	
2.	1♣	6	to 1♡ . . . 2♡
	1♢	6	to 1♠ . . . 2♠
	1♡	7	
	1♠	7	
3.	1♣	13	to 1♡ . . . 2 N.T.
	1♢	13	to 1♠ . . . 2 N.T.
	1♡	12	
	1♠	12	
4.	1♣	10	to 1♡ . . . 3♡
	1♢	9	to 1♠ . . . 1 N.T.
	1♡	10	
	1♠	9	
5.	1♣	12	to 1♣ . . . 2 N.T.
	1♢	12	to 1♢ . . . 2 N.T.
	1♡	12	to 1♡ . . . 2 N.T.
	1♠	12	to 1♠ . . . 2 N.T.
6.	1♣	12	to 1♣ . . . 3♣
	1♢	11	
	1♡	11	
	1♠	11	
7.	1♣	9	to 1♣ . . . 1 N.T.
	1♢	9	
	1♡	9	
	1♠	9	
8.	1♣	11	to 1♡ . . . 4♡*
	1♢	11	to 1♠ . . . 4♠
	1♡	14	
	1♠	14	

*Note that you should raise ♡, not mention spades.

	Opening Bid	*Responder's Point Value*	*Responses*
9.	1♣	12	to 1♢ . . . choice of 2
	1♢	12	N.T. and 3♢.
			2 N.T. is the best.
	1♡	12	to 1♡ . . . 2 N.T.
	1♠	12	to 1♠ . . . 2 N.T.
10.	1♣	13	to 1♡ . . . 4♡
	1♢	12	to 1♠ . . . 2 N.T.
	1♡	13	
	1♠	12	

CHAPTER 6

No Trump Theory—Both Sides of the Table

♠♡♣◇♠♡♣◇♠♡♣◇♠♡♣◇♠♡♣◇♠♡♣◇♠♡♣◇

OPENING bids in No Trumps are also Limit Bids because, as opposed to suit opening bids which can vary from 13 to 20 points, No Trump opening bids are made on specifically defined and limited counts. In common with responder's Limit Bids they announce both the upper and lower limit of strength, are not forcing and **do not promise a rebid.** Indeed, opener will *not* bid again without a very good reason.

There are different schools of thought as to the strength required for an opening Limit Bid in No Trumps. "Weak throughout" means using a count of 12-14 points all the time, "strong throughout" means that the count is 15-17 points and "variable" means 12-14 points when *not* vulnerable and 15-17 points when vulnerable. If you learn "variable" you will know the requirements for both weak and strong, so will be able to accommodate your partner whatever he demands. "Weak throughout" is by far the most satisfactory as well as the easiest to handle but, alas, too many die-hards still cling to the "strong No Trump", so for your own sake you must learn both. Meanwhile, in practice, we suggest that you should use a 12-14 point No Trump throughout. Such a count will be dealt to you time after time while you may wait all the evening for a suitable 15-17 count. A weak No

Trump opening bid gets you out of trouble time after time when otherwise you would have to think of a suitable rebid and thirdly, time after time it will be difficult, or even impossible, for your opponents to compete. Be that as it may, make sure you learn the counts required for "variable".

One No Trump Opening Bids: Ideally these bids should only be made on evenly balanced hands containing "something in everything". You are suggesting to your partner that you should play the hand without any trump suit, that is, suit with added trick-taking power so you try to have a "stop" in every suit. An Ace, a King with one guard, K-x, or a Queen with two other cards, Q-x-x are, in reasonably favourable circumstances, stops, but you can't have everything in this life and will learn to look on your prospective No Trump hands with the eyes of hope.

"Evenly balanced" means with no predominating suit and ideal "shapes" are 4–3–3–3 in each suit, 4–4–3–2 or sometimes, when the 5-card suit is a minor, 5–3–3–2. In No Trump bidding a 10 counts as ½ point, so for two 10's you can count a full point but you must *not*, if contemplating a No Trump opening bid, add "long card" points.

You will remember the magic formula, 26 points between the combined hands for a game. If you make an opening bid which says that you have 12-14 points in an evenly balanced hand your partner is in a strong position to know your combined count within very close limits. Similarly, of course, if your No Trump is strong, you will have promised 15-17 points. It is most important to be accurate about this and to remember that 15 or 16 points makes you *too strong* to bid a weak No Trump while 14 points is *not strong* enough if you are using a strong No Trump. 18 or more points makes the hand *too strong* whichever variation you are using.

Responses: If partner himself has an evenly balanced hand, he will be able to judge pretty accurately what, in terms of a No Trump contract, the combined hands are worth. Here is a table of responses for you:—

If opener bids 1 N.T. weak, showing 12–14 points in a balanced hand:—	Responder raises to 2 N.T. on 11–12 points and raises direct to 3 N.T. on 12+ or 13 points.
If opener bids 1 N.T. strong, showing 15–17 points in a balanced hand:—	Responder raises to 2 N.T. on 8–9 points and raises direct to 3 N.T. on 9+ points.

If you do a little mental arithmetic you will see the logic of these raises. If responder knows you have a minimum of 12 points and he has 12 himself, he knows your minimum combined count is 24. He tells you this by raising to 2 N.T. which *invites* you to advance to 3 N.T. if you hold the maximum rather than the minimum. If he has a good 12 or 13 points himself he knows the combined hands must be in the 26 point-range, so he bids game direct, not putting the onus on you. In exactly the same way, if a strong No Trump is being used, 8 or 9 points will bring the combined minimum up to about 24 points and you are requested to advance to 3 N.T. if you hold the maximum. Over 9 points brings the combined hands into the 26-point range, worth the immediate game raise.

These counts apply to both opener's and responder's evenly balanced hands but responder could have an unbalanced hand, either weak or strong, quite unsuitable to play in No Trumps. Again, his very precise knowledge of the strength of his partner's opening bid comes to his aid.

With an unbalanced but *weak* hand, one which he knows will not bring the combined count up to 26 points, he can make a **weak take-out** into *two* of a suit. Make no mistake about it, because a lot of people get this wrong, the weak take-out operates over either a weak or a strong No Trump opening bid. Whether or not to make a weak take-out will depend on the known strength of the No Trump bid, as a responder's count which won't bring the combined total up to 26 points if partner holds 12-14 may well bring it up to that figure if partner has 15-17. But it is a golden rule that if a player makes a weak take-out in response to an opening No Trump, opener will not bid again. If your partner bids 1 N.T. and you bid 2♡ you say you have an unevenly balanced but weak hand, not good enough to make the count up to 26 points, which you think would play more comfortably with your long suit as trumps than in No Trumps—quite a comprehensive and explicit message for the two words "Two Hearts".

Carrying the logic of this one stage further, responder could hold a strong but unevenly balanced hand with a good suit he would like to suggest as trumps for a game contract. If he raises in No Trumps he gets no chance of playing in his good suit and if he bids two of his suit, partner will take it for a weak take-out and pass. So he bids *three* of his suit, a bid which is **unconditionally forcing to game,** and opener must rebid. He has a choice, according to his hand, of rebidding 3 N.T. if his partner's suit is his own least favourite (only a doubleton) or, if he likes it, holding 3 or 4 cards in it, he can raise to game in your suit.

Lastly, please note that the very first question you must ask when you sit down opposite to a strange partner is "What No Trump shall we use?" It is, as you can see, vitally important for both of you to know whether an opening No Trump bid contains 12-14 points or 15-17 points. And don't lie about your No Trump openings. Once you have agreed what strength you are going to use, stick to it.

♠ Q 9 x **♡ K x x** **◇ A J x** **♣ Q J 10 x**	13½ points, a typical 1 N.T. bid if you are using "weak". If you are using "strong" you must not open 1 N.T. as it would not be true and would bid 1♣. Top the hand up by two points, say by substituting the ♠**A** for the ♠**Q** and you have 15½ points. Too *strong* for a weak No Trump opening, but just right for a strong No Trump.
♠ Q x x **♡ Q J x** **◇ Q x x** **♣ A K x x**	14 points—an excellent weak No Trump opening bid which shows your full values all in one bid. It is not strong enough for a strong No Trump opening, and you would bid 1♣. Top the hand up again, say by the inclusion of the ◇**K**, and it would make an excellent strong No Trump opener but be too good for a weak No Trump opener.
♠ K J x x **♡ Q J x** **◇ Q 10 x** **♣ A K Q**	18½ points are *too strong* for 1 N.T. whichever variation you are using. Open 1♠ which is your 4-card suit. You will be learning to rebid in No Trumps to show your full count very soon now.
♠ J 10 x **♡ A x x** **◇ Q x x** **♣ K x x x**	This time partner opens 1 N.T. Count your points—10½—and see how important it is for you to know your partner's value. If he has 12–14 you *can't* total 26 between you,

so you pass with a clear conscience. If he has 15–17 you can't total less than 25½ points, so you jump direct to 3 N.T.

♠ K x x
♡ J x x x
◇ A x x
♣ J x x

Partner opens 1 N.T. You have 9 points. If partner has 12–14 you pass without a second thought. If he has 15–17 you bid 2 N.T. inviting him to go on to 3 N.T. if his hand is maximum.

♠ 6
♡ Q 9 8 6 4 3
◇ K 7 3
♣ 8 4 3

If your partner opens 1 N.T. it doesn't matter whether you know it is weak or strong, you know you can't make the combined hands up to 26 points or anything like it. Also your hand is completely unsuited to a No Trump contract but your hearts, if you are allowed to use them as trumps, will be invaluable, so bid 2♡. Partner will pass and you have a very good chance of making eight tricks in this denomination.

♠ 7
♡ J 10 9
◇ A K 9 x x
♣ J 10 x x

Here is another case where the known strength of the opening No Trump will affect your bid. If it is 12–14 points, you can't make it up to 26 and your hand is too unbalanced, with the singleton spade, for you to fancy No Trumps at all, so you make a weak take-out into 2◇. If, however, partner has a strong No Trump of at least 15 points you have a minimum combined count of 25 as well as a nice-looking 5-card suit. Bid 3 N.T. even though you are so unbalanced. 9 tricks are likely to be easier to make than the 11 required for a diamond game. Take exactly the same hand, though, except that the 5-card suit is now in spades.

♠ A K 9 x x
♡ J 10 9
◇ x
♣ J 10 x x

It's interesting to notice what a difference little details can make. Opposite to a weak No Trump you still can't make up to 26 points and you prefer to play in spades, so you make a weak take-out into 2♠ which your partner will pass and which you have every expectation of making. Opposite to a strong No Trump you have the values for game though you personally would still prefer to play in spades so you bid 3♠, not 2♠ which your partner would pass. The jump bid is *game forcing*, and your partner will either raise to 4♠ if he has good support or rebid 3 N.T.

Two No Trump Opening Bids:

There is very little new theory for you to learn about 2 N.T. opening bids, the only vital things being the necessary point count and that vulnerability makes no difference at all.

As before, you require an evenly balanced hand with a guard in every suit but *a count of 20-22 points*. Not *less* than 20 points and not *more* than 22. Honesty is as essential here as it was with 1 N.T. openings and your partner, hearing a 2 N.T. opening, will know that five, possibly even four points, will bring your combined total up to the magic 26 and will raise to 3 N.T. As responder to a 2 N.T. opening you must learn to look on six or seven points as a positive gold mine, knowing it faces a minimum of 20 points.

♠ A Q x ♡ A J x x ♢ K x ♣ A K x x	Here you have a balanced 21 points, making an excellent 2 N.T. opening bid. It has "something in everything" and is far too strong to consider opening 1 N.T.
♠ K Q 10 ♡ A K x ♢ Q J 10 x ♣ A J 10	Here again you should open 2 N.T. As an opening bid it is *not* forcing and your partner may pass on less than four points. But you need so very little help to be able to make 9 tricks!

♠ x x x
♡ Q 10 x
◇ Q J x x
♣ 10 9 x

If your partner opened 2 N.T., you would not look at this hand in disgust but with the eyes of hope. It cannot fail to bring a minimum of 20 points up to 26, so raise to 3 N.T.

♠ Q J 10 x x x
♡ x
◇ x x x
♣ x x x

Until you get well beyond the learner stage, *there is no weak take-out* of an opening 2 N.T. which means that if you respond at all you must reach a game contract. Even with only 3 points you would not pass on this hand. Your partner must have some spade support in his "evenly balanced 20–22 points" and, with spades as trumps, you have a very good chance indeed of making a game. So bid 3♠ over 2 N.T., take out into 4♠ if he rebids 3 N.T., and pass if, instead, he raises to 4♠.

Three No Trump and Four No Trump Opening Bids:

In the Acol system there are both 3 N.T. and 4 N.T. opening bids, but both these have what are known as "conventional" meanings—special meanings which are not what they would appear to be. As a beginner you can forget about them.

In addition to the two conventional opening bids mentioned above there are several "conventions" which are widely used in conjunction with No Trump bidding. Here again, useful as they undoubtedly are, they have no place in a book for beginners. You cannot learn to run before you can walk, so get your basic theory in good working order before you even consider starting to add the "frills". You can do very well without them.

One final word on the strength of 1 N.T. opening bids. We have quoted the correct Acol counts of 12-14 points for a weak no-trump and 15-17 points for a strong no-trump. Many players of the old, or "kitchen bridge "school still stick like adamant to a 16-18 point no-trump. Don't let this worry you—your responses are merely based on the knowledge of the 16-point minimum which has been announced.

QUIZ ON CHAPTER 6

1. If you have agreed to use the weak No Trump (12–14 points) what opening bid would you make on the following hands ?
   (a) ♠ Q x x: ♡ K J x x: ◇ A J: ♣ Q x x x:
   (b) ♠ Q 10 x: ♡ K J x x: ◇ A J: ♣ A x x x:
   (c) ♠ A Q x: ♡ K J x x: ◇ A J: ♣ A x x x:
   (d) ♠ K Q 10 x x: ♡ A x: ◇ A x x: ♣ x x x:
   (e) ♠ A K J: ♡ K J 10: ◇A J x: ♣ K Q x x:

2. If you have agreed to use the strong No Trump (15–17 points) what opening bids would you make on the following hands ?
   (a) ♠ Q x x: ♡ K J x x: ◇ A J: ♣ Q x x x:
   (b) ♠ K Q x: ♡ Q J 10: ◇ A x x x: ♣ K J x :
   (c) ♠ A Q x: ♡ K J x: ◇ A Q 10 x: ♣ A 10 x :
   (d) ♠ K x x: ♡ A Q x: ◇ A J x x: ♣ K x x:
   (e) ♠ K x: ♡ A Q: ◇ A J 10 x x x: ♣ A x x:

3. If your partner opens 1 N.T. weak, what would you bid in response on the following hands ?
   (a) ♠ K J x: ♡ Q x x x: ◇ K J x: ♣ x x x:
   (b) ♠ K J x: ♡ Q x x x: ◇ K J x: ♣ J 10 x:
   (c) ♠ K J x: ♡ Q J x x: ◇ K J x: ♣ J 10 x:
   (d) ♠ Q J 10 x x x: ♡ K x x: ◇ Q x: ♣ x x:
   (e) ♠ A K x x x x: ♡ K Q x: ◇ x x: ♣ x x:

4. If your partner opens 1 N.T. strong, what difference would this make to your responses, if any, on the hands in Question No. 3 above ?

QUIZ ON CHAPTER 6—ANSWERS

1. (a) 1 N.T., ideal for this bid, 13 points, evenly balanced.
   (b) 1♣. 15½ points, too strong for 1 N.T., so you bid one of the lower of your two *divided* 4-card suits.
   (c) 1♣ again, because you are too strong for 1 N.T. whether using weak or strong.
   (d) 1♠, and we hope you did not fall into this trap. This is just a straightforward opening one-bid in a 5-card major suit.
   (e) 22½ points, just that shade more than you need for 2 N.T. but still the best bid on the hand.

2. (a) 1♣. Not strong enough for 1 N.T. so the lower of your divided 4-card suits. You may not like it much, but you really must open.
   (b) 1 N.T. This hand is just right for a strong No Trump.
   (c) A perfect 2 N.T. opening bid at any vulnerability.
   (d) 1 N.T., again perfect for the bid, top limit of 17 points.
   (e) 1♢. Apart from the count which is too good for 1 N.T., you have a 6-card diamond suit to show.

3. (a) No Bid. Even if partner has 14 you cannot make up 26 points.
   (b) 11½ points, so raise to 2 N.T. If partner has 13 or 14 you have 26.
   (c) 12½ points, so a direct raise to 3 N.T. Worth chancing that he hasn't got the barest of the bare 12 points.
   (d) 2♠. It would need a near miracle to make 9 tricks at No Trumps or 10 tricks in spades, but eight in spades shouldn't be too hard.
   (e) 3♠. Now you have high game ambitions, but would prefer to play in spades, so say so.

4. (a) 2 N.T. Note the difference. This time if partner has 17, as he may well have, you add up to 26 between you.

(b) 3 N.T., knowing that you can't be *under* 26 points anyhow.

(c) 3 N.T. again, though even more confidently !

(d) 3♠. Although you have only 8 high-card points you have 10 counting distribution, which should be good enough for a game in spades.

(e) 3♠ again. No doubt in your own mind, but if partner prefers 3 N.T. you will pass.

CHAPTER 7

Change-of-Suit Responses

WE now come to the wide class of responding hands where your holding is unsuitable for a Limit Bid, either in a suit or No Trumps, and you have to respond in a new suit. You may have only a moderate hand, but you may also have enough to make you think a game contract is possible if you can find the right fit, and if you have to take violent action such as direct jump bids to make sure of getting there you will be unable to explore for the best possible contract, for which you may need to hear opener's rebid.

A RESPONSE TO AN OPENING BID MADE IN A NEW SUIT IS UNCONDITIONALLY FORCING FOR ONE ROUND UNLESS RESPONDER HAS PREVIOUSLY PASSED. You will know, therefore, that if you change the suit your partner will bid again.

Responses at the One-level:

(*a*) If you have a suit you can show at the one-level, as 1♠ over 1♡, you may show it on as little as 6 points. When counting your points, don't add extras for shortages in side-suits when you don't "agree" opener's suit—the worst tragedy you can meet on two otherwise excellent hands is a 'misfit". You may add extra values for long cards in your own suit provided it is good enough to become the trump suit or, later, when you learn to revalue your hand in the light of partner's bid.

♠ x x x	If partner opens 1♣ or 1◇, bid 1♡.
♡ K 10 x x	If he opens 1♡, bid 2♡. If he opens 1♠,
◇ A x x	bid 1 N.T.
♣ x x x	

(*b*) You may not bid at the two-level without a minimum of 8 points but if it is possible within these terms of reference you should always bid a longer suit before a shorter.

♠ K 10 x x	If partner opens 1♣ you can bid 1◇, your
♡ x x	longest suit, but if partner opens 1♡ you
◇ K x x x x	cannot, with only 6 points, bid 2◇ so you
♣ x x	bid your 4-card suit, spades, which you can
	do at the one-level. If partner bid 1♠ you
	would raise to 2♠.

(*c*) As responder you must bid first the *lower-ranking* of two equal and adjacent suits, not the higher ranking as you did as opener.

♠ Q J 10 x	If partner opens 1♣ or 1◇, bid 1♡, not 1♠.
♡ K J x x	He may have either a heart or spade suit as
◇ x x	well as his first bid, so this gives the best
♣ x x x	means of finding a fit in either. An opening
	1♡ or 1♠ bid you would raise to two of
	that suit.

(*d*) A change-of-suit response at the one level promises no more than would be required to bid 1 N.T. in the same position, i.e., 6-9 points.

♠ x x x	Over an opening 1♣ you can bid 1◇.
♡ Q x	Over 1♡ or 1♠ you are too good to pass
◇ K x x x x	with 7 points, but not good enough to bid
♣ Q x x	your diamonds at the two-level, so would
	bid 1 N.T.

Responses at the Two-level:

To make a simple change-of-suit response at the

two level you need a minimum of 8 points. You should also try to avoid bidding 4-card suits at the two-level unless you have a strong hand or need to make a temporising bid. You may, of course, still bid at the one-level in appropriate circumstances, but the extra points permit you to bid at the two-level if expedient.

♠ x x x ♡ K Q x x x ♢ A 10 x ♣ x x	Over 1♣ or 1♢ you would respond 1♡, but over 1♠, for which you have no direct raise, you are strong enough to bid 2♡. An opening 1♡ you would, of course, raise to 3♡. Remember that, opposite 1♡, your doubleton club counts one extra point.
♠ K Q x x x ♡ Q 10 x x ♢ Q x ♣ x x	Over 1♣ or 1♢ bid 1♠, your longest suit. Over 1♡ raise to 3♡ in preference to bidding spades. Over 1♠ raise to 3♠. Opposite to an opening bid in either major suit, your two doubletons count one extra point each.
♠ K 10 x ♡ K 10 x x ♢ A x x ♣ J 10 x	Over 1♣ or 1♢ bid 1♡. Over 1♡ bid 3♡. Over 1♠ it is best to make a Limit Bid of 2 N.T. because your hearts are not worth bidding at the two-level. Give yourself one less spade and one more heart, and you would bid 2♡ over 1♠.
♠ K 10 x ♡ x ♢ A Q x x x ♣ K J x x	Here is an example where, if partner opens at all, you want to get to game if possible. Over 1♣ bid 1♢, as the change of suit forces him to rebid. Over a 1♢ opening you are in a little trouble and your safest " try " is 2♣, a temporising bid to see what he says next. If he shows hearts you can bid 3 N.T. If he opens 1♡ you can safely bid 2♢, and if he rebids 2♡ again you will jump to 3 N.T. If his opening is 1♠ you bid 2♢ and, once he rebids spades, showing a minimum of five, you can raise him to 4♠. In this way you give yourself the best chance to explore for your final contract.

Forcing Bids:

If you have a really good hand and your partner, perhaps even somewhat to your surprise, opens the bidding, you are immediately *certain* of a game between you, and possibly a slam. You've got to tell your partner this at once. There must be no gentle exploring to start with or, later, you may find it impossible to convince your partner of how strong you are. In fact if you *don't* make a forcing bid he will always know that you have less than 16 points—which in turn means that with 16 points or more you must always force.

The way to do this is to make a *jump bid*, that is, a bid of one more level than is necessary, in a new suit. Over 1♡ you could *force* with 3♣ or 3♢ instead of making a simple 2♣ or 2♢ response, or bid 2♠ instead of a simple 1♠. Don't be alarmed at this idea—it does not commit you to more than a game contract at the moment, but it is **unconditionally forcing to game,** which means that your partner is ordered not to let the bidding die until at least a game contract has been reached. *Now* you can take your time exploring because you no longer fear being left in a part-score contract.

♠ K J 10 x x **♡ x** **♢ A K Q J 10** **♣ A x**	This hand may be an extreme example but it could happen. Partner opens 1♠ and immediately you are certain of at least a spade game. If you can find out that he has both the **♠A** and **♡A** you would expect to make 7♠ and if he has only one of them, at least 6♠. Bid 3♢—don't jump to 4♠. Now you can explore at leisure.
♠ x **♡ Q 10 x x** **♢ K x** **♣ A K Q x x x**	Partner opens 1♡ in support of which you have 17 points. This is *too good* for the Limit Bid of 4♡ showing 13–15 points, so you force with 3♣, thereafter taking

your time to discover whether to bid a slam or stop in 4♡.

When you have a fit for the suit your partner opens and, at the same time, want to pass on this message of extra strength, you should try to make your forcing bid in a suit ranking below the one opened. Just very rarely this may not be possible, but it won't happen often enough for you to have to trouble about it at the moment.

♠ K J x x **♡ K Q J x** **◇ A x x** **♣ K x**	If partner opens 1♡ or 1♠ you are certain of at least a game, and a slam if his hand is not a bare minimum. If you jump direct to game he may well pass. Force with 3◇, a suit in which you have first round control. This jump demands at least a game contract and suggests slam hopes if the opening bid is strong.
♠ Q x x **♡ K Q 10** **◇ K Q x** **♣ K Q J x**	Partner opens 1♠ and with 18 points you are *certain* of game. Force with 3♣ which makes sure of the bidding continuing at least to game and will give you time to find out if he is strong or weak, and has three or four of the missing Aces.

As your experience grows you will extend the use of these forcing bids. For the present you need do no more than remember that if your responding hand is good enough for you to know that **game is certain and slam is possible,** you should make an immediate game-forcing bid of a jump in a new suit which will warn your partner of the position. He in turn, if he has a good opening bid as opposed to a minimum, may well be the one to initiate slam investigations.

On pages 79 and 80 you will find a summary table of these responses but first there is one more point to be emphasised. Rules were made to be broken. As a learner, break them as seldom as possible. You will, however, undoubtedly meet situations where your hand does not come into any of the clear-cut categories illustrated, in which case choose the bid which breaks the least of the rules whilst, at the same time, making the greatest sense of your hand. This situation will arise most frequently when you are bidding over an opponent's intervening bid.

♠ K Q x
♡ x x x
♢ Q x x x
♣ J x x

If your partner opened 1♠ you would, normally, with this evenly balanced 8 point hand, bid 1 N.T. If your right-hand opponent intervened with 2♡ over your partner's 1♠ you can no longer bid 1 N.T., and you certainly can't bid 2 N.T. on 8 points. In any case, a bid in No Trumps over an intervening bid shows a good stop in the suit bid against you. Your natural bid being unavailable, you still can't pass on this hand and a bid of 2♠ is the nearest to truth that you can get.

TABLE OF RESPONDING BIDS

Raise	Points	Comments
1♠ to 2♠ or 1♡ to 2♡	6–9	Provided you have primary, that is, 4-card trump support for a major suit bid, you make a Limit Bid in that suit in preference to
1♠ to 3♠ or 1♡ to 3♡	10–12	any other bid, as the best final denomination is already known, and all that remains is to find out at what level the final contract
1♠ to 4♠ or 1♡ to 4♡	13–15	should rest. As responder, with this primary trump support, you value *short* side-suits, that is, suits other than the trump suit, adding 3 for a void, 2 for a singleton, and 1 for a doubleton.
1♠ or 1♡ to 1 N.T.	6–9	On an evenly balanced hand which does *not* contain primary trump support as above, you may
1♠ or 1♡ to 2 N.T.	10-12	make a Limit Bid in No Trumps based on the exactly similar scale given here. The demarcation
1♠ or 1♡ to 3 N.T.	13–15	between 10 and 11 points is so slight that you should be able to judge whether you have a *good* 10 (2 N.T.) or a *bad* 11 (1 N.T.)
		The above are all **Limit Bids** and **not forcing.**
In the minor suits		The same point values apply with the exception that the raise direct to four (1♣–4♣ or 1♢–4♢) is omitted as this cuts out the possibly better level of 3 N.T.

Table of Responding Bids—*cont.*

Raise	Points	Comments
Over one of a suit, new suit bid at the one-level	Not less than 6 points	At the one-level a change-of-suit response can be made in preference to bidding 1 N.T. A response at the one-level does not promise more than the 6–9 points required to bid 1 N.T. but it may be much stronger, which the subsequent bidding will show.
New suit bid at the two-level	Not less than 8 points	A change of suit response is **unconditionally forcing for one round unless the bidder has previously passed.** To raise the level by bidding a new suit at the two-level, responder promises a minimum of 8 points. Otherwise the same rules hold good, and the bid is forcing unless preceded by a pass.
Jump bid in a new suit	16 or more points	A jump bid in a new suit is **unconditionally forcing to game** and opener must keep the bidding open until at least a game and possibly a slam is reached. As experience develops you will find that you will make forcing bids of this type on less than 16 points, according to the "shape" of your hand.

QUIZ ON CHAPTER 7

1. If your partner deals and opens 1♢, what do you bid on each of the following hands ?

(a) ♠ K J x x: ♡ x x x: ♢ Q x x x: ♣ J x:
(b) ♠ K J x: ♡ x x x: ♢ Q x x x: ♣ J x x:
(c) ♠ K J x x: ♡ K 10 x x: ♢ Q x x x: ♣ J:
(d) ♠ K J x: ♡ K 10 x: ♢ Q x x: ♣ J 10 x x:
(e) ♠ K J x x: ♡ x x: ♢ x x: ♣ K x x x x:
(f) ♠ K J x: ♡ K 10 x: ♢ x x: ♣ K 10 x x x:
(g) ♠ K J x x: ♡ K 10 x x x: ♢ Q x: ♣ x x:
(h) ♠ K J x x x: ♡ K 10 x x: ♢ Q x: ♣ x x:
(i) ♠ K J x: ♡ K Q x: ♢ K Q x x: ♣ A x x:
(j) ♠ K J x: ♡ K J x: ♢ Q x x x: ♣ A x x:

2. If your partner deals and opens 1♡, what do you bid on each of the following hands ?

(a) ♠ K J x x: ♡ K J x: ♢ x x x: ♣ x x x:
(b) ♠ K J x: ♡ K J x: ♢ 10 x x x: ♣ x x x:
(c) ♠ K J x x: ♡ K J x x: ♢ x x x: ♣ x x:
(d) ♠ K J x: ♡ K J x: ♢ A K x x x: ♣ x x:
(e) ♠ A K Q J: ♡ 10 x x x: ♢ K J x: ♣ x x:
(f) ♠ A K Q: ♡ 10 x x: ♢ K x x x: ♣ Q J 10:

3. On each of the following hands, what response would you make if partner made the opening bid indicated ?

	Hand		Opening bid
(a)	♠ K J x x	(i)	1♡
	♡ Q 10 x x	(ii)	1♠
	♢ Q x x	(iii)	1 N.T. (12–14 points)
	♣ x x	(iv)	1♢
(b)	♠ x x x	(i)	1♣
	♡ K 10 x x x	(ii)	1♢
	♢ K x x x	(iii)	1♡
	♣ x	(iv)	1♠
(c)	♠ K J x x x	(i)	1♡
	♡ Q 10 x x	(ii)	1♠
	♢ x x	(iii)	1♢
	♣ Q x	(iv)	1 N.T. (12–14 points)

QUIZ ON CHAPTER 7—ANSWERS

1. (a) 1♠. Your alternative is a Limit Bid of 2♢ but 1♠ is more constructive and may enable partner, with a strong hand, to go to game in No Trumps.
   (b) 2♢. Without a 4-card major but with a 4-card fit for your partner, it is best to make the Limit Bid in diamonds. Note that you have exactly the same count but a rather different "shape".
   (c) 1♡, the lower of adjacent and equal suits in response. In support of diamonds you have 12 points, as also you have if partner bids spades next. A moment to hold back and wait for partner's rebid.
   (d) 2♣. This is a difficult hand, with no direct diamond support, no suit to bid at the one-level, and too good for 1 N.T. while too weak for 2 N.T. 2♣, your 4-card suit, is a temporising bid.
   (e) 1♠. You are not strong enough to show your long suit, and even on this weak hand, 1♠ is more constructive than 1 N.T.
   (f) 2♣. Now you are good enough to show your 5-card suit, which you bid on the principle that you show your longest suit first if your count is good enough.
   (g) 1♡. No question about this—not only is your heart suit the longer of the two, but it is also the lower-ranking.
   (h) 1♠, your 5-card suit in preference to the 4-card one.
   (i) 3♣. This is a forcing bid, telling partner your hand is so good that you are certain of a game and may possibly be able to bid a slam, depending on how good his opener is.
   (j) 3 N.T. The count justifies a jump to 4♢ but this, you may remember, is not a good bid in a minor suit. With stops in each suit it is much better to show your "shape" and count by the Limit Bid.

2. (a) 1♠, the 4-card major you can show at the one-level. Partner won't think you have a wonderful hand for certain.
   (b) 1 N.T. You have not got a respectable suit to bid at the one-level, can't bid at the two-level, can't support

hearts directly, yet must keep the bidding open on 8 points.

(c) 2♡. You have 9 points in support of hearts and a 4-card fit so you can use the ready-made Limit Bid.

(d) 2◇. An excellent hand of your own, ample points to bid at the two-level, though no direct heart support. A typical moment to await opener's rebid because, if he repeats his hearts you will know he has a minimum of five and can raise to game in this suit.

(e) 4♡. You didn't make the mistake of bidding spades, did you? With 4-card heart support and 15 points (1 for the doubleton club as responder), you raise direct to game in hearts.

(f) You have a choice here of temporising with 2◇ because you know this change of suit will compel partner to bid again, or bidding a direct 3 N.T. The latter is a better bid on a hand of this sort, on which, as you will learn when we get to the play section, you would prefer the lead to come *up* to your hand rather than *through* it.

3. (a) (i) If partner opens 1♡ you make a direct Limit Bid of 2♡.

(ii) If partner opens 1♠ you do exactly the same in spades, 2♠.

(iii) If partner opens 1 N.T. you pass. Even if he has the maximum of 14 you can't make up 26 between you.

(iv) If partner opens 1◇ you bid 1♡, showing the lower of two equal and adjacent suits.

(b) (i) If partner opens 1♣ you bid 1♡—a bid at the one-level showing your longest suit.

(ii) If partner opens 1◇ you still bid 1♡. You have a possible choice of a 2◇ Limit Bid and would use this if your right-hand opponent bid either 1♠ or 2♣, when you would *not* be good enough to bid 2♡ over him.

(iii) If partner open 1♡ you have no hesitation in raising to 2♡.

(iv) If partner opens 1♠, you have a difficult choice. You can't bid at the two-level to show your hearts but you could bid 1 N.T. With the singleton club, though, on the whole it is better to lie a little and bid 2♠. If partner curses you afterwards your alibi is that you have a choice of evils.

(c) (i) If partner bids 1♡ you raise to 3♡, the Limit Bid on 10 pts.

(ii) If partner bids 1♠ you make the Limit Bid of 3♠.

(iii) If partner bids 1◇ you bid 1♠, the 5-card suit.

(iv) If partner bids 1 N.T. your best course is to make a weak take-out into 2♠, a contract far better suited to your hand.

CHAPTER 8

Second Round Bids

THIS is the last chapter on the every-day bidding sequences, but it is important because it deals with opener's rebid, that is, his second bid, when he clarifies the strength of his opening.

You will remember that you need a minimum of 13 points to open one of a suit, but that the upper limit of the hand could be as high as 20 points, so an opening bid of 1 ♡ announces a count of 13-20 points. If Responder bids 1♠ he shows a minimum of 6 points and, because he did not force, a maximum of 15. This indicates a possible combined total of as little as 13+6=19, or as much as 20+15=35. With 26 points required for a game the first combination will yield nothing but a part-score whilst the second will, if a "fit" is found, probably yield a slam. The time has now come for this situation to be clarified.

A Sign-Off Rebid: If you have opened on a minimum hand and partner has responded with a simple change-of-suit bid which, you will remember, is forcing for one round, you must bid again. Responder's hand may be as good or better than your own and he wants to hear your rebid before he decides on the final contract. So to show your minimum you "sign off" by rebidding two of your suit if it is five or more cards in length, by rebidding 1 N.T. or by making a bid *at the two-level only* in a second suit.

♠ x x x
♡ A K 10 x x
♢ K x x
♣ Q x

You open 1♡ and partner responds 1♠. You have a minimum hand, but this change of suit is forcing. Sign off by rebidding 2♡. Note, if your partner had previously passed, his 1♠ would not have been forcing and your best course would be to pass.

♠ Q J x
♡ A Q x
♢ A J x x
♣ x x x

Playing strong No Trump you must open 1♢. If partner responds 1♡ or 1♠ you rebid 1 N.T., *not* 2♢.

♠ K J x x x
♡ A J x x x
♢ K x
♣ x

You open 1♠, the higher ranking of two equal and adjacent suits. If partner bids 2♣ or 2♢ your rebid is 2♡ which does *not* show additional strength. It merely offers two possible trump suits and asks partner to show his preference between them.

♠ K J x x x
♡ x
♢ K x
♣ A J x x x

Here you will have opened 1♣ so your rebid to 1♡ or 1♢ would be 1♠, again showing the second suit at an economical level. Notice that, had you opened 1♠ partner would have had to bid 2♡ or 2♢ and, to show your clubs, you would have had to take the bidding to the three-level which you must not do without a far stronger hand. In the same way, had you opened 1♡ in the previous example and partner had responded 2♣ or 2♢, you would have had to say 2♠ to show your second suit. If your partner liked your hearts and hated your spades he would have to bid 3♡ to put you back to that suit and this you are not strong enough to tolerate—or risk telling your partner you can tolerate.

There is one other opener's rebid which is virtually equivalent to a sign-off, and that is a *single* raise in the suit your partner bids.

♠ K J x
♡ x x x x
♢ A x x x x
♣ A

You open 1♢ and partner responds 1♡. You are, remember, forced to bid again. It would be foolish to rebid your diamonds with the 4-card heart fit so your best rebid is 2♡. Note that had your partner previously passed you would yourself pass his 1♡ bid, confident that no game existed.

♠ x x ♡ A Q x x x ◇ K 10 x x ♣ K x	In this last example you open 1♡ and partner responds 1♠. Your correct rebid is 2◇, not 2♡. 2◇ does not show extra strength but merely offers a second possible suit in your mutual search for a "fit".

Two important Acol rules fall into place here:—

1. *Opener's* **simple change-of-suit rebid is not forcing and does not show additional strength.**

2. **If opener has additional strength he must show it by means of a jump rebid.**

In the first of these rules the difficulty for beginners is to remember the difference between opener and responder. Responder's simple change of suit *is* forcing (unless he has previously passed) but opener's is not. Compare these sequences:—

South	*North*	
1♠ ?	2◇	South opens 1♠ and North changes the suit to 2◇ which is forcing, so South must make a rebid.
 1♠ ?	No 2◇	This time North passed originally, so when North bids 2◇ over South's 1♠ it is not forcing and South may pass if he wishes.
1♠ 2♡	2◇ ?	South opens 1♠, North changes the suit to 2◇ which is forcing, and South rebids 2♡, showing a second suit. But this bid is

not forcing and North may pass if he sees fit.

The natural corrolary to this, of course, lies in Rule 2, that if opener has additional strength he must show it by a jump rebid. Before we examine these jump rebids, let's take a look at opener's sign-off rebids from responder's point of view.

Responder's Eye View of Opener's Rebids:

Your partner opens 1♡ to which you respond 1♠ and he rebids 2♡.

♠ K J x x **♡ x x x** **♢ A x x x** **♣ x x**	On this hand you pass without a second thought. Your 1♠ response was a near minimum, so you see no future beyond a possible part score, and you're glad to have even as good a "fit" as three hearts.
♠ K J 10 x **♡ Q x** **♢ A x x x** **♣ K 10 x**	You make a rebid of your own of 3 N.T. After all, partner has promised you 13 points and must have something outside his hearts to help you. You are the one who knows you have a minimum of 26 between you, so it is up to you.
♠ A Q J x x x **♡ x** **♢ x x** **♣ x x x x**	Now you sign off yourself by taking partner's 2♡ out into 2♠. You have no hope of game, you hate his hearts, and his support, for your suit can hardly be worse than your's for his!

On these next examples your partner opens 1♢, you bid 1♠ and his rebid this time is 1 N.T., indicating about a 15-point hand with no particular enthusiasm for diamonds—probably a 4-card suit.

♠ K J x x **♡ K x x** **♢ Q x** **♣ x x x x**	On this hand you pass. Partner's maximum count is 15 points so you cannot have a combined 26. A part-score, therefore, is the best you can hope for and No Trumps as good a contract as any.
♠ K J x x **♡ K x x** **♢ Q x** **♣ Q J 10 x**	You raise opener's rebid to 3 N.T. Even if his hand is the barest minimum 13 points you have 25½ between you which, with only a little luck, may well produce game.
♠ A K J x x x **♡ x** **♢ Q x** **♣ x x x x**	Here you take the 1 N.T. bid out into 2♠ which, in the light of your knowledge of his hand, is a weak take-out. Your suit is bound to be valuable if used as trumps but it is most unlikely that you can make a game.

♠ K J x x x ♡ x ◇ x x ♣ K J x x x	This time you rebid 2♣ over 1 N.T. This second suit bid is *not* forcing and it will warn your partner that your hand is both unbalanced and weak. At his next turn he will show you which of your two suits he prefers.

On these four hands your partner opens 1◇, you respond 1♡, and his rebid is to raise to 2♡.

♠ x x ♡ A Q x x x ◇ x x x ♣ Q J x	You pass, rightly feeling that you would need a lot of luck to make ten tricks and must content yourself with a part-score.
♠ x x x ♡ A Q J x x ◇ A Q x ♣ Q x	Here you bid 4♡. You have a good enough hand to have opened 1♡ yourself, so if partner can open and then support your suit, even if his hand is minimum you should have a good chance for game.
♠ A x x ♡ K J x x ◇ J 10 ♣ K 10 x x	This time you show your count by yourself rebidding 2 N.T. Opener will know that you have 10-12 points and could have made a first response of 2 N.T. but preferred to show a major suit first. He can pass this, convert to 3♡ or, if the omens seem good, bid 4♡.
♠ Q 10 x ♡ A K x x ◇ K 10 x ♣ Q J x	A rebid of 3 N.T. from you is now in order. You could have bid this as your first response on your count of 15 points, but made a change-of-suit bid first knowing you would get another chance to bid.

Gradually, you see, both partners will be building up a picture of the combined power of their hands. Opener's rebid clarifies his first bid and if, as in all these examples, it is a near minimum, he shows this by signing off. Responder can then himself pass or bid again as he sees fit.

There is an important item which has been mentioned several times, an explanation of which falls into place here, and that is showing preference.

Preference:

Showing "preference" operates at any level of the auction, but most frequently at these low levels, so if you learn about it now you will be able to apply the rules whenever the situations arise.

If a player bids a suit and his partner raises that suit, it is said to be "agreed" and no question of "preference" will arise. If a player, however, bids two different suits, he is showing that he holds two possible trump suits and is asking his partner to choose between them. This is the main object of the careful selection of which of two suits to bid first—the facilitating of the rebid to show the second suit.

Opener bids 1♠, you respond 2♣ and he rebids 2♡ not, you will remember, showing extra strength but suggesting a minimum or near minimum opener with the choice of two suits for trumps. Here are four possible responding hands:—

♠ Q x x
♡ x x x
◇ Q x
♣ K J 10 x x

Although you have three of each you actually prefer the spades and you show this preference by rebidding 2♠. **This does not constitute a raise in spades.** It merely shows that, of the two, you prefer spades to hearts. Even with two little spades and one little heart you would still *prefer* spades, so a return to the first bid suit at the lowest available level is a simple preference bid. Your 2♣ response was minimum and you have no justification for doing more.

♠ x x
♡ Q x x
◇ Q x x
♣ K J 10 x x

Your 2♣ response was minimum and of your partner's two suits this time you prefer hearts, which you show *by passing* his 2♡ bid.

♠ A x x
♡ Q 10 x x
◇ x
♣ A K x x x

You bid 4♡. If this surprises you, note that if partner had opened 1♡ you would have made a 4♡ Limit Bid, so even if his opening is minimum, with this hand you want to play in game. You not only *prefer* hearts, but have a marked desire to play in game in that denomination, so give a jump preference bid.

♠ A Q 10
♡ K x
◇ x x x
♣ K J x x x

Your hand is too good to give a simple preference bid to 2♠ but you are not yet certain whether opener has a 5-card spade suit. Although you have 13 points you cannot make the final decision yourself. Give a jump preference to 3♠ which opener will interpret as showing a good strong 2♣ response and less than four spades *or you would have had a Limit Bid raise in the first place.* Though not forcing, this jump preference bid is highly encouraging, and opener will go to game if he can find any justification for doing so.

♠ Q x x
♡ K Q 10 x
◇ A J 10 x
♣ x x

Partner opens 1♣ to which you respond 1◇ and he rebids 1♠. Now your common-sense bid is 3 N.T. No question of preference arises when you have a "stop" such as this in the unbid suit, hearts. If opener simply cannot bear this contract he will bid 4♣, which will be asking you for preference and you, preferring it, will convert to 4♠.

♠ A 10 x x
♡ K Q x x
◇ x x
♣ Q 10 x

Here you bid 1♡ over partner's opening 1♣ and he rebids 1♠. You immediately revalue your hand seeing that, opposite a 1♠ opening, you would have had a Limit Bid raise of 3♠. This you now give—a jump preference as well as a Limit Bid.

♠ Q x x
♡ K J x x
◇ x x
♣ Q x x x

Again you bid 1♡ over the opening 1♣ and partner responds 1♠. Show your preference by bidding 2♣, all your hand is worth. Put the ♠A in place of the ♠Q, and you would be strong enough for a jump preference to 3♣.

♠ x x x x
♡ K J x x
◇ Q x
♣ x x x

For the last time you bid 1♡ over 1♣ and partner rebids 1♠. You show your preference for spades by passing. Your 1♡ was completely minimum and, let's face it, you would have been glad if you'd been allowed to pass 1♣. Rightly you didn't, so have found this far more acceptable suit to play in.

When your partner opens the bidding in one suit and rebids in a second you do not *know* that the two suits are equally long. The second suit may be as long as the first, or it may be shorter. Whichever it is it won't be *longer* than the first because the rule is that, with two suits to show, you bid the longer first. From this it follows that if you have equal support for both suits, either equally good or equally bad, you should return your partner to his first bid suit, not leave him in his second, however poor your hand. This, of course, will *not* constitute a raise. Suppose your partner opens the bidding with 1♡. On each of the following hands you would respond 1♠, and then partner rebids 2◇.

♠ K J x x
♡ 10 x x
◇ Q x x
♣ x x x

You have three cards in each of partner's suits and the diamonds are actually stronger. You must, however, give him preference to 2♡ as there is a chance that his first suit is longer than his second.

♠ K J x x
♡ x x
◇ Q x x x
♣ J 10 x

Show your marked preference for diamonds by passing the 2◇ bid. You have at least found a 4-4 trump fit.

♠ A Q x x
♡ K J 10
◇ x x x
♣ Q x x

This time you can give a jump preference bid to 3♡. Your partner won't expect 4-card heart support as you did not make a Limit Bid in hearts in the first place, but he will know your 1♠ was far from minimum. He may pass, or he may try 3 N.T. or 4♡.

♠ **A K Q x x x**	Repeat your own suit, spades, with a jump
♡ **K x**	to 3♠. As you did not force in the first
◇ **x x**	place opener will get a very accurate
♣ **x x x**	picture—no support for his red suits, much

better than a minimum 1♠ bid in the first place though not enough for a force. With the particular opening hand we are considering, he would pass 3♠, but give him the ♣A in place of the ♣K and he would raise you to 4♠ which you would have a very good chance of making.

Earlier in this chapter you learned that if opener has a strong opening hand he must find a way to show it which, of course, means *avoiding* making a sign-off rebid. Occasionally this is unavoidable, but more usually opener can find an expressive rebid. Here No Trump Limit Bids may well come to his aid.

Opener's Limit Rebids in No Trumps:

These Limit Bids, like the responder's Limit Bids we have already studied, give the strength of the bidder's hand, both upper and lower limit, within a very close range. As responder making a No Trump Limit Bid, your values were tabulated from 6 points upwards to 15 (page 56). As opener you have already guaranteed 13 points, so quite a different set of values operates. In fact there are two slightly differing sets of values, depending on whether responder has bid at the one-level or the two-level.

These rebids may be made, according to strength, on hands where either opener has no long suit he wants to repeat, or where responder's bid fills a gap in his hand.

Here is a table setting out the counts required in detail:—

1.	If responder bids at the *one-level* (1♡–1♠ or 1♣–1◇)	Opener's rebid of 1 N.T. shows 13–15 points.	This will be a hand on which, because using a strong No Trump, you could not open 1 N.T. or you did not fancy it for No Trumps because it was completely lacking in the suit responder has now bid.
2.	Do.	Opener's rebid of 2 N.T. shows 16–18 points.	Here you will have one of the stronger hands, either evenly balanced or happy to play in No Trumps once responder has shown a holding in its danger-suit.
3.	Do.	Opener's rebid of 3 N.T. shows 19–20 points.	This will be the same only stronger still, opener being unwilling to play below game level if responder can bid at all.
4.	If responder bids at the *two-level* (1♡–2♣ or 1♡–2◇)	Opener's rebid of 2 N.T. shows 15–17 points.	This is a very frequent use of the bid to avoid making a sign-off on a 15 or 16 point hand. Sometimes one even takes a chance on one suit to avoid a sign-off.

5.	Do.	Opener's rebid of 3 N.T. shows 18 or more points.	Again, opener is unwilling to play in less than a game contract.
6.	If responder bids 1 N.T. over a suit opening.	Opener's rebid of 2 N.T. shows 17–18 points, and Opener's rebid of 3 N.T. shows 19 points.	The raises are made because, in the first case, it is possible that responder has nearer 9 pts. than the minimum of 6, in which case he will bid 3 N.T. In the second, opener is unwilling to play below game level if responder has even 6 points.

Like every other bid in the Acol system there's sound logic behind these, so they should fall easily into place in your mind. In Nos. 1, 2 and 3 in the table, responder's bid in a new suit at the one-level promised only the minimum of 6 points. Opener now tells his own count, within very fine limits, leaving responder free to judge the final contract. If he knows opener's possible maximum is 15 points and he is weak himself, he can pass. With a stronger hand he can take further action. If responder is told, as in No. 2, that his partner has 16-18 points, he needs only 10 himself to be *certain* of a combined 26, and even with 8 or 9 will probably chance the possible shortage of 2 points and bid game. In No. 3 opener has bid game anyway, so responder's only consideration will be whether to leave the contract in No Trumps or take out into a suit.

The reason for the different counts in Nos. 4, 5 and 6 is simply that, if responder has bid at the two-level, he has a guaranteed minimum of 8 points and opener, therefore, needs fewer to achieve a combined count of 26. In No. 4 responder needs only 9 points for the target and in No. 5 the promised 8 is enough.

The same reasoning applies if responder has bid 1 N.T., as in No. 6. If opener rebids 2 N.T. he asks responder to go to game if he holds maximum rather than minimum for his bid, and with 19 points opener obviously bids 3 N.T. direct.

You will remember that responder's 1 N.T. over 1♣ showed 8-10 points, not the usual 6-9, so if the sequence has, in fact, been 1♣–1 N.T., opener's values for his raises may be scaled down to allow for 8-10 in responder's hand.

♠ Q 10 x
♡ K J x
◇ Q J x
♣ A Q x x

Too strong for a weak 1 N.T. bid so open 1♣. Rebid 1 N.T. over any change-of-suit response. Add one point, say by substituting the ◇K for the ◇Q and your rebid would be 2 N.T. Top it up still further by making the diamonds ◇ A K x and you would rebid 3 N.T.

♠ K J x
♡ A Q 10 x x
◇ K x
♣ Q 10 9

You open 1♡ and responder bids 2◇. You are too strong to sign off in 2♡, especially when you know responder has a minimum of 8 points and holds your shortest suit. Rebid 2 N.T., showing a minimum of 15 points, and avoiding a sign-off.

♠ K J x x
♡ A 10 x
◇ K Q x
♣ K J x

17 points. Open 1♠ and, if partner bids two of any other suit, rebid 2 N.T. Add one point, say the ♡J in place of the ♡10, and your rebid would be 3 N.T. If partner responds 1 N.T. to your 1♠, rebid 2 N.T.

So much for opener's No Trump Limit Bids. If you happen to be in responder's seat you have a choice of showing no further interest by passing, or of signing off by repeating your own suit at the lowest available level, telling partner that, in spite of knowing his count, you are not interested in a game contract. Alternatively, you can raise to game, either in opener's original suit, in No Trumps, or your own suit, but never forget that a player who has made a Limit Bid will not bid again unless forced, so any further action is strictly up to you.

♠ Q 10 x x x x **♡ x x** **◇ x x x** **♣ K J**	If partner opens 1♡ you respond 1♠. If he rebids 2♡ you take out into 2♠. If he rebids 2 N.T. you take out into 3♠. If he rebid 3 N.T. you take out into 4♠, the only contract with any hope in it for your hand.
♠ K J x x **♡ x x** **◇ Q x x x** **♣ J x x**	Partner opens 1♡ and you respond 1♠ to which he rebids 2 N.T. Your sign off is to pass. Even if he has the maximum of 18 points you have only 25 between you.
♠ A K x x x x **♡ x x** **◇ x x x** **♣ K J**	In contrast to the first of these hands above, after 1♡ — 1♠ you are not at all unhappy when opener rebids 2 N.T. showing 16–18 points. You feel pretty certain of making game if you play in spades, but if you rebid 3♠ opener will take the hint and pass, so your rebid must be 4♠.
♠ K J x x **♡ x x x** **◇ A J x** **♣ J 10 x**	Here, over 1♡ — 1♠ — 2 N.T. you know for certain that the combined hands contain a minimum of 26 points, so you raise to 3 N.T.

Opener's Jump Rebids: There are three divisions in this category of jump rebids which are used to show additional strength not of the No Trump type. The first of these, a jump rebid in the suit he has opened, is a Limit Bid, therefore *not* forcing though highly encouraging.

♠ x x ♡ A K J x x x ◇ A x ♣ K x x	Opener bids 1♡ and, over 1♠, 2♣ or 2◇, rebids 3♡. This shows a minimum of a 6-card trump suit and approximately seven playing tricks with this suit as trumps. Here there are only 15 honour card points

but the hand is far too strong for a sign-off rebid of 2♡.

Responder will, of course, review his hand in the light of this knowledge, a major feature of which will be that even a doubleton in hearts will probably be adequate trump support. On a bare minimum responder will exercise his right to pass a Limit Bid, but should accept the encouragement if he possibly can and bid to game.

The second division covers a jump bid in *responder's* suit, which is also a Limit Bid.

♠ K J x x ♡ A Q x x x ◇ K x ♣ Q x	Partner has bid 1♠ to your opening 1♡. You must accept the fact that he may have responded on 6 points and a 4-card spade suit and *ask* him if he has done this or if he is stronger. You rebid 3♠, a jump bid but

still a Limit Bid. If responder is weak he can pass and if reasonably good he can advance to 4♠.

The third division of opener's jump rebid is a jump bid in a new suit. This is a very important one to remember as it **is unconditionally forcing to game** and shows that the hand is very strong, probably in the upper region of the 13-20 points for an opening bid.

♠ A Q x x x ♡ A J 10 x x ◇ A x ♣ K	You open 1♠ and partner bids 2♣. Clearly this hand is very different from the sign-off types we examined at the beginning of this chapter. Partner has a minimum of 6 points and you want to be in game for certain, so your rebid is 3♡.

If you are responder when this sort of bid is made

by your partner you must judge what action to take. Remember you must take some action as the bid is forcing to game, and you must not pass. You must judge between raising partner's second suit, giving simple or jump preference to his first suit, repeating your own suit if length in that is your only asset, or bidding 3 N.T. if you have a stop in the fourth, as yet unbid, suit.

Opener's Rebid if Responder has Forced:

Finally, we must take a brief look at opener's rebid if responder makes an immediate game force to the opening bid, that is, a jump of one more level than necessary for a simple change-of-suit bid in a new suit. This is not as difficult as you may be thinking. Just look at your hand and decide what you had intended to rebid if partner had made a simple change-of-suit bid instead of a jump, *and make this same response at the forced higher level.* If you have opened 1♠ intending to rebid 2♠ over your partner's 2♣, 2♢ or 2♡ response, instead of which he forces with 3♣, rebid 3♠. This is still a sign-off bid but at least confirms length in spades. If you have opened 1♠ intending to rebid 2♡ over 2♣ or 2♢ and partner forces with 3♣, show your hearts as you had intended but at the forced higher level of 3♡. If you had intended a Limit Bid in No Trumps, make the same bid again at the forced higher level. That is to say, if you intended to bid 1 N.T. after an opening of 1♣, over any response from partner and he forces with a bid of two in any suit, rebid 2 N.T. If you had intended to rebid 2 N.T., make your rebid 3 N.T.

If you had intended to make the very strong rebid of 3 N.T. it's another story, because now you will know that the combined hands must go slam-hunting, which is too much to ask of you here.

QUIZ ON CHAPTER 8

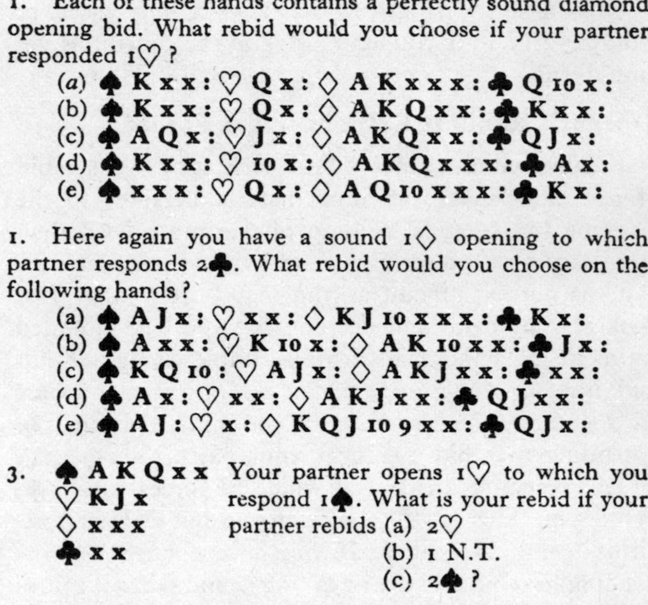

1. Each of these hands contains a perfectly sound diamond opening bid. What rebid would you choose if your partner responded 1♡?

(*a*) ♠ K x x : ♡ Q x : ◇ A K x x x : ♣ Q 10 x :
(b) ♠ K x x : ♡ Q x : ◇ A K Q x x : ♣ K x x :
(c) ♠ A Q x : ♡ J x : ◇ A K Q x x : ♣ Q J x :
(d) ♠ K x x : ♡ 10 x : ◇ A K Q x x x : ♣ A x :
(e) ♠ x x x : ♡ Q x : ◇ A Q 10 x x x : ♣ K x :

1. Here again you have a sound 1◇ opening to which partner responds 2♣. What rebid would you choose on the following hands?

(a) ♠ A J x : ♡ x x : ◇ K J 10 x x x : ♣ K x :
(b) ♠ A x x : ♡ K 10 x : ◇ A K 10 x x : ♣ J x :
(c) ♠ K Q 10 : ♡ A J x : ◇ A K J x x : ♣ x x :
(d) ♠ A x : ♡ x x : ◇ A K J x x : ♣ Q J x x :
(e) ♠ A J : ♡ x : ◇ K Q J 10 9 x x : ♣ Q J x :

3. ♠ A K Q x x
♡ K J x
◇ x x x
♣ x x

Your partner opens 1♡ to which you respond 1♠. What is your rebid if your partner rebids (a) 2♡
(b) 1 N.T.
(c) 2♣?

4. ♠ K Q x
♡ K x x
◇ x x
♣ A Q J x x

Again your partner opens 1♡, to which you respond 2♣. What is your rebid if partner rebids (a) 2♡
(b) 2◇
(c) 3♣?

5. ♠ K Q x x
♡ J x x
◇ x x x
♣ J x x

For the third time your partner opens 1♡ and here you respond 1♠. What is your rebid if partner rebids
(a) 2♡
(b) 2◇
(c) 2 N.T.?

QUIZ ON CHAPTER 8—ANSWERS

1. (a) 1 N.T. You have "something in everything" and partner has bid your weakest suit.
   (b) 2 N.T., the Limit Bid which tells your partner you have 16–18 points.
   (c) 3 N.T., showing a minimum of 18 points.
   (d) 3♢. Your hand is not very safe to suggest No Trumps, but your partner may be able to bid 3 N.T. once he knows how good your diamonds are.
   (e) 2♢, the simple sign-off bid on a weak hand which only managed to add up to 13 because of the fifth and sixth diamonds.

   Remember that, on each of these hands, your partner promised you only that he had a minimum of 6 points. He will take further action if he can.

2. (a) 2♢, the sign-off bid on a near minimum hand with a 6-card suit.
   (b) 2 N.T., the Limit Bid showing, in this situation, 15–17 points.
   (c) 3 N.T., the Limit Bid showing 18 points.
   (d) 3♣. You can't offer No Trumps but you can raise your partner's club bid in preference to signing off in diamonds.
   (e) 3♢, the jump bid showing seven playing tricks at diamonds.

   Remember that, with your partner having responded at the two-level, he has promised you a minimum of 8 points.

3. (a) 4♡. Once partner has rebid his hearts your hand is worth this bid.
   (b) 3 N.T. If partner has 13 your total is 26 and your spade suit should prove invaluable.
   (c) 4♠. The combined hands should produce a game but if partner likes your suit that is clearly the best contract.

4. (a) 4♡. Your own hand is of opening strength and once partner has rebid his suit you can go straight to game in it.

(b) 3 N.T. Again, the combined count justifies a game contract and if partner stops both red suits this should be the best spot.

(c) 5♣. A lot of tricks to make, but no one has mentioned a diamond stop so don't try No Trumps.

5. (a) No bid. You responded on a bare minimum and, not having been forced, pass as soon as you can.

(b) 2♡, giving partner preference to his first bid suit which does *not* constitute a raise in hearts.

(c) No Bid. Even if partner has the maximum of 18 you don't total 26 between you, and your hand is depressingly barren to think of taking a chance on 3 N.T.

CHAPTER 9

The Acol Strong Two Opening Bids & Responses

♠♡♣◇♠♡♣◇♠♡♣◇♠♡♣◇♠♡♣◇♠♡♣◇♠♡♣◇

SOMETIMES you will pick up a hand so good that you feel you really must open something better than a one-bid in a suit. Very strong hands fall into two classes, the first of which is called the Acol Strong Two.

You have already learned how to open one of a suit and make your rebid a jump to three in it, to show a 6-card suit and seven playing tricks in that suit. With one trick more, that is, eight playing tricks, you may open with a Strong Two. This immediately tells your partner that you have an exceptionally strong hand *based on suit length rather than high card points*.

Note: You **cannot** open a Strong Two of this sort in Clubs. Two Clubs as an opening bid has a special meaning which we shall be dealing with in the next chapter. So Strong Two opening bids can be made in Spades, Hearts and Diamonds.

As your experience grows you will learn to extend the use of these bids but, for the present, you should think of them as suitable for two types of hands:—

1. Strong single-suited hands containing eight playing tricks at the suit bid.
2. Powerful two-suiters which, though they may not

contain the full eight playing tricks on their own, are likely to do so if a fit with partner can be found.

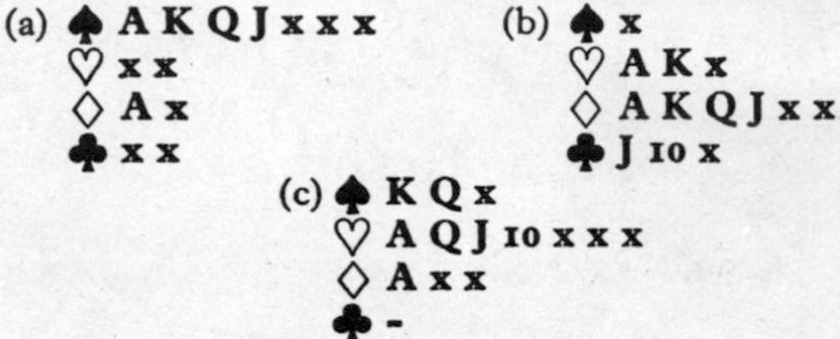

These three hands all qualify in the first class, (a) for an opening of 2♠ because you fully expect to win seven spade tricks and the ♢A. The second qualifies for a 2♢ opening because only very bad luck will prevent you from making six diamond tricks plus the ♡A-K, and (c) is a 2♡ opening bid. You are morally certain to make at least six hearts, one spade and the ♢A. Note that all three are based on *distribution*, which includes one unusually long and strong suit.

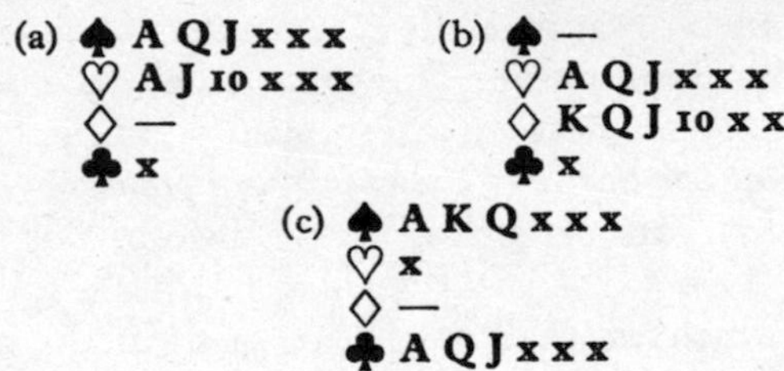

These three hands qualify under the second class, being extremely strong two suiters. On (a) you would open 2♠ intending to show hearts on the second round. On (b) you would open 2♡ intending next to bid the diamonds, and on (c) you would open 2♠ again, intending to show clubs on the next round.

From responder's point of view, when he hears his partner make a Strong Two opening bid, he does not know which class it is in and for this reason **opening Strong Two bids are unconditionally forcing for one round.**

Even with nothing at all in your hand you must keep the bidding open for one round, for which there are, actually, two reasons:—

1. Opener may have more than eight certain tricks in his hand, even enough to make game on his own, but he wishes first to investigate your hand to see whether you could, between you, bid a slam.
2. He may have a hand from Class II, where he is anxious to find the best fit with your hand, however weak it is.

♠ A K Q J 10 x x
♡ A Q J x
♢ x
♣ x

Even with the worst possible luck, declarer could only lose four tricks on this hand, but if responder holds as little as the ♡10 he will only lose three tricks. If he weren't certain you would respond to an opening 2♠ he would have to open 4♠ and risk missing a possible slam. If he is sure, he can open 2♠ without fear.

♠ x
♡ x x x x
♢ x x x x
♣ x x x x

Perhaps this is your hand when your partner makes an opening Strong Two bid in spades. Suppose his hand is either (a) or (c) in the group of hands to illustrate class II. You have 4 card support for any suit except spades, so give partner his chance to show his second suit if he has one.

The Negative Response: If your hand does not contain one of the "positive" responses we shall be discussing in a moment, you must respond with the "negative" of 2 N.T. Thereafter you are permitted to pass opener's rebid *unless* this is a jump in a new suit below game level.

South	*North*	
2♡	2 N.T.	As North in this sequence, you may pass South's rebid of 3◇ on a blank hand, or,
3◇	?	if you have it, give him preference to his first suit by bidding 3♡.
2♠	2 N.T.	This time South's rebid shows he is two-suited and, as it is a jump in a new suit
4◇	?	below game level, is **forcing to game.** The rules for showing preference may come in useful here, but bid again you *must*.

South	*North*	
2♠	2 N.T.	Here South's jump rebid is already at game level so you are not compelled to
4♡	?	bid again. You would, however, show preference for spades if you have it by converting 4♡ to 4♠. Even with an equal number of hearts and spades, return him to his first bid suit.

Positive Responses:

With as little as one certain trick in your hand and a biddable suit, you may show the suit if it does not raise the level of the bidding, that is, you could bid 2♡ over 2◇, or 2♠ over 2♡. If you have to *raise* the level (2♡—3◇) you must have at least a trick and a half and a 5-card suit. This is merely an extension of bidding at a lower level, where you needed 6 points to bid at the one-level and 8 at the two-level.

If it is possible, however, it is usually best to give partner a direct raise in his suit. You've seen the sort of suit—or suits—he will have and probably the best news you will be able to give him is that his suit is o.k. by you. Three to an honour or even any three of the suit will be adequate support.

You must *not* give an immediate raise of partner's suit, even if you like it, unless your hand contains the requirements for a positive response. You must bid the negative 2 N.T. first and then, when he rebids, put him up in his suit.

There are two important classes of hands suitable for a direct raise in opener's suit and these are:—

1. A double raise, that is, 2♡—4♡, or 2◇—4◇. This shows good trump support, a count of 10-12 points **and no ace or void.**
2. A single raise in opener's suit (2♡—3♡, or 2◇—3◇). This is an unlimited bid and may be either strong or weak, but it guarantees trump support **and at least one Ace or void.**

You can see from these two rules that a single raise may be weaker than a double raise, or it may be much stronger, agreeing the suit while you know that you propose to go slam-hunting later.

Any positive response is forcing to game, so, as responder, you know opener will rebid.

If you have an evenly balanced hand of about 10–12 points without adequate trumps to give a direct raise, and provided you have **no Ace or void,** you should respond 3 N.T., not 2 N.T. which would be the negative, to an opening Strong Two. If your 10–12 points include an Ace or void you must show a suit instead.

There is one other immediate response you should know and that is an immediate jump in a new suit. This shows a solid self-supporting suit of your own with which you don't need any help and also, by inference, denies support for your partner's suit.

Here are the responses set out in the form of a table, which you may find helpful.

Positive bid	Holding	Comments and Examples
Single raise in opener's suit:— (2♡—3♡)	Trump support plus **at least one Ace or void**	Trump support may be only a doubleton-honour or x x x as it will be opposite a powerful suit. You may have more than one Ace or void but must have at least one. ♠ **x x x:** ♡ **K x x:** ◇ **x x x:** ♣ **A x x x:** Raise 2♠, 2♡ or 2◇ to three of that suit.
Double raise (2♡—4♡ or 2◇—4◇)	Good trump support, 10—12 points and **no Ace or void**	The double raise specifically *denies* any first-round control, while the single raise is unlimited and may have one or more first round controls. ♠ **K x x x:** ♡ **K x x x:** ◇ **Q J x:** ♣ **x x:** Raise 2♠ or 2♡ to four of that suit.
Take-out into new suit at same level (2◇—2♡ or 2♡—2♠)	8 or more points and a biddable suit	If there is a choice between a direct raise of opener's suit or showing a new suit, make the direct raise. ♠ **K x x:** ♡ **KQ x x x:** ◇ **x x x:** ♣ **x x:** If opener bids 2♠ or 2♡, raise to game in either. If he opens 2◇ bid 2♡.

Positive bid	Holding	Comments and Examples
Take-out into new suit at three-level (2 ♢—3 ♣ or 2 ♡—3 ♢)	At least a 5-card suit and 9 or more points.	As at the one-level, you need a slightly beiter hand to raise the level of the bidding than to bid at the same level. ♠ **K x x:** ♡ **x x:** ♢ **A J x x x:** ♣ **J 10 x:** Raise 2 ♠ to 3 ♠, the best news for your partner, showing trump support and at least one Ace or void. Over 2 ♡ bid 3 ♢.
Jump bid in a new suit	A suit of your own as good as seven headed by A-K-Q or six headed by A-K-Q-J	This shows a solid self-supporting trump suit of your own which does not require support and by inference denies support for partner's suit. ♠ **A K Q J x x:** ♡ **x:** ♢ **x x x x:** ♣ **x x:** If partner opens 2 ♡, bid 3 ♠. Transpose the hearts and diamonds, and you would bid 3 ♡.
3 N.T.	An evenly balanced hand with 10—12 pts. and **no Ace or void.**	As with the other direct bids to game, this also guarantees **no Ace or void.** It also, by inference, denies good trump support. ♠ **x x:** ♡ **K Q x x:** ♢ **K J x x:** ♣ **K x x:** Over 2 ♠ bid 3 N.T. Over 2 ♡ bid 4 ♡ or over 2 ♢ bid 4 ♢.

QUIZ ON CHAPTER 9

1. What opening bids would you make on the following hands?

(a) ♠ x x: ♡ A K Q J x x: ◇ x x x: ♣ A K:
(b) ♠ x x: ♡ A K Q 10 x: ◇ x x x: ♣ A K x:
(c) ♠ A Q J 10 x x: ♡ A K Q x x: ◇ x x: ♣ —:
(d) ♠ A Q x x: ♡ K 10 x: ◇ K x x: ♣ J 10 x:
(e) ♠ K J 9 x x x: ♡ A x: ◇ A Q x: ♣ K x:
(f) ♠ A x: ♡ x: ◇ A K Q J x x x: ♣ x x x:
(g) ♠ x: ♡ K Q J 10 x x: ◇ A K Q x x x: ♣ —:

2. If your partner opened the bidding with 2♠ what would you bid on the following hands?

(a) ♠ K x x x: ♡ J x x x: ◇ K x: ♣ Q J x:
(b) ♠ K x x x: ♡ A x x x: ◇ K x: ♣ Q x x:
(c) ♠ K x x x: ♡ x x x x: ◇ x x: ♣ Q x x:
(d) ♠ K x x: ♡ A x x x x: ◇ K x: ♣ Q x x:
(e) ♠ K x: ♡ K Q J x x: ◇ K x: ♣ Q x x x:
(f) ♠ x x: ♡ x: ◇ A K Q J x x x: ♣ x x x:
(g) ♠ 10 x x x: ♡ K Q J x: ◇ K x: ♣ x x x:

3. You deal and open the bidding with 2♡ to which your partner responds 2 N.T. What do you rebid on the following hands?

(a) ♠ x x: ♡ A K Q 10 9 x: ◇ A K x: ♣ x x:
(b) ♠ A 10 x: ♡ A K J x x x x: ◇ —: ♣ A x x:
(c) ♠ x: ♡ A K Q 10 x x: ◇ A K Q J x: ♣ x:

QUIZ ON CHAPTER 9—ANSWERS

1. (a) 2♡, because you are confident that, with any luck at all, you can win 8 tricks at hearts.
   (b) 1♡, a perfectly normal opening bid.
   (c) 2♠, because you want to be sure of a chance to show your hearts if partner can't support spades.
   (d) 1 N.T., again, a perfectly normal hand.
   (e) 1♠. It is a good strong hand, but not good enough for any other bid.
   (f) 2◇. This time you are sure of seven diamond tricks and the ♠A.
   (g) 2♡, to make certain of playing in at least a game. If partner responds 2 N.T. you intend to rebid 4◇, the forcing jump bid.

2. (a) 4♠, a double jump on good trump support, about 10 points and no Ace or void.
   (b) 3♠ on a stronger hand, please note, than the double raise above. This shows spades support and at least one Ace or void.
   (c) 2 N.T. In spite of your spade support you must deny "positive" values on the first round.
   (d) 3♠, giving direct support which is better than bidding your own hearts.
   (e) 3♡. You can't give an immediate spade raise but are strong enough to show your own suit at the three-level.
   (f) 4◇, the jump response to show a solid and self-supporting suit of your own.
   (g) 4♠, again the double jump on good spade support, " positive " honour values and no Ace or void.

3. (a) 3♡. You have no more than your opening bid but responder, knowing the sort of hand you have, may be able to put you to game on the second round. With a very bad hand he will pass.
   (b) 4♡. This time you need so little help from partner that however weak he is you want to try to make a game.
   (c) 4◇, the forcing jump bid. If partner has any diamonds he will raise to 5◇, otherwise he will put you back to 4♡.

CHAPTER 10

Conventional Bids
The Acol Opening Two Club
Bids & Responses
and " Blackwood "

♠♡♣◇♠♡♣◇♠♡♣◇♠♡♣◇♠♡♣◇♠♡♣◇♠♡♣◇

UP to now all the bids you have learned have been strictly related to the cards in your hand, that is, if you have a good spade suit you bid spades, if you have an evenly balanced hand you bid No Trumps, and so on. Now you have to learn something quite new, the "conventional" bids. Up to a point any bid could be said to be conventional as it aims at indicating a specific holding or type of hand, but a true conventional bid is purely artificial and carries a meaning other than the apparent natural one.

The Acol Opening Two Club bid is an artificial conventional one and could, in fact, be made without a single club in your hand. It is used to show a "rock-crusher"—a hand of enormous power virtually capable of producing game on its own strength. It is also unconditionally forcing and the negative or "bust" reply is 2◇ which, equally, bears no relation to the diamond holding but denies the requirements for a "positive" response. Before we consider responses, however, we'll have a look at some 2♣ opening bids, of which there are two distinct classes, powerful No Trump hands and powerful suit hands.

Class I. No Trump Type Hands:

If you turn back to p. 68 and make sure you know what you have already learned about Two No Trump opening bids, you will be well on the way to knowing a No Trump type of 2♣ opener when you meet one, because all you need is a few extra points. On 20–22 points in an evenly balanced hand you open 2 N.T. On 23–24 points you open 2♣ ("I have a superb hand, partner!") and make your *rebid* 2 N.T. ("and it is evenly balanced with 23–24 points!"). Remember your partner is *bound* to respond to a 2♣ opening so you are certain to have a chance to give the second part of your message. *This is the only 2♣ opening bid which is not unconditionally forcing to game* and responder, with a genuine mess of pottage, may pass the 2 N.T. rebid.

Don't, as responder, let this be a stumbling-block to you even from your earliest days. What might be a moderate or even poor hand in response to a 1 N.T. opening bid may well be a slam-going gold mine when partner has opened 2♣. All you have to do is, once again, remember the magic formula, 26 points for a game, so if your partner opens 2♣ and rebids 2 N.T., you need only three points to make his minimum of 23 points up to what he will need for his game, which makes raising him to 3 N.T. on 3 points somewhat less crazy than you might at first think.

If, after the 2♣ opening, the rebid is 3 N.T., this shows a minimum of 25 points, and as this is already a game contract, responder need take no further action unless his hand warrants it for some reason.

Unfortunately a "negative" rather than a "positive" response to a 2♣ opening is the most frequent, so looking at a few examples to make these openings and responses clear, we will consider for the moment that responder bids the almost inevitable 2◇ which, as you will soon be learning, shows less than one Ace and one King, or any nine points.

♠ A K x
♡ A Q x x
◇ K x
♣ A K x x

23 points, and as nearly evenly balanced as you could wish. Open 2♣ and when partner responds 2◇, rebid 2 N.T., which pinpoints your values very precisely. Top it up a bit more, say by making the diamonds ◇ A-K, and your rebid over the 2◇ would be 3 N.T.

♠ A Q x
♡ K J x x
◇ A Q x
♣ K Q J

As it stands, this is a straight 2 N.T. opener, showing 20-22 points. Give it one extra point—say the ♡Q in place of the ♡J, and it becomes a 2♣ opener with a 2 N.T. rebid. Increase that again by substituting the ◇K for the ◇Q and it would count 25 points, a 2♣ opener with a 3 N.T. rebid.

♠ x x x
♡ Q 10 x
◇ Q x x x
♣ x x x

If your partner opens 2♣ your hand contains only the negative response of 2◇. If he then rebids 2 N.T., showing 23-24 points do you pass, because you have such a dreadful hand? Of course you don't! Your 4 points must more than make up the 26 he needs for game, so raise to 3 N.T. Obviously, had his rebid been 3 N.T., you would pass.

♠ Q J x x x x
♡ x
◇ x x x
♣ x x x

As with the opening 2 N.T. bids there is, at this stage, no weak take-out, which again means that if responder bids at all when he is not in a forced position a game contract must be reached. On this hand you would respond 2◇ to an opening 2♣ and over a 2 N.T. rebid would say 3♠. If opener then bids 3 N.T. take out into 4♠, the only contract you really have any hope of making.

This covers Class I of the 2♣ openers, the evenly balanced No Trump hands of a very high count. Summarised briefly the rules are:—

Holding:	Opener bids:	Responder bids:
An evenly-balanced 23-24 points	2♣ and then *rebids* 2 N.T.	2◇ on a "negative" holding and may pass 2 N.T. on a completely blank hand, but should raise to 3 N.T. on 3 points or show a long suit.

An evenly-balanced 25 or more points	2♣ and then *rebids* 3 N.T.	As this is already at game level, responder may pass 3 N.T., or take out into a suit if he thinks fit.

One must not discount the possibility of responder having a "positive" holding opposite the 2♣ bid, in which case things may proceed quite differently. Generally, if opener's hand is of the No Trump type, it is better for him to show this with the appropriate No Trump rebid, the exception to this being if responder's "positive" bid comes in opener's four-card suit. But such hands are rare and difficult to bid to the best advantage even for experts, so, as a beginner, don't let it worry you too much.

Class II. Very Strong Unbalanced Hands:

By "unbalanced" we only mean hands which you would clearly prefer to play at a suit contract rather than in No Trumps. You've met them many times already in this book, in our discussions on opening bids, rebids, and responses. Now, however, we are dealing with the exceptionally strong hands, the "rock-crushers" of game-going strength, and for these you have to make yourself familiar with a slightly different method of hand valuation, the Quick Trick count.

As the name suggests, a Quick Trick is a card or combination of cards likely to win a trick quickly and easily, and the important ones for you to know are:—

Ace = 1 Q.T.	A-Q = 1½ Q.T.
A-K = 2 Q.T.	K-x = ½ Q.T.
K-Q = 1 Q.T.	Other honour cards and combinations, + values.

There are eight Quick Tricks in the pack, the A-K in each suit, and for a Two Club opening bid you require a minimum of five. If you turn back to the example hands on p. 114 you will see how this works. On the first, the ♠A-K = 2 Q.T., the ♡A-Q = 1½ Q.T., the ◇K = ½ Q.T. and the ♣A-K = 2 Q.T., a total of 6 Q.T., well-qualifying the hand for a 2♣ opening. On the second, the ♠A-Q = 1½ Q.T., the ♡K = ½ Q.T., the ◇A-Q = 1½ Q.T., and the ♣K-Q = 1 Q.T., a total of 4½ Q.T., enough only for a 2 N.T. opening until we added the ♡Q which made the ♡K-Q = 1 Q.T. bringing the total up to 5 Q.T.

By opening 2♣ you *guarantee* to your partner that you have a minimum of five Quick Tricks and—here is the vitally important rule—if you make your rebid in a suit and not in No Trumps, your bid is **unconditionally forcing to game.** Responder must *not* allow the bidding to die until at least a game contract has been reached.

♠ A K J x x **♡ A x** **◇ A J 10 x x** **♣ A**	5+ Quick Tricks and a perfect 2♣ opener. If partner bids 2◇ you show your spades by bidding 2♠, *knowing* he will respond again however weak his hand so that you will be able to offer your diamonds too, thus being sure of reaching the best available game contract.
♠ K Q J 10 x **♡ A x** **◇ K Q x** **♣ A K x**	5 Quick Tricks and plus values, so open 2♣. True you *might* be unable to make a game, but you certainly don't want to risk being unable to try. Responder needs so very little to make it an odds-on bet.

You won't, let's face it, get this sort of hand very often—unless you're a good deal luckier than I ever am!—but you don't want to waste them when they do turn up. If your partner produces a positive response you may really be going places in the slam line, so now let's turn to responder's side of the table.

Responding to Opening Two Club Bids:

As already mentioned, the immediate "negative" response to a 2♣ opening is 2♢, and this shows a holding of *less than* one Ace and one King or any eight points. The bid is just as artificial and conventional as the opening 2♣, and bears no relation whatsoever to responder's diamond holding. All it does is deny the requirements for a positive response.

Once having shown his negative, responder is at liberty to show anything helpful that he has on the next round, but this, of course, may be nothing at all. If opener has rebid in a suit, which you will remember is forcing to game, responder must produce a second bid, and his second negative is the lowest available bid in No Trumps:—

2♣—2♢ or 2♣—2♢
2♡—2 N.T. 3♢—3 N.T.

In the first of these sequences, opener will be showing his best suit and responder, unable to raise any enthusiasm, merely keeps the bidding open with 2 N.T. In the second sequence, opener's best suit is clearly diamonds, which he has to bid at the three-level. *Don't* confuse this with "support" for the 2♢ response which does *not* show a diamond holding. Over 3♢ responder, with nothing constructive to offer, must keep the bidding open with 3 N.T.

♠ x x
♡ J x x x
♢ x x x
♣ x x x x

Partner opens 2♣ and you respond 2♢. Partner rebids 2♠ so you produce the second negative of 2 N.T. Had he chanced to bid 2♡ instead of 2♠ your best effort would be to raise to 3♡.

♠ Q x x x
♡ K x x
♢ x x x
♣ J x x

To an opening 2♣, respond 2♢. If partner rebids 3♣ or 3♢, bid 3 N.T. If he bids 2♡ or 2♠, raise to three of his suit. Unlike an opening suit bid of one for which you require 4-card support, you may consider three to an honour adequate when the opening has been 2♣.

♠ J 10 x x x x
♡ x
◇ x x
♣ A J 10 x

Although it's a very good hand in its way you must make your first response to 2♣ a negative. If you don't your partner is bound to place you with at least 1½ Q.T. and bid too high. You must, however, realise that if *opener* can produce support for your long suit there is almost certainly a slam available. It will be up to you subsequently to show that, in spite of being "negative", you have a very good hand.

Sometimes you will find you have a "positive" response to an opening 2♣ bid. An Ace and a King will always add up to 1½ Q.T., and to 2 Q.T. if they are in the same suit, and the other requirement for a "positive", any 8 points, will also come to about the same in combined plus-values. Adding responder's 1½ Q.T. to his own minimum of 5 Q.T. will generally make opener pretty sure of a slam and he will immediately explore as to the best final denomination. Responder must, of course, know how best to show his values, and may always show a biddable suit if he has one in addition to the necessary points. A biddable suit is just the same as it was at the lower levels, four cards headed by one or more high honours if it can be shown at the two-level and a five-card suit if it has to be shown at the three-level. A few examples will be the best way to make this clear.

♠ K x x
♡ A J 10 x
◇ x x x
♣ x x x

Over an opening 2♣ you have a "positive" holding and a biddable heart suit, so your response should be 2♡, from which your partner will know that you have at least 1½ Q.T. and a biddable heart suit.

♠ K x x
♡ x x x
◇ A J 10 x
♣ x x x

This is the same hand as the above except that the hearts and diamonds have changed places. You still have a positive response but if you bid 2◇, it will be the negative. Your suit is not good enough to bid 3◇, so bid

2 N.T. This shows the requirements for a positive response but no biddable suit.

♠ K x x
♡ x x x
♢ A J 10 x x
♠ x x

This is practically the same hand except that now the diamonds *are* good enough to show at the "positive" level of 3♢.

♠ K x x
♡ Q J 10
♢ K x x
♣ J x x x

10 points—a gold mine opposite to a 2♣ opener. Don't make the error of bidding 3♣ in the mistaken belief that you are supporting partner's suit—he may be void in clubs. You have no biddable suit, so respond 2 N.T.

♠ 10 x x x x
♡ A K x
♢ x x x
♣ x x

You clearly have a positive response to 2♣ as your ♡A-K are 2 Q.T., and you also have a perfectably biddable 5-card suit. Respond 2♠ and don't get scared if opener gets enthusiastic. Remember that you have 2 Q.T. and he has 5 Q.T. so only one is missing, so he just *must* have one or more in spades.

Here is a beautiful hand which was actually dealt in a match a little time ago:—

West	*East*
♠ A K x x x x	♠ Q 10 x x x
♡ A Q J	♡ K x x
♢ A Q J	♢ x x
♣ x	♣ A x x

West dealt and, of course, opened 2♣ to which East, his partner, had the positive response of 2♠. This, as perhaps you can imagine, was beyond West's wildest hopes—not only a positive response, but one in his own splendid suit. It remained only to check up whether East's bid was made on an Ace and a King or on eight assorted points without an Ace. If the former, 7♠ would be the correct contract, and if the latter they would have to stop in 6♠. At this point an astute reader will be asking how West can do this checking up, which brings us quite painlessly to:—

The Blackwood Convention:

"Blackwood" is what is known as a Slam Convention, and is a method of finding out how many Aces and Kings your partner may have. Its use need not be confined to opening 2♣ hands, and either partner may employ it any time he has reason to suspect a slam may be available if the necessary number of Aces and Kings are opposite to his own hand.

It might be as well to point out here that there are a number of such Slam Conventions, and in your career as a bridge player you will certainly meet—and may even find you prefer—one of the others. "Blackwood", however, is the easiest of all and the most widely known, and you are not likely to come across a partner who will be unable to play it with you. This is how it works:—

Once the final trump suit has been agreed, either directly or inferentially, either partner, without any specific holding but because he suspects a possible slam, may initiate a slam try by a bid of 4 N.T. This asks his partner to show the number of *Aces* he holds by the use of the following scale:—

With no Ace	bid 5♣
With one Ace	bid 5♢
With two Aces	bid 5♡
With three Aces	bid 5♠
With four Aces	bid 5♣

You will notice that the response of 5♣ shows either no Ace or all four, but this cannot give rise to any confusion. Only on exceptionally rare occasions will the 4 N.T. bidder have no Ace himself and, if it should happen, his hand will be so rich in Kings and Queens that it will be perfectly obvious that his partner could never have bid at all if also Aceless.

Having got the reply to his question about Aces, the 4 N.T. bidder may then enquire about his partner's King holding by bidding 5 N.T. This asks for Kings on a similar sort of scale:—

With no Kings	bid 6♣
With one King	bid 6♢
With two Kings	bid 6♡
With three Kings	bid 6♠
With four Kings	bid 6 N.T.

This bid of 5 N.T. asking for Kings should only be used when the previous 4 N.T. bid has shown that the partnership holds all four Aces, and also when the response, which must necessarily be at the 6-level, will not embarrass the 5 N.T. bidder.

Finally, it can happen that the 4 N.T. bidder will get a nasty disappointment, discovering that between them he and his partner have two Aces missing when he knows that they need three to make their slam. This is all right if the final contract is to be in a major suit, as he can just bid 5♡ or 5♠ over responder. The trouble comes if the final contract is to be in No Trumps, because the 4 N.T. bidder can't just bid 5 N.T. over the response—this, you will remember—would be the conventional bid to ask for Kings. The way out of this difficulty is for the player who has made the 4 N.T. bid and got the unsatisfactory answer to bid five of any previously unbid suit, which asks *responder* to convert to 5 N.T.

None of this is really as confusing as it sounds, so let's sort it out against a few bidding sequences. Firstly, the question of agreeing a suit "inferentially" may have puzzled you. As you gain experience you will meet several conventional ways in which a suit may be agreed inferentially but don't let this worry you at present. Here's just one simple example—your partner, much to your surprise, deals and opens 1♡ and you have this hand:—

♠ x
♡ K Q J x x
◇ A K Q J x
♣ K Q

Clearly you are happy to play in hearts and if your partner has two of the three missing Aces, 6♡ will be your contract. If he has all three, you will play in 7♡. You bid an immediate 4 N.T. which, though it is not a raise in hearts, will tell him that all you want to know is his Ace holding and that you are happy to play in his suit. If he should disappoint you by bidding 5♣ (no Ace) or 5◇ (one Ace) you will bid 5♡. If he bids 5♡ (two Aces) you will raise to 6♡ and if he bids 5♠ (three Aces) you will bid 7♡.

The matter of agreeing the trump suit directly is easier to understand.

West	*East*	
1♡ 4♢ 5♡	3♢ 4 N.T. 6♢	West's raise to 4♢ agrees diamonds as trumps, East bids 4 N.T. asking for Aces. West responds 5♡ showing two which is enough for East's purpose and he bids 6♢.
1♡ 4 N.T. 5♡	3♡ 5♢	East's 3♡ bid is a direct strong Limit Bid and gives West hopes of a slam. Hearts are directly agreed and he bids 4 N.T. 5♢ showing one Ace is not enough, so West bids 5♡.
1♡ 4 N.T. 6♡	3♡ 5♡	The same sequence, except that East shows two Aces, enough for West who bids 6♡.
1♡ 4 N.T. 5 N.T. 7♡	4♡ 5♢ 6♡	Here the strong Limit Bid of 4♡ encourages West to bid 4 N.T. and he finds (he has three Aces himself) that East has the missing one. He now wants to know how many Kings East has and when he hears that East has two, he bids 7♡.
1♡ 4♢ 5♢ 5 N.T.	3♢ 4 N.T. 5♠	Diamonds are agreed, but East actually wants to play the hand in No Trumps. He hopes for a slam and asks for West's Aces, being disappointed to find he has only one. This is not enough for a slam and he can't bid 5 N.T. himself as this would be the conventional request for Kings. Wanting to play in No Trumps, therefore, he bids five of a previously unbid suit, 5♠, and West dutifully converts to 5 N.T., which is passed.

QUIZ ON CHAPTER 10

1. What opening bid would you make on the following hands?

(a) ♠ K Q x: ♡ A J x: ◇ A Q 10: ♣ K Q x x:
(b) ♠ K Q x: ♡ A K J: ◇ A Q 10: ♣ K Q x x:
(c) ♠ A Q x: ♡ A K J: ◇ A Q 10: ♣ K Q x x:
(d) ♠ K J x: ♡ A J x: ◇ A Q 10 x: ♣ K J x:
(e) ♠ A K J x x: ♡ A K x: ◇ x x x: ♣ x x:
(f) ♠ A K J x x x: ♡ A K x: ◇ x x: ♣ x x:
(g) ♠ A K Q J x x: ♡ A K x: ◇ x x: ♣ x x:
(h) ♠ A K Q J x x: ♡ A K x: ◇ A Q: ♣ x x:
(i) ♠ A K: ♡ A K Q x x: ◇ x: ♣ A Q J x x:
(j) ♠ A Q J 10 x: ♡ A K Q x x: ◇ A K x: ♣ —:

2. Go back over the hands given in No. 1 above and pick out the ones on which you were told to open 2♣. If your partner responded 2◇, what would your rebid on them be?

3. Your partner opens the bidding with 2♣. What would you respond on the following hands?

(a) ♠ x x x x: ♡ J x x x x: ◇ —: ♣ x x x x:
(b) ♠ K Q J x x: ♡ x x x: ◇ x x x: ♣ x x:
(c) ♠ K Q J x x: ♡ A x x: ◇ x x x: ♣ x x:
(d) ♠ x x: ♡ J 10 x x x: ◇ A x x: ♣ K x x:
(e) ♠ Q x x: ♡ J 10 x: ◇ K J x: ♣ Q x x x:
(f) ♠ Q x x: ♡ x x: ◇ K J 10 x x: ♣ J x x:
(g) ♠ Q x x: ♡ x x: ◇ K J 10 x x: ♣ K x x:
(h) ♠ A K J x x: ♡ x x x: ◇ x x x: ♣ x x:

4. The bidding has gone as shown in each case. What would you bid next on each of the following hands?

(a) 1♠—4♠ ♠ K J x x: ♡ A x x: ◇ x: ♣ K Q J x x:
4 N.T. — ?
(b) Ditto. ♠ K J x x: ♡ A x x: ◇ x: ♣ A Q J x x:
(c) On both, opener next bids 5 N.T. What do you bid?

ANSWERS TO QUIZ ON CHAPTER 10

1. (a) 2 N.T. 21 points, and evenly balanced—an excellent hand for the bid.

(b) 2♣. The addition of the ♡K brings this up to 24 points, which qualifies.

(c) 2♣ again, the hand counting 25 points which is even stronger.

(d) 1♢, which we hope did not catch you. With 19 points the hand does not qualify for either 2 N.T. or 2♣.

(e) 1♠, a perfectly normal good opening one-bid.

(f) 1♠ again—nothing about this hand makes it worth more than a one-bid, but on the second round you would be entitled to rebid 3♠.

(g) 2♠, the opening Strong Two bid which you met in Chapter 9.

(h) 2♣. This time you have 5½ Q.T. so need have no other thoughts.

(i) 2♣. 5½ Q.T. and even plus values, with two suits to show later.

(j) 2♣. 6+ Q.T. as well as a void in clubs. Remember the 2♣ bid has nothing whatever to do with your holding in that suit.

2. Taking only the hands from Question 1 on which you opened 2♣, your rebids would be:—

(b) 2 N.T., showing the evenly balanced 23-24 points. Responder may pass.

(c) 3 N.T., showing the extra values, still evenly balanced.

(h) 2♠. No need to hurry—your partner will go on bidding till a game contract is reached.

(i) 2♡. Here with two suits to show you are certain to get the chance of finding the best fit for your contract.

(j) 2♠. Another two-suiter and if partner doesn't support spades you are sure of a chance to show your hearts.

3. (a) 2♢. Even with none at all in your hand you must give this "bust" reply.

(b) 2♢. Although you have a nice spade suit you have not enough to give a positive response on the first round. Show your spades when opener has rebid.

(c) 2♠. Now you have certainly got a positive response and make it in your excellent biddable suit.

(d) 2♡. Another positive response with an Ace and a King (1½ Q.T.) and a biddable suit.

(e) 2 N.T. With 9 points you are too good to give a negative but have no biddable suit.

(f) 2♢. Just under strength for a positive response, but you will bid strongly later.

(g) 3♢. Here you are strong enough to give a positive response, but your suit is diamonds and 2♢ is the negative, so you must bid 3♢.

(h) 2♠. A positive response with 2 Q.T. and a good biddable suit.

4. (a) 5♢, showing one Ace.

(b) 5♡, showing two Aces.

(c) 6♡ on the first hand, which shows two Kings in addition to the one Ace you have already shown, and 6♢ on the second, showing one King.

CHAPTER 11

Intervening Bids & Overcalls

♠♡♣◇♠♡♣◇♠♡♣◇♠♡♣◇♠♡♣◇♠♡♣◇♠♡♣◇

UP to now we've allowed the opening bidder and his partner to have things virtually all their own way without interference from the opposition, but this happy state of affairs is, you will find, the exception rather than the rule. Frequently one side will open the bidding and the other will want to compete, or at least try to put a spoke in their opponents' bidding sequence. So for a little while you must, as it were, change your seat and learn the fundamental rules for making "intervening bids" or "overcalls", when one of your opponents has opened the bidding before you.

The first thing to realise is that if the opponent on your right opens the bidding he announces, both to his partner and to the table at large, that he has enough strength to make an opening bid. You, therefore, bidding after him, may find yourself sandwiched between two good hands. This does not mean that you must sit back mute every time the opposition gets a bid in first. One gets nowhere in this life without taking a few risks, but at least let the measure of your risk be worth the measure of your possible gain. In other words, don't thoughtlessly put yourself in the position of being caught by an over-expensive business double from the hand on your left, a course of action you will find good players extremely prone to taking.

There are four good reasons for making an intervening bid or overcall:

1. To investigate whether or not you and your partner have enough strength to gain the contract for yourselves.
2. To suggest a good lead to your partner in the event of becoming the defenders.
3. To offer some opposition in the hope that the other pair may be forced to bid too high and thus go down.
4. To prepare the way for a possible "sacrifice", that is, win the auction though in a contract you have no real expectation of making, to keep the other side out. This applies most usually when they are vulnerable and you are not, your aim being to stay in the game with another chance to win the rubber later.

A Simple Intervening Bid in a New Suit:

There is a marked difference between the type of hand suitable for an intervening bid and the thirteen points required for an opening bid. In fact it is more the *type* of hand that matters, the chief requirement being a sound suit of your own.

An intervening bid at the one-level (1♠ over 1♡) may be made relatively freely as the danger of being doubled at this level is not very great, but more often than not the opening bid will force you to bid at the two-level (1♡—2◇), when more care is required.

A hand which is below strength for an opening bid may well provide a reasonable intervening bid, and conversely a hand suitable for an opening bid may be totally unsuitable for an intervening bid. Take these two hands:—

♠ A J 10	♠ A J x
♡ x x x	♡ K 10 x
◇ A x x x	◇ Q J x
♣ A x x	♣ Q x x x

On both these hands you would open, if given the chance, 1 N.T., but you must not be tempted to make an intervening bid. Both are good defensive hands but not attacking ones in the light of an opening bid. Bide your time and hope that your opponents will bid too high, which you might well prevent them from doing if you made a bid at this stage.

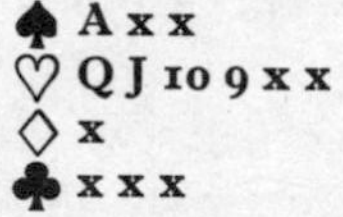
♠ A x x
♡ Q J 10 9 x x
◇ x
♣ x x x

This hand has an excellent heart suit, strong enough to show at the one-level over either of the minors or at the two-level over 1♠. Only a disastrously unlucky distribution against you could cause you any serious harm.

When considering an intervening bid, rather than counting points, look at your distribution and "shape". Whichever level your contemplated bid may be at, try to see that, in terms of playing strength, you are not more than two tricks short of your bid if vulnerable and not more than three if not vulnerable.

Other important points to remember are never to make an intervening bid at the two-level on *less* than a five-card suit, to make the bid in a suit in which you can afford to play if you win the auction, and also in a suit you would like your partner to lead if you become the defenders. Note here too, by the way, that as your intervening bid virtually guarantees a five-card suit, your partner is at liberty to raise you on three-card support.

Lest these strictures should have frightened you off trying to make an intervening bid at all, consider one other side of the picture, the nuisance value it may have for your opponents. If, for example, your right-hand opponent opens 1 ♢ or 1 ♡ and you intervene with 2♣, you prevent opener's partner from responding at the one-level. Over either opening he might have wanted to bid 1♠ but not be strong enough to bid 2♠ over you, so the best fit and safest game or part-score contract may be lost to them for ever.

There is one very important "don't" to be learned at this stage, and that is *don't* be tempted into trying to make an intervening bid if your only length and strength is in the suit opened by the other side. There is nothing you can do about it at the moment except to pass and hope that things will develop to your advantage later in the auction.

Lastly, remember that whatever the vulnerability, whatever the agreed strength for an opening No Trump bid, a No Trump bid used as an intervening bid **is always strong, guaranteeing a minimum of 16 points plus two stops in the suit opened.** Look at the two example hands at the top of p. 128, which were suitable to open 1 N.T. but not to make an intervening bid—they are *not* strong enough to *intervene* with 1 N.T. They completely lack the playing strength requirements for an intervening bid.

♠ x x
♡ K Q x x x
♢ A x x
♣ Q x x

If an opponent bids 1♣ or 1♢ this hand is worth an intervening bid of 1♡. Over an opening 1♠ it would be a reasonable risk for a 2♡ bid if not vulnerable but a wiser pass if vulnerable. If your opponent opens 1♡, *pass.* If you feel like doubling, wait till you've read the section on Take Out Doubles later in this chapter, to see why you can't do this.

♠ K J x x x
♡ Q x x
◇ x x x
♣ A x

Over an opening 1♣, 1◇ or 1♡ you would be perfectly correct to come in with an intervening bid of 1♠ but if the opening bid should be 1♠, again you must pass. Add, say, the ◇K bringing you up to 13 points and over 1♠ you must still pass. You are not strong enough to bid 1 N.T. which would promise 16 points and your best hope is to await developments. You may be able to double their final contract or, if your partner shows a suit, offer No Trumps.

♠ K J x
♡ x x
◇ A 10
♣ K Q 10 x x x

On this hand your club suit is good enough to show at the two level over any other suit opened by the opposition. Particularly over an opening spade bid you have an excellent hand, as your ♠K-J lie over the call.

♠ K J x
♡ A 10 x x
◇ K Q x
♣ K J 10

Whatever suit is opened against you, this hand is worth an overcall of 1 N.T. It has a stop in every suit, the required minimum of 16 points and, most important of all, a good stop in whichever suit is opened. Over an opening of 1♣ or 1◇ you could, it is true, bid 1♡ as you don't guarantee a five-card suit if bidding at the one-level, but your hand could be much weaker than it is and 1 N.T. is your best way of telling your partner of your "shape" and values.

The Take-Out Double:

In these hands illustrating simple overcalls you have, once again, been bidding what you actually hold. Now you have to learn an extremely useful conventional bid, the Take-Out or, as it is sometimes called, the Informatory Double, which *asks* your partner to show you his own best suit.

The moment to think of using this bid is if you feel you would like to *ask* your partner rather than *tell* him which suit should be trumps. You should have a minimum of about 13 points, strength in the *other* three suits and "shape" by way of a shortage (not more than a doubleton) in the suit opened. In addition, a take-out double of a major suit implies willingness to play in the unbid major suit. Again this is not as complicated as it sounds, and a few examples will soon give you the idea. Remember your chief clue, when you want to *ask* your partner rather than *tell* him.

♠ x	Over an opening 1♠ you obviously can't
♡ A Q x x	possibly pass on this hand, but which
◇ K Q x x	suit are you to choose? You can't
♣ A x x x	guarantee a five-card suit that you

haven't got and you can't bid 1 N.T. on 15 points and no stop in spades. You *double*, which requires your partner to show you his own best suit.

The situation need not be quite as clear-cut as in the hand above, which is ideal for the use of a take-out double.

♠ A J x x	Over a 1♣ opening it is far better to double, asking your partner to show his best suit, than it is to make a guess at either hearts or spades. He may, of course, bid diamonds, but at least you have three good ones in the suit of his choice.
♡ K 10 x x	
◇ A J x	
♣ x x	

♠ A K J x x	It is better to double an opening 1◇
♡ K J x x	than it is to bid your spades. Your
◇ x	partner, even with a weak hand, may well
♣ A x x	have four or more hearts, but if he

chooses clubs nothing will be lost as you can then bid 2♠.

Another point which often puzzles learners is how to tell whether a double is "business" or for a take-out, so here are your clues:—

If your partner has not yet bid, (except to pass), a double made at the first opportunity of doubling and at not more than the two-level, is for a take-out.

If partner has made a bid, either in a suit or No Trumps, the double is a business one, made in the expectation of defeating the opponents' contract.

Compare these sequences:—

	N.	*E.*	*S.*	*W.*	
1.	1♠	Dbl.			Clearly a take-out double by East.
2.	1♠	—	2♠	Dbl.	Also clearly a take-out double, this time by West who has had no previous opportunity to bid. East's only bid has been a pass.
3.	1♠	2♡	3♠	—	A business double by East who bid hearts on the first round and clearly now expects to defeat the 4♠ contract.
	4♠	Dbl.			
4.	1♠	2♡	Dbl.		A business double by South whose partner, North, opened with 1♠. South does not think that East will be able to make 2♡.

Finally, a double of an opening 1 N.T. bid is *not* asking for a take-out and is intended primarily for penalties. Such a double should only be made holding the *upper* limit of the strength of the announced opening No Trump, and the partner of the doubler will only take out if his hand is so weak that he sees no chance that they hold the balance of power and is, therefore, afraid that the 1 N.T. doubled will be made.

There are several other types of intervening bids we shall be coming to shortly, but first let's run over the rules for responding to your partner when he has made a take-out double.

Responding to a Take-Out Double:

A Take-Out double is forcing. In other words, it asks a question which demands a reply, but there are two situations in which you may exercise discretion and pass. The first of these is if the opponent on your right makes a bid between you and your partner's take-out double.

N.	*E.*	*S.*	*W.*	
1♡	Dbl.	2♣	?	In this sequence you are West and your partner, East, doubles North's opening 1♡. South's bid of 2♣ lets you off the hook

as it were. You need not bid as South's action leaves the auction still open when it gets back to your partner.

It follows, therefore, that if you *do* bid over such an intervening bid as South's, it becomes a "free" rather than a "forced" bid, and shows positive values. A redouble in South's position, by the way, counts as a bid which lets you off, but if you have any five-card suit you should most definitely show it, and if you have a four-card suit you can show at the one-level you should bid that too. Your partner has elected to *ask* your views on the possible trump suit so don't, if you can possibly avoid it, throw the onus of a guess back on to him.

The second situation in which you may pass a take-out double is if you have length and strength in the suit doubled so that, from your point of view, your holding of the opponent's trump suit plus the 13 or more points promised by your partner's double suggest that your best result will be to defeat their doubled contract rather than play for one of your own.

N.	*E.*	*S.*	*W.*
1♡	Dbl.	—	?

As West in this sequence you find you have next to nothing in your hand except ♡ **QJ 10 x x x** so your best bet is to pass the double for penalties. You are particularly happy to do this if your opponents are vulnerable as the penalty should be worth collecting, especially when you are not likely to be able to make a game yourselves.

If there is no intervening bid on your right to let you off, and if you haven't the sort of hand worth passing for penalties as explained above, you are forced to find a response to your partner's double, and here are the rules:—

1. On a hand of less than four points bid your

longest suit at the lowest available level but at all costs keep the bidding low.

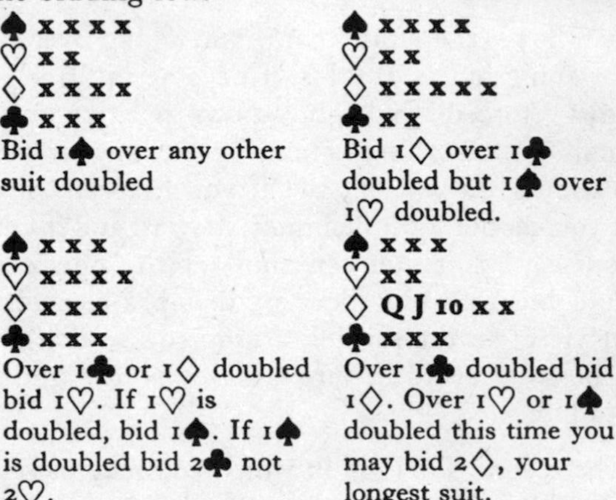

♠ x x x x ♡ x x ♢ x x x x ♣ x x x Bid 1♠ over any other suit doubled	♠ x x x x ♡ x x ♢ x x x x x ♣ x x Bid 1♢ over 1♣ doubled but 1♠ over 1♡ doubled.
♠ x x x ♡ x x x x ♢ x x x ♣ x x x Over 1♣ or 1♢ doubled bid 1♡. If 1♡ is doubled, bid 1♠. If 1♠ is doubled bid 2♣ not 2♡.	♠ x x x ♡ x x ♢ Q J 10 x x ♣ x x x Over 1♣ doubled bid 1♢. Over 1♡ or 1♠ doubled this time you may bid 2♢, your longest suit.

2. On a somewhat stronger hand, one counting between 4–8 points, take out the double into your longest suit, though you should still bid a four-card major rather than a five-card minor if this keeps the level of the bidding lower.

3. With a balanced hand and a minimum of 8 points you may bid 1 N.T., but this does *not* promise a stop in the opponent's bid suit. It merely promises at least 8 points and no biddable suit.

♠ **Q J** x ♡ x x x ♢ **K J** x ♣ **J** x x x	Respond to a double of any opening suit bid with 1 N.T. on this hand. Change it, though, by adding one spade in place of one of the hearts and your best response to a double of any lower ranking suit will be 1♠, and still 1 N.T. to 1♠ doubled.

4. On a balanced hand of 9–10 points *including a good stop in the suit opened*, bid 2 N.T. Without such a stop, jump the bidding by one step in your longest suit keeping, if you have any choice, to the rule about

bidding the higher-ranking of equal and adjacent suits first.

♠ x x x
♡ J 10 x x x
◇ A Q x
♣ K x

If partner doubles 1♣ or 1◇ bid 2♡, not 1♡, to distinguish your hand from the hopelessly weak ones we have considered earlier. Remember that 10 points opposite to the minimum required for a double is pretty strong and that, in any case, your partner won't misunderstand your jump bid.

♠ K J 10 x
♡ A Q x x
◇ x x x
♣ x x

If partner doubles either 1♡ or 1♠, bid 2 N.T. If he doubles either minor bid 2♠, not 1♠, selecting the higher-ranking of your two suits.

5. On very strong hands offering a choice of contract you have a new conventional bid to learn, what is known as a cue bid in the opponent's suit. This is best explained by an example, as usual.

♠ A 10 x x
♡ K Q 10 x
◇ x x
♣ A J x

If partner doubles 1◇, bid 2◇. This does *not* announce good diamonds, but passes the buck back to him. He asked by his double which suit you would prefer as trumps, and your view is that the best choice will be *his* best suit. This is your way of telling him so. Even if he doubles 1♣, 2♣ will be your best response. Your partner is almost morally certain to bid one of the majors, which you can raise and if he *should* bid diamonds, you can jump to 3 N.T.

Jump Overcalls:

Back now to immediate overcalls, and this time we are going to look at hands which are too good for a simple overcall and not suitable for a take-out double. These are the hands where most of your strength is concentrated in one, or perhaps two good suits, in which case your overcall should be a jump bid of *one* more level than is necessary for a simple intervening bid (i.e., 1♡—2♠ or 1♡—3◇). This jump bid is *not* forcing but your partner will understand that your hand is strong, and will do his best to respond. Here are a couple of examples:—

♠ x x ♡ A K x x x x ◇ A x ♣ K Q x	You are too strong to make a simple intervening bid here but the hand is quite unsuitable for a take-out double as your only interest is in a heart contract. Over an opening 1♣ or 1◇, bid 2♡. Over an opening 1♠ bid 3♡.
♠ A K x x x x ♡ A Q J x x ◇ x ♣ x	Over an opening minor suit bid you are again too strong for a simple intervening bid and quite unsuitable for a double. Bid 2♠ and later, if expedient and you get a second chance, show hearts asking for a preference.

Note that these strong "shape" hands promising a 6-card suit, are shown by a jump bid of *one* more level than is necessary for a simple overcall, just as a responder's force is made by jumping one more level than is necessary for a simple response. What, then, is the meaning of a jump bid of two or more levels?

Pre-emptive Overcalls:

Jump bids of two or more levels are what is known as "pre-emptive" which, in plainer English, means a bid made solely in an effort to put a spanner in the works for the opposition. You may make a pre-emptive overcall or, for that matter, a pre-emptive opening bid or direct response (of which more anon) when you think that your hand, though containing a very long suit of its own, is useless if played in any other denomination and equally useless in defence.

♠ K Q x x x x x x ♡ x x ◇ x ♣ x x	Suppose the player on your right opens 1♡. Can you dream of any other contract than a spade one ? Can you have any hope at all of defeating a heart or, indeed, any other contract ?

The answer to both questions is no. You cannot make a jump bid to 2♠ as this would promise your partner a strong hand so you jump one extra step, to 3♠, which tells him the whole story. Increase the strength of your hand just a little, say by including the ♠J or one extra spade, and your best "pre-empt" would be a jump of three levels to 4♠.

Game Forcing Overcalls:

Finally, you need in your armoury a game-forcing overcall, one which will tell your partner that, in spite of the opposition opening bid *you* have an exceptionally good hand—probably one on which you would have liked to have opened 2♣—and want to reach a game contract. This is another moment for a cue-bid in the suit opened. Don't be frightened by this idea. It is merely another conventional bid on the same lines as the opening 2♣ because it bears no relation to the cards actually in your hand *except* that you should not have more than one loser in the suit opened.

♠ A K Q J x x x
♡ x
◇ A x
♣ K Q x

If your right-hand opponent opens the bidding with, for instance, 1♡, bid 2♡. This bid has two advantages over a take-out double here. First, there is no risk of partner leaving a double in for penalties, and secondly, the take-out double is forcing for one round only. Your partner might well pass a jump bid to 2♠—the last thing you want—and if you jump to 3♠ or 4♠ he will take it as pre-emptive and weak so he will pass and you may well miss a slam. If you cue-bid opponent's suit, however, he will know how strong you are and will keep the bidding open at least to game.

♠ A K Q x x
♡ —
◇ A J 10 x
♣ K Q x x

Again if your opponent opens 1♡, bid 2♡. This time, however, you are not so emphatic about a spade contract but want time to explore for the best fit with your partner. The main thing you don't want is to be left to defend a low doubled heart contract!

As your experience grows you will learn other and more sophisticated methods of intervening, but at this stage they would only muddle you. So learn these elementary methods before you spread your wings.

QUIZ ON CHAPTER 11

1. At Love All your right-hand opponent opens the bidding with 1♢. What bid would you make on each of the following hands?

(a) ♠ x x: ♡ A Q J x x: ♢ K x x: ♣ x x x:
(b) ♠ x x x: ♡ x x x: ♢ K x: ♣ A J x x x:
(c) ♠ K x x: ♡ Q x ♢ x x: ♣ A K J x x x:
(d) ♠ K Q x: ♡ K x x: ♢ x x x: ♣ A x x x:
(e) ♠ K J x x: ♡ A Q J: ♢ x x: ♣ A Q x x:
(f) ♠ K Q J x x x: ♡ A Q: ♢ x x: ♣ K J x:
(g) ♠ K Q x: ♡ x x: ♢ A Q x x x: ♣ Q x x:
(h) ♠ A K: ♡ A Q J x x x: ♢ K x: ♣ A x x:
(i) ♠ K J x: ♡ A Q x: ♢ K J x: ♣ K x x x:
(j) ♠ x x: ♡ K Q x x x x x: ♢ x x: ♣ K x:

2. Your partner has doubled the dealer's opening bid of 1♢, next hand has passed and it is your turn. What do you bid on these hands?

(a) ♠ J x x x x: ♡ x x x: ♢ x x: ♣ Q x x:
(b) ♠ Q J x x x: ♡ A x x: ♢ x: ♣ Q x x x:
(c) ♠ Q J x x: ♡ Q x x: ♢ K J x: ♣ J x x:
(d) ♠ Q J x x: ♡ K J x: ♢ J x x: ♣ x x x:
(e) ♠ Q J x x: ♡ A Q x x: ♢ x: ♣ K J x x:
(f) ♠ Q J x: ♡ K J x: ♢ x x x: ♣ J 10 x x:

ANSWERS TO QUIZ ON CHAPTER 11

1. (a) 1♡, a simple intervening bid on a reasonable suit. Your ♢K is worth more than its face-value of 3 points lying over the bid.

   (b) No Bid. Even allowing for the ♢K over the bid, your hand is not worth a call at the two-level.

   (c) 2♣. Here you are well worth the intervening bid, having an opening hand of your own.

   (d) No Bid. A typical hand for lying low, not getting into trouble, and possibly causing trouble later.

   (e) Double. This is a take-out double of course, asking partner to show his best suit.

   (f) 2♠. Too good a hand for a simple over-call, but the bid is not forcing so it merely warns partner that you are strong in shape as well as points.

   (g) No Bid. Your main strength is in the suit opened, so pass and bide your time.

   (h) 2♢, the game-forcing bid which makes sure that your partner will keep the auction open for you.

   (i) 1 N.T., with a double stop in diamonds and a count of 18 points in an evenly balanced hand.

   (j) 3♡. Pre-emptive, and trying to interfere with the opponents' bidding sequence. Also warning partner that you are good for nothing if not hearts.

2. (a) 1♠, showing your best suit which, happily, is quite a good one.

   (b) 2♠, showing your best suit and distinguishing your hand from the miserable lot you had in (a).

   (c) 2 N.T., showing a count of 9-10 and a good stop in diamonds.

   (d) 1♠, not quite good enough for a jump to 2♠.

   (e) 2♢, passing the buck back to partner. You have a good hand and prefer him to choose anyway.

   (f) 1 N.T., showing 8 points, no biddable suit, and *not* confirming a stop in diamonds.

CHAPTER 12

Loose Ends

THIS is the last chapter on bidding and in it we are going to try to tie up various loose ends—points which have been touched on but not yet explained, and others which it may have occurred to you to question as you were reading, none of which merit a chapter on their own at this stage of your career as a bridge player. First, the pre-emptive bids which appeared in the section on intervening bids.

Pre-emptive Opening Bids and Responses:

In case you haven't already realised it for yourself it is worth pointing out that all opening bids made at the one-level or responses made at the lowest available level (1♡—1♠ or 1♡—2◇), are simple ordinary bids. Opening bids made at the two-level, one level higher than is necessary, whether 2♣, two of a suit or 2 N.T., are very strong bids and responses made at one level higher than necessary (1♡—2♠ or 1♡—3◇) are also very strong and forcing. In other words, a bid at *one* level more than necessary shows strength. A bid at *two* or more levels than necessary shows weakness coupled with "shape", and these bids are known as pre-emptive. You've already met the pre-emptive intervening bids where you jump not one level to show strength, but two or three levels with the object of disrupting the opposition's bidding sequence. Now you must meet pre-emptive opening bids, though for the time being it is more necessary for you to know that these bids exist than how to make or counter them as they are difficult, even for highly experienced players to handle. Briefly, however, you should know that, particularly if not vulnerable against vulnerable opponents, an opening bid made at the level of three or more can often play havoc with the other pair's bidding sequence and so be well worth your while. You won't be intending to make your contract (except by a miracle!) but you will be hoping to make life very difficult for the other side.

You don't count points at all for this sort of bid and, indeed, if you have anything like a fair number your hand won't qualify for a pre-emptive opening. Suitable hands are single-suited with one very long suit of seven or eight cards, containing no reasonable support for any unbid major suit, and virtually worthless in defence.

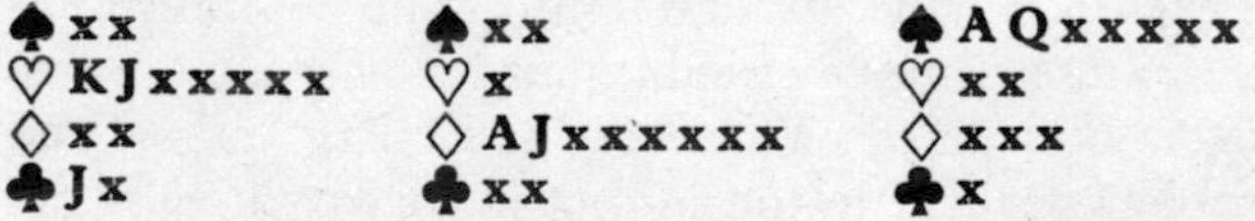

♠ x x	♠ x x	♠ A Q x x x x x
♡ K J x x x x x	♡ x	♡ x x
◇ x x	◇ A J x x x x x x	◇ x x x
♣ J x	♣ x x	♣ x

The three hands above are typical opening three-bids, each in its own suit. Imagine the trouble this may cause an opponent with a moderately good or even very good hand. He'll be forced to start his bidding at an extremely high level and even if he dares to do this, may never have time to find out his best contract.

The best position for an opening pre-emptive bid is third in hand after two passes, as by then you will know that neither your partner nor the next player was strong enough to open and, if your hand is something like one of the above, it's a pretty fair guess that fourth hand, on your left, will be strong. The very high level of a pre-emptive opening just before him may put him completely on the spot.

Never make a pre-emptive bid fourth in hand after three passes. There is no point in trying to obstruct the bidding of a strong hand which you know doesn't exist!

If you make a pre-emptive opening bid as dealer or second in hand *before* your partner has passed, he may be the one with the strong hand. He will know the character of your hand, and probably the wisest course for a beginner who is in responder's seat is to pass unless holding a real rock-crusher with at least three and a half or four certain tricks in it. As already pointed out, judgment in such cases is frequently difficult even for really experienced players.

Countering Opening Pre-emptive Bids:

This is another department of the game which can be extremely difficult—and rightly so because, as you've seen, a pre-emptive opening bid is solely intended to create difficulties. You will find many pages and chapters devoted to the subject in advanced books, all of them far too complicated for inclusion here. From a learner's point of view, with a splendid hand and a good suit of your own, bid it even at the four-level, remembering that it is just to prevent you from doing this that the high opening bid was made.

If you have a very strong hand of the take-out double type, that is, something in everything except the suit opened and 16 or more points, you may bid 3 N.T. which takes the place of a take-out double at this level, and is a request to partner to show his best suit. Lastly, as you have this 3 N.T. bid in place of a take-out double you can, on a suitable hand, make a *business* double of the opening pre-emptive bid.

Just as you have already learned that there are a number of different Slam Conventions, so there are a number of different methods of dealing with opening pre-emptive bids. You are bound to come across them and may even find you prefer one of the others. Using 3 N.T. for a take-out is, however, widely used and easy to remember.

That is as much as you need to bother about for the present, so now let's turn to a few other points which will crop up far more often, all of which are covered under the broad heading of responding after an intervening bid.

Responding After an Intervening Bid:

As mentioned previously, an opponent's intervening bid may prevent you from making the responding bid you had intended, for example:—

♠ **K x x x** ♡ **Q x x** ♢ **K x x** ♣ **x x x**	Your partner opens 1♡ and your intended response would be 1♠. If you have to contend with an intervening bid of 2♣ or 2♢ you are not strong enough to bid 2♠ and short of passing, which would be

madness, you will have to tell a little lie. Your only possible course is to bid 2♡ even though you have not got primary, or 4-card heart support. Your partner will know that you may have been forced into such a position, so don't be too scared at what you are doing. Remember that to pass would be a lie too, so to bid 2♡ is merely the lesser lie.

With 6–9 points and no biddable suit you have learned to keep the bidding open for your partner with 1 N.T. An intervening bid relieves you of this responsibility because the auction will get round to your partner again anyway. This does not mean, of course, that you need never find a response over an intervening bid, and if you have any values worth showing you must always try to show them. What it does mean is that a response of 1 N.T. over a one-level intervening bid becomes "positive" rather than just a keep-open bid, and guarantees a guard in the suit intervened. On the example above, for instance, if the intervening bid over your partner's 1♡ opening were 1♠ instead of 2♣ or 2◇, you could bid 1 N.T. Move the ♠K into another suit and you *could not* bid 1 N.T. as you would not have the spade stop you were promising.

A bid of 2 N.T. over an intervening bid at either the one or two level (1♡—1♠—2 N.T. or 1♡—2♣—2 N.T.) still carries the same basic meaning as it would do without the intervening bid, that is, 10–12 points in an evenly balanced hand, but in addition to this it also guarantees a good stop in the suit intervened.

♠ A Q x
♡ x x x
◇ Q 10 x x
♣ K J x

Over partner's opening 1♡ you would, without any intervention to cope with, respond 2 N.T. If the intervention is either 1♠, 2♣ or 2◇ you can also bid 2 N.T. as you have all the requirements, an evenly balanced 12 points and a stop in which ever suit your opponent bids.

If your hand contains a suit limit bid in response to your partner, the intervening bid is unlikely to damage it and you will be able to use it in the normal way. If, however, the intervention forces you to change your line of action you will simply have to find the best bid you can in the circumstances. If you have to lie, make the lie as small a one as possible.

A Business Double:

You have been warned about the danger of getting your intervening bid caught by a business double by the player on your left, and now we come to the point when *you* may be "the player on the left". You must, in fact, learn when to make a business double of an intervening bid in preference to any other response.

A business double at the one-level is infrequent because this low contract has to be defeated by so many tricks to make it worth while, which means, almost inevitably, that the other side could have scored a game, but a business double at the two-level, especially if your opponents are vulnerable, can be most profitable.

You must not, unless in extremely exceptional circumstances, double an intervening bid if you have support for your partner's bid suit. The logic of this is that the more you and your partner hold of the suit, the less your opponents will have and, therefore, your top cards in it, with which you are hoping to take defensive tricks, will probably get nipped in the bud by being trumped by declarer. The further logical extension of this is that a business double of an intervening bid categorically *denies* support for partner's bid suit. It also promises a damaging holding of the suit intervened—as good as four or five to two honours, and a count of 8 or 9 points.

♠ **x**
♡ **K J x x x**
◇ **A J x x**
♣ **x x x**

If your partner opens 1♠ and next hand intervenes with 2♡, your hand is tailor-made for a business double which warns your partner of your lack of spade support and tells him of the character of the rest of your hand. Your partner will only disturb your double if he has the weakest of weak opening bids or, if vulnerable against non-vulnerable opponents, your double makes him sure of a game (probably in No Trumps as you can't support spades).

♠ **A J x x**
♡ **K J x x x**
◇ **x**
♣ **x x x**

But on this hand, which is exactly the same except that the spades and diamonds are transposed, you must *not* double a 2♡ intervention. You can support spades and your best bid is the natural limit response of 3♠.

Bidding Over Opponent's Take-Out Double:

Quite often the intervening bid will be made, not in a suit, but by way of a take-out double. This is an *asking* bid, asking the partner of the doubler to show his best suit, and this completely changes the complexion of responder's bids. Firstly, if your hand contains a natural limit bid in partner's suit, that is, 4-card trump support plus some points, make the limit bid anyway, but devalue it in order to make it as difficult as possible for your left-hand opponent to answer the question he has been asked, which means erring on the side of overbidding rather than underbidding. If, however, you have a full strength raise of a one-bid to the 3-level, use a conventional bid of 2 N.T. which means exactly the same as, for example, 1♡—3♡ would do, and your partner will treat it as a strong limit bid, merely converting to 3♡ or 4♡ direct if he sees fit.

Following an intervening take-out double, a simple change of suit bid (1♡—Dbl—1♠) is no longer forcing and is more generally used as a rescue bid when you have a long suit of your own and little or no support for partner's. By implication, therefore, in the sequence above, heart support is *denied*.

1 N.T. after a double may be used to show in the region of 7-8 points. This can be very obstructive if the suit doubled is a minor, as it prevents a reply at the one-level.

A count of 9 or more points is reserved for a *redouble*, which does not promise support for partner, but rather the probability that you would like the chance to make a business double of whatever the opponents bid. It guarantees action on the next round and opener should pass unless he does not fancy the idea of defending a low-level contract.

A genuine change-of-suit can be shown by a jump bid (1♡—2♠) and is only a one-round force. You will use this for hands with a good suit of your own, little or no support for partner's suit and one which is unsuitable for a redouble.

QUIZ ON CHAPTER 12

1. As third hand after two passes, not vulnerable against vulnerable opponents, what opening bid would you make on these hands?

   (a) ♠ A J 10 x x x x: ♡ x x: ◇ x x: ♣ x x:
   (b) ♠ A Q 10 x x x x: ♡ Q x x x: ◇ x: ♣ x:
   (c) ♠ A J 10 x x x x: ♡ A Q x: ◇ x x: ♣ x:

2. The player on your right deals and opens 3♡. What action do you take?

   (a) ♠ A Q J x x x: ♡ K x: ◇ A x x x: ♣ x:
   (b) ♠ A Q J x: ♡ K x: ◇ A K x x: ♣ K Q x:
   (c) ♠ A Q x: ♡ K J 10 x: ◇ A K x: ♣ K Q x:

3. Your partner, North, deals and opens 1◇ over which East bids 1♡. What do you bid on these hands?

   (a) ♠ A x x x: ♡ x x x: ◇ x x x: ♣ K J x:
   (b) ♠ A x x: ♡ x x x: ◇ Q 10 x: ♣ J 10 x x:
   (c) ♠ A x x: ♡ K J x: ◇ x x x: ♣ J 10 x x:

4. Your partner, North, deals and opens 1◇ over which East bids 2♣. What do you bid on these hands, and what would you have bid if East had not intervened?

   (a) ♠ A x x: ♡ K x x: ◇ Q 10 x x: ♣ x x x:
   (b) ♠ A x x: ♡ K x x: ◇ x x: ♣ K J x x x:
   (c) ♠ A x x: ♡ K x x: ◇ x x x: ♣ x x x x:

5. Your partner, North, opens 1♡ and East doubles. What do you bid on these hands?

   (a) ♠ Q J x x x x: ♡ x: ◇ x x x: ♣ x x x:
   (b) ♠ Q J x: ♡ K J x x: ◇ x x x: ♣ x x x:
   (c) ♠ A Q x: ♡ x x: ◇ K J x x: ♣ Q J x x :

QUIZ ON CHAPTER 12—ANSWERS

1. (a) 3♠, a perfect hand for this pre-emptive opening.
   (b) 1♠. With such good hearts you should not "pre-empt", but it is better to open on such a hand, and go on bidding spades ad lib. unless partner bids hearts.
   (c) 1♠, for which you are fully up to strength.

2. (a) Bid 3♠. You are too good to let him get away with 3♡ uncontested.
   (b) Bid 3 N.T., asking partner to show his best suit.
   (c) Double—a business double at this level.

3. (a) 1♠, a natural bid you would have made without the intervention.
   (b) 2◇. You cannot bid a second suit, nor can you bid 1 N.T., so your only alternative to a pass (unthinkable!) is the slight lie of a direct raise.
   (c) 1 N.T. Now your heart holding *over* the intervention justifies this bid.

4. (a) Over 2♣ you bid 2◇, a simple raise which is all you can offer. If East had not intervened you would have made the same response.
   (b) Double the 2♣ intervention, a business double. East has taken the words out of your mouth because you had intended to bid 2♣ yourself.
   (c) No bid over 2♣. You have nothing constructive to say and are not strong enough to double. Without the 2♣ intervention you would have bid 1 N.T.

5. (a) 1♠, the natural bid you would have made without the double.
   (b) 3♡, upgrading the natural limit bid to obstruct next hand.
   (c) Redouble, telling your partner that you have at least 9 points outside the heart suit opened by him and that he is not to let the double frighten him. You promise to take action on the next round and should collect a good penalty from doubling your opponents' contract.

SECTION III
The Play of the Cards

CHAPTER 13

Techniques of Suit Management

WE have now reached the point where the auction is over, the contract is known, and the cards have to be played. One player has become declarer, and we are going to look at things first from his point of view.

It does not take any particular skill to win a trick with the Ace of Trumps nor, for that matter, a second trick if you have the King of Trumps too. But you cannot hope, even between the combined hands of declarer and dummy, always to find all the sure winners required to make the contract. Some cards, unless your bidding has gone very much astray, will be ready-made winners, but the rest will have to be developed or "established", so as to make the best possible use of the resources at your disposal. For this purpose there are various basic techniques you will have to acquire but before we examine these, let's spare a little time to get one or two points clear.

If you are South, declarer, with the ♠A K Q J facing four small ones in dummy, it is easy to see that you can expect to win four spade tricks without undue difficulty. You have the four top cards in the suit which are, therefore,

♠ A Q x x

	N	
W		E
	S	

♠ K J x x

equal from a trick-winning point of view. Suppose, however, that you have this combination instead. Can you see that you still have exactly the same four spade tricks? The ♠A-Q in dummy and the ♠K-J in your own hand are still of equal trick-taking capacity, and you can play South's two little ones on North's Ace and Queen, and North's two little ones on South's King and Knave. You also have an added advantage which the first combination did not give you—you have two entry cards to dummy and two to your own hand, which may prove invaluable.

In both these examples you had the same number of spades in both hands, but frequently you will find that one hand will have more of a suit than the other, in which case it is often possible to use the *long* suit for valuable "discards" of losers—cards which can never take a trick. In this example South has one spade only, opposite to the four top ones. This means that a lead of the small one will be won in dummy (North), and South, having no more spades, may throw away, or discard, three cards he doesn't want on North's other three winners. Here North's spades were all "tops", ready-made established winners, but such a comfortable situation is, you will find, the exception rather than the rule, and far more often you will have to set about *establishing* your winners, thus providing yourself with a spot to park your losers.

♠ A K Q J

	N	
W		E
	S	

♠ x

Let's take a look at some of the more frequent suit combinations and discover what we mean by establishing a suit. In the ones we've seen so far, no establishing was necessary.

(a) ♠ x x x x

	N	
W		E
	S	

♠ A K Q x

Now the ♠J is missing. With eight cards between North and South, there are five outstanding. If these are divided 3 and 2 between East and West, your three tops will draw them all, and you will have established the last for a fourth trick, just as the four tops produced four tricks before. But if the outstanding cards are divided 4—1, there will be one big one left when you've played your A-K-Q, and you will not be able to establish the last.

(b) ♠ x x x x

	N	
W		E
	S	

♠ A K x x

Now South is missing the ♠Q as well as the ♠J, and it will never be possible to win four tricks by leading out top spades, because one opponent must hold at least three to a high honour which will be good once your ♠A-K are gone. If, however, you play out the ♠A-K and the outstanding cards are divided 3—2, playing a third spade, even though it is a loser, will draw that last good one, and you will have established your own fourth.

(c) ♠ x x x

	N	
W		E
	S	

♠ A K Q x

This time there are only seven spades between the two hands, so your ability to establish more than the three sure tops depends entirely on the "break". If the outstanding six are divided 3—3 they will fall on your A-K-Q and your fourth will have become established as the last and, therefore, best spade. If they are divided 4—2 you will not be able to establish your own fourth and it will be a loser.

(d) ♠ x x x

	N	
W		E
	S	

♠ A K x x x

Here you are back to holding eight spades between the two hands as you had in (b), but they are divided differently. If you play out your Ace and King and the outstanding five are divided 3—2, the play of a third losing card will establish *two* "little x's" as winners in your own hand.

(e) 

Adding the ♠Q to your seven spades gives you an extra chance. A 3—3 break will establish your two little ones without loss, meaning five spade winners. A 4—2 break would mean that you had to play off a fourth losing round before your own fifth spade became established as a winner, giving you four tricks in the suit. You might, of course, discover a 5—1, or even a 6—0 break, so you can't be certain of the number of your winners until you investigate the suit.

(f) 

This time you have a total of nine spades so there are four to be located. If they break 2—2, falling on your Ace and King, your four little ones will have become established for no loss. If they break 3—1 you will have to give up one trick to establish three of your small ones, and a 4—2 break would mean two losers in the suit.

We could go on all day with variations on this theme, but you will soon learn to work out the trick-taking possibilities for yourself. The point you have to understand is that you don't have to content yourself with winning only with the Aces and Kings, but that you can often develop, or "establish" tricks from the "little x's" too.

Considering No Trump contracts only for the time being, if you hold, for instance, the ♠K Q J 10 you can't win four tricks, because one of your opponents holds the ♠A, but once this has been played you *will* have *three* spade tricks. In other words, once you can knock out the ♠A you will have established three spade tricks for yourself, and generally, if this has to be done, it is better to do it sooner than later. With a solid holding such as this, missing only the Ace, you can go on playing your spades until one opponent parts with his ♠A. Once again, however, your suits will not always be so obliging, and we have now come to the basic techniques which will help you to convert possible losers into winners, that is, to establish a suit. There are four of these, Ducking, Unblocking, Finessing, and Holding Up. Another, Ruffing, you will learn about later when we come to consider trump suit contracts.

Let's just recap for a moment. On p. 26 you learned that the hand which actually wins any particular trick is the one to lead to the next trick. Thus if dummy's card wins the trick, the dummy hand leads next, and if South's card wins, South leads next. It frequently happens that, as declarer, you *want* to lead from a particular hand for a specific purpose, so you deliberately win the trick in that hand. Cards which enable you to win where you choose are called "entry cards". Sometimes they are ready-made and sometimes they have to be contrived with skill and care. One way, which contrives the entry card as well as helping to establish the suit, is called "ducking".

Ducking:

Ducking means playing a low card deliberately when you could play a high one, and its basic use is to create an entry card where, otherwise, this vital possession is lacking. Suppose you are playing a No Trump contract and the *only* helpful thing in dummy is the club suit.

There is no visible entry and you need four club tricks to make your contract. You could play the ♣A and ♣K and then a little one which, as you can see in this case, would clear out the last high club from the defenders leaving you two good clubs in dummy. This would be all right if you had another Ace or something so that you could get into dummy to play them now they're established. But you haven't, and you also haven't another club left yourself to lead. How can you cope? Well, you can do this by *ducking* the first round of clubs. Play a low club, both from your own hand *and from dummy*. East will win, but all you've done is bring his winner forward by two tricks—he had to win with his ♣Q anyway. Now, however, next time you win a trick in the South hand, you have a club—two clubs in fact—left to lead. The outstanding clubs fall and you will make a total of four tricks in the suit.

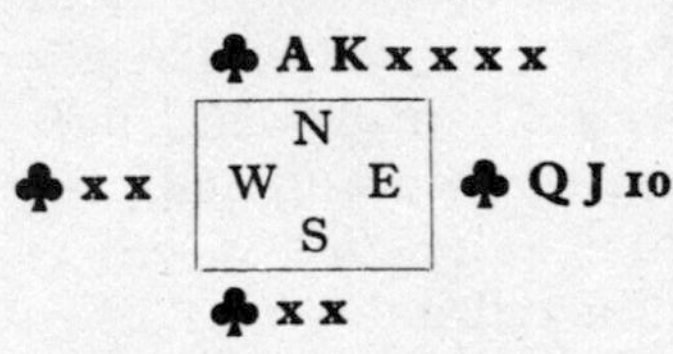

Here you have virtually the same situation. If you don't duck the first round of clubs when you have no entry to dummy you have no hope at all of making more than the Ace and King in the suit. Your opponents have five between them, one of which must be a winner. Let them make this early, keeping that vital second club in your own hand as an entry card, so that you can sweep in and make five club tricks instead of only two—not to mention the fact that you will be able to discard three useless cards from your own hand in the process.

Sometimes ducking requires more self-control than this, which was clearly a case of needs must when a club trick had to be lost anyway.

♣ A K Q x x

	N	
W		E
	S	

♣ x x x

With no outside entry to dummy, how do you play if you need four tricks in the suit? You have a total of eight, so, with any luck, the outstanding five will be divided 3–2 and will fall on your A-K-Q. Suppose they're not divided 3–2, though, but 4–1. Look at a possible full division of the suit:—

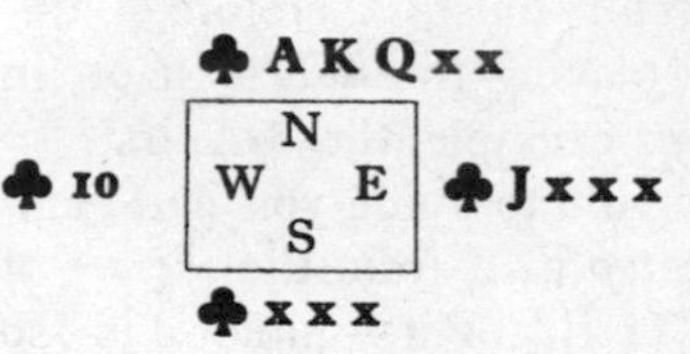

Needing four club tricks you must duck the first round, as a safeguard against a 4–1 break. Needing only three club tricks, you could afford to play out the top three, hoping that the others would fall which, if they did, would simply give you extra tricks.

Unblocking:

This is another important technique also based on the need to create entries which, in turn, is related to suit establishment. To block yourself means that you let yourself be caught with a high card which must win the trick, leaving you with no re-entry to the established suit.

♣ K Q J x x

	N	
W		E
	S	

♣ A x

If, just because you happen to be in dummy at the time, you play the ♣K first, you will be left with the ♣A in your own hand. This cannot help winning the second club trick and you will have no card left to lead to dummy's winners. This particular example might not catch you because beginners have a very strong tendency to play out Aces before Kings, Kings before Queens, and so on, not always realising that as long as they have these cards themselves they are of the same value for trick-taking purposes. So change the cards a little, still leaving yourself the Ace, King, Queen and Knave, though divided differently:—

♣ A Q J x x

	N	
W		E
	S	

♣ K x

If you play out the ♣A first, you will be left with the ♣K which must win the second trick and no way back to dummy. You must, therefore, "unblock" by playing the ♣K first or, in the previous example, the ♣A first.

There is a simple little rule to guide you here, and this is always to lead the *top* card from the *shorter* of the two holdings first. Get rid of it—unblock it—so that you retain a small one to use as an entry card later. If, for instance, you hold A K x x opposite to Q x, you can only win three tricks, but remember to play the Queen first from the short holding so that you have a small one left to lead to your A-K. The temptation, particularly if you happen to be leading from the hand that holds the A-K, is to grab for the high ones first. Try it out, assuming that you haven't got any other entry card, and see where it gets you. Similarly, with the A-x in one hand and the K Q x x or perhaps K Q J x in the other, it is essential to play the Ace first. Take away the fourth card in this last holding, making it K Q J opposite A x and, although you have the four top cards they will only win you three tricks as two of them must fall together. If you block the suit by not getting rid of the Ace first, you may well find you only make two tricks, not being able to get back to make the third.

Just before we go on, can you see how to handle this

♣ A Q J 10 9

	N	
W		E
	S	

♣ K

combination assuming, again, no other entry in dummy? Yes, full marks if you saw it. All these cards, as they run in a complete sequence, are of equal trick-taking capacity. Therefore you should play the ♣K and *overtake it with the ♣A*, which will give you the full five tricks in the suit.

All the way through the play of a hand this unblocking principle has to be watched. Remember it's the hand with the short suit from which you must get rid of the high card or cards first.

♣ A J x x x

	N	
W		E
	S	

♣ K Q x

In this example you have two high cards, the King and Queen, in the short hand, and both these must be played off before you touch the ♣A in dummy. Otherwise you'll be left with the King and Queen and no little card to get back to the dummy hand.

♣ A K Q x x

	N	
W		E
	S	

♣ J x x x

With nine cards in the suit and only four out against you, and as you have the four top cards yourself, you are sure of five winners as long as you don't block yourself. The ♣J must be played from the short hand first. Suppose you forget this and carelessly start by playing out the Ace and King from dummy. You've still got time to recover as long as you've discovered that there is not a 4–0 club break against you. With even a 3–1 break all the opposition's clubs must fall on your A-K-Q, so you can afford to throw away your ♣J on the ♣Q, leaving yourself with a little one which won't overtake dummy's fourth card.

Change the club holding again, making it ♣A K x x x

in dummy and ♣J x x x in your own hand. You have not got a sequence of honours and you can't unblock. If you need five club tricks all you can do is pray for a 2–2 break which will drop the opponent's Queen. If this happened you would be careful to win the third trick with the ♣J in your own hand, keeping a small one to lead back to dummy. Let's take a final example, making the suit even more awkward, and see how to handle it.

♣A K 7 5 4

N
W E
S

♣J 9 8 3

You are still hoping for a 2–2 break—which let's assume you get. But if you have carelessly played out dummy's ♣A and ♣K and dropped your own two smallest ones, the ♣3 and ♣8 on them, you will still have blocked yourself. Even though the ♣Q has fallen, dummy will have the ♣7 5 4 and you the ♣ J 9, which blocks the re-entry to dummy just as effectively as an Ace or King would do. The solution is to play the ♣8 and ♣9 on dummy's ♣A–K. Now if the club break materialises you will be able to win the third round with the ♣J and still have the little ♣3 left to lead to dummy's remaining ♣7 5.

As beginners you can't expect to notice and prepare for these situations every time, but it can do no harm to try to remember right from the start that you may need such a return ticket to an established suit. You'll be surprised at how quickly you'll find yourself able to cope, so that you don't get yourself stuck in the wrong hand.

Finessing: Next on our list of techniques comes finessing, which might be described as the art of winning more tricks than you obviously can in any specific suit. If you turn back to the examples of suit distributions given on pages 151 and 152 you will see that, in each case, you have touching cards in the suit, but you won't always be lucky enough to hold such combinations. More often your suits will be headed by broken honour combinations with one or more of the pretty pictures missing. You might well hold the A–Q, the A–Q–J, the A–K–J, or A–Q–10 and so on. All these *broken* honour holdings are called "tenaces" and we shall refer to them by that name in future.

♣ A Q

	N	
W		E
	S	

♣ x x

Let's take the simplest tenace of all, the A–Q, which is in dummy opposite two little ones in your own hand. You have no idea who has the other cards in the suit, but can you see that, if you play out the ♣A, it doesn't matter where they are because whoever has the ♣K to start with will still have it, and will be able to win the second club trick with it ? It is, however, a 50–50 chance whether East or West has the ♣K, so suppose, instead of playing out your ♣A, you lead a low card from the South hand *towards* the tenace. If West has the ♣K he will either play it, in which case you will crown it with the ♣A and your ♣Q will take the second trick, or he will refrain from playing it in which case, as it is still in his hand, your ♣Q will win the trick and your ♣A will be ready to win the second trick. If East has the ♣K there is nothing you can do about it—he is sitting *over* your tenace and, when you play the ♣Q his ♣K will pop out to win. By "finessing" the ♣Q, however, you are working on the 50–50 hope that West has the missing King.

Now let's extend this situation a little further and put in all thirteen cards in the suit:—

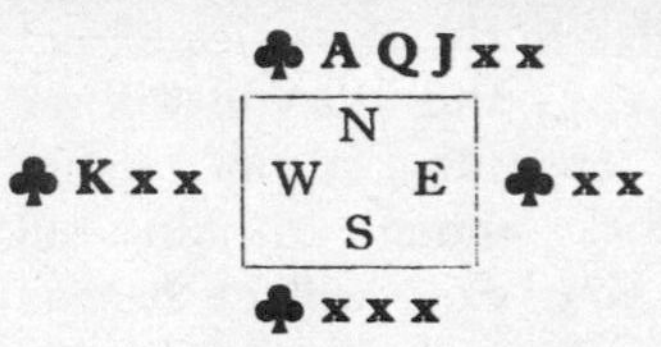

Get a pack and lay out these cards, turning them over as you play them, to be absolutely sure you understand. If you play out the ♣A, West's ♣K is bound to win a trick. Now try playing *from* your hand *towards* the tenace and hoping that West has the ♣K. If he plays a little card on your lead, you play the ♣J from dummy—which wins the trick. If you next play out the ♣A, West's ♣K will still be alive to take the third club trick, so you bide your time, wait till you can win a trick in the South hand, and then lead another small club and *finesse again*. This time the ♣Q will win and West's ♣K will drop helplessly on the ♣A when you play it for the third round.

Here's another combination, missing the ♣Q. If you play off the ♣A and K and West holds the ♣Q x x, he is sure to win a trick. If you lead low from the South hand *towards* the tenace and play the ♣J, this will win if West has the ♣Q and, still more, if the six outstanding cards are divided 3–3, it will win you four tricks in the suit—try it and see.

This time you are missing the ♣K and ♣J and, as usual, want to make as many tricks as possible, so you play *towards* the tenace and if West plays a small one, you play dummy's ♣10. If East plays low you know that West has both the ♣K and ♣J, so you get back to your own hand and finesse again. Had East played the ♣J on your ♣10 you would still have finessed the ♣Q against the ♣K next time. If, however, East had produced the ♣K when you played the ♣10, you would know that West held the ♣J. To see how this might help you, give North the ♣9. Your first finesse would be low towards the ♣9 and, if this drew the ♣K from East, the next time you were leading from the South hand you would play a second small club and finesse the ♣10. This would ensure that West never won a trick with his ♣J, even if he started with four cards in the suit.

♣ A Q 10 9

N

S

♣ x x x

It is worth noting something of fundamental importance here—another of the major reasons for not playing out all your Aces and Kings as soon as you gain the lead as declarer. Apart from being control cards, that is, cards which will win tricks in the suit and prevent your opponents from doing damage in it, **you will almost certainly need them as entry cards, either to your own hand or to dummy,** so that you can take essential finesses or run off winners in established suits.

Communications:

This matter of entries from one hand to the other—what is known as "communications" between the two hands, can present difficulties. Sometimes the entries are there, ready made, sometimes nothing you can do will provide them, but sometimes you can find a way around the situation by thoughtful planning.

♠ A J 10 9

	N	
W		E
	S	

♠ Q x x

In this combination the ♠K is missing, you want to finesse in an attempt to "catch" it without loss of a trick but, if you lead low from South and the ♠9 wins, indicating that West holds the ♠K, you are short of entries back to the South hand to take the finesse again. The way to handle this is to lead the ♠Q in the first place. Now, if no one produces the ♠K, you are still in the South hand with the winning ♠Q and can lead a low spade and finesse the ♠10. Change the cards to A J x x in one hand and Q 10 x in the other and you would lead the Queen or 10—they are of the same value as the Knave is sitting opposite—letting it run if not covered.

This combination needs more care. You must lead the ♠9 first from the South hand. If this wins you will be able to "run" the ♠Q, to catch West's ♠K even if he started with ♠ K x x x. If you lead the ♠Q first and it wins, you will be unable to avoid overtaking either the ♠9 or your "x" in North's hand, so will either have to find an entry back to take the finesse again or risk losing a trick to the King.

There are countless variations on this theme and you will learn to recognise and handle them as your experience grows. Meanwhile, your golden rule is to try to lead *towards* honour holdings, not away from them. Even if your only holding is K x opposite x x, if you lead *towards* the King you have a 50–50 chance of finding the Ace on its left and so of winning one trick in the suit. This principle applies to all honour holdings unless they are solid.

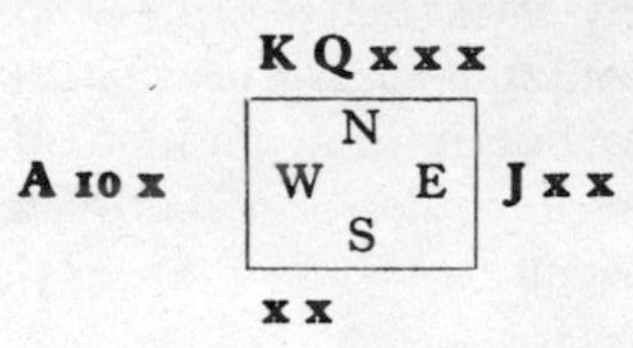

Here, if you lead the King, the Ace will win, and though you will be able to win the second trick with the Queen, East's Knave will be good for the third round. If you can contrive to lead twice *towards* the K–Q, you will only lose one trick. On whichever round West elects to play his Ace, your King and Queen will subsequently drop East's Knave and West's 10 without further loss to yourself.

Q x
N
S
A x x

This time you lead first *towards the Queen*. If West has the King he will either play it, leaving your Queen good and, later, your Ace will win, or he will hold it up, in which case your Queen will take the trick. If you played out your Ace first, of course, your Queen would be left sitting all naked and bare with no hope of winning wherever the King was, but add another "x" or so to the Queen, and you could play the Ace first if expedient.

Whatever the combination the principle holds good —lead *from* nothing *towards* something, which gives you the best chance of making extra tricks. It is also worth remembering to look for these situations early in the hand so that you can plan to keep any necessary entry cards intact for use when required.

Holding Up:

The last of this selection of play techniques we are going to examine here is "Holding Up", which means keeping a high card and refusing to part with it at the first opportunity. This is always difficult for beginners, whose reaction is to win any trick that can be won regardless of the possible consequences. *Communications* loom large again here, but it is a question of communications between the defenders, not between declarer and dummy at this stage.

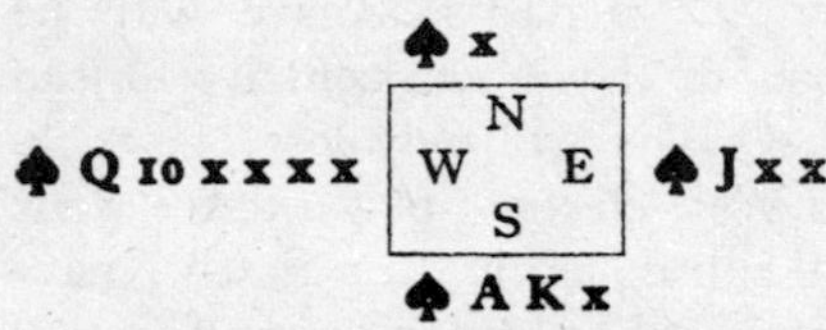

You are South playing in 3 N.T. and West leads a low spade. Your natural reaction with that lovely ♠A and K, is to win the trick. Let us, however, complete the full picture, which will also take us back to finessing:—

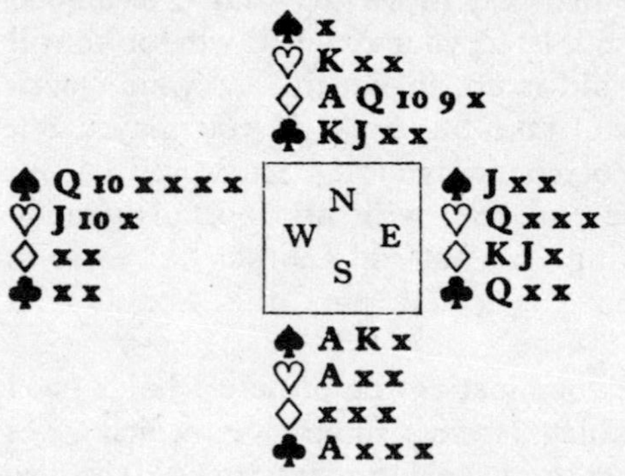

You can count the ♠A and K, the ♡A and K, a questionable number of diamonds and the ♣A and K, so you have work to do to produce nine tricks. If you win the first spade trick and finesse the diamond, playing the ♢9 to East's ♢J, East will return a second spade which you also win and finesse the diamond again. This loses to East's ♢K, East leads his third spade, taken by West who has three "established" spades to win. These, plus the two diamonds already won by East–West, make a shambles of your 3 N.T. contract. Now look at it again and realise this danger and how to cope with it. If you **hold up** on the first spade lead, allowing East's ♠J to win the trick he will, of course, return a second spade. South wins and finesses the diamond which loses as before, East leading his third spade. South wins and finesses the diamond again but this time, when East wins with the ♢K, *he has no spade left to lead.* It doesn't matter which suit he tries because South has established his nine tricks and has also *exhausted* the communications between the defenders.

The situation is not always as clear-cut as this. Here once again you are South playing in 3 N.T. against which West leads the ♢K.

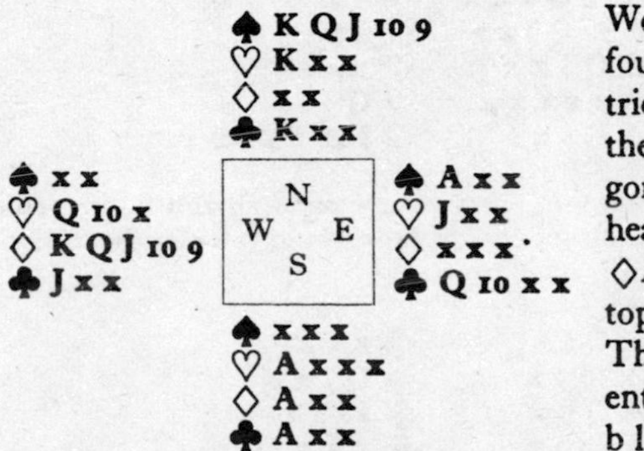

We can count four spade tricks once the ♠A has gone, two top hearts, the ♢A and two top clubs. There are no entry problems as dummy's two Kings face South's two Aces, but the unfortunate diamond lead finds South with only one "stop" in the suit. The only hope is that East holds the ♠A and that his stock of diamonds can be exhausted before he wins his spade trick. So South *holds up* the ♢A at trick 1 and also at trick 2, playing it at trick 3 when he can't avoid it. Then, with fingers crossed, he leads a spade and—joy of joys !—East wins. He has no diamond to lead and he can't get his partner in again, so South now makes his 3 N.T. in comfort.

As a tailpiece to this chapter it is worth pointing out that these techniques are also available to the defenders, about whom you will be learning in Section IV.

QUIZ ON CHAPTER 13

1. Leading from your own hand towards dummy, and needing a certain four tricks in hearts to make your contract, how would you play to give yourself the best possible chance if you had no outside entry card at all to dummy?

	Dummy	*You*
(a)	♡ **A K Q x x x**	♡ **x x**
(b)	♡ **A K Q J x x**	♡ **x x**
(c)	♡ **A Q J x x**	♡ **x x x**
(d)	♡ **A 9 x x x x**	♡ **Q J 10**
(e)	♡ **A K 8 x x**	♡ **J 10 6 x**

2. If you have no entry problems at all and no immediate danger from the opponents, how would you play the following combinations?

	Dummy	*You*
(a)	♣ **K Q J x**	♣ **x x x**
(b)	♣ **A 10 9 x**	♣ **Q J x x**
(c)	♣ **A Q 9 x**	♣ **10 8 x**
(d)	♣ **A J 10 9**	♣ **x x x**

3. Again with no entry problems or dangers, how would you play these combinations to give yourself the best possible chance of the maximum number of tricks?

	Dummy	*You*
(a)	◇ **A x x x**	◇ **Q J 10 9**
(b)	◇ **A x x x**	◇ **Q 10 9 8**
(c)	◇ **K J 10 x**	◇ **x x x**
(d)	◇ **Q x x**	◇ **K 10 9 x**

4. The lead is in dummy for the first and last time—you have no other entry apart from the good suit you now propose to play. How do you plan the management of it?

	Dummy	*You*
(a)	♠ A K J x x	♠ Q x
(b)	♠ A K J 6 3	♠ Q 10 9 2
(c)	♠ K J 10 9 x	♠ A Q x
(d)	♠ K J 10 9 x	♠ A x x
(e)	♠ A J 10 9 x	♠ K x x

5. Returning to Question No. 2 above, to which you have now found the correct answers:—

(a) Having led towards the ♣K Q J x, the ♣J wins. What would you plan to do?

(b) The ♣Q has won the first round. What would you do next?

(c) The ♣8 has won the first round. What would you do next?

(d) The ♣9 lost to the ♣Q. What would you play when next on lead?

QUIZ ON CHAPTER 13—ANSWERS

1. (a) Lead a small one and play small from dummy, i.e., "duck", to guard against a 4—1 break.
   (b) Lead a small one and win in dummy, then leading out the three other tops. You make your four tricks this way, and only a 5—0 break will prevent you from making six.
   Note: If the player on your left fails to follow suit to your first lead, you should duck. You will know of the 5—0 break in time and can ensure five heart tricks anyway.
   (c) Lead small from your own hand and finesse, playing the ♡J. If this wins, return to your own hand via another suit and finesse again. With any luck at all you'll catch the ♡K in this way.
   (d) Lead the ♡Q from your own hand and run it *whether your left-hand opponent covers or not.* If he puts the ♡K on your Queen and you win with the ♡A, you will have blocked the suit. You have no other entry, remember and once your ♡A has gone, your ♡J-10 will be the highest. Let the ♡K win then next time you are in your hand play the ♡J and a small one from dummy. Lastly play the ♡10 and *overtake it* with the ♡A for your entry.
   (e) Lead the ♡J and run it. If it is covered on your left you can afford to win in dummy and then lead back towards your ♡10.
2. (a) Lead *from* your hand *towards* dummy's K-Q-J-x.
   (b) Lead your ♣Q. If covered on your left, win with the ♣A. If not covered, let it run.
   (c) Lead the ♣8—this is important—towards dummy's holding. Try to work out why.
   (d) Lead small and finesse dummy's ♣9.
3. (a) You would lead the ◇Q from your own hand and run it unless covered. If not covered you would continue with the ◇J and so on.
   (b) Play the ◇A from dummy first and then lead low back towards your ◇Q 10 9. If nothing helpful appears on your right you have a guess to make, but probably the best is to play the ◇9.

(c) Lead from your hand towards the honours, of course. If your left hand opponent plays low, play the ♢10.

(d) First round, lead a low diamond towards the ♢Q. If she wins, lead a low one back and finesse the ♢9.

4. (a) Low from dummy and win with your ♠Q, then your little one back to dummy's high honours.

(b) You've got to watch the unblocking here. The safest way will be to lead from dummy and win with the ♠Q first. Then win with the ♠10 and lead the third back to dummy for the rest.

(c) Low from dummy first, win with the Ace *and* Queen, and then your last little one back to dummy's remaining high cards.

(d) Low from dummy towards your ♠A first, then lead a little one and finesse the ♠9. You want to avoid losing a trick to the ♠Q if you can, and if your right hand opponent started with ♠ x x you can do this.

(e) Exactly the same card combination except that the ♠A and ♠K have changed hands. Low to the ♠K and then finesse the ♠9 hoping to catch the ♠Q. If the ♠Q wins this trick you will still have a little one to lead to dummy's remaining ♠A J 10.

5. (a) You would plan to return to your own hand via another suit and lead *towards* the remaining ♣K Q x.

(b) If the ♣Q wins, lead the ♣J. You're still hoping to catch the ♣K without loss of a trick and have got him placed on your left.

(c) This was a rather hard one, but if you think about it you will see why it was necessary to play that ♣8 on the first round. If it wins, marking the ♣K on your left, you want to finesse again so next you play the ♣10 and, if not covered this time, let it run again and you still have a third club to lead from your hand to finesse the ♣Q. If you lead the ♣10 on the first round you will be unable to avoid over-taking the ♣8 with the ♣9 on the next round so, if your left hand opponent started with ♣ K x x x, you won't catch the ♣K without returning to your own hand before finessing again.

(d) Lead low and finesse the ♣10, hoping for the ♣K to be on your left.

CHAPTER 14

Planning No Trump Contracts

♠♡♣◇♠♡♣◇♠♡♣◇♠♡♣◇♠♡♣◇♠♡♣◇♠♡♣◇

IN the previous chapters you have met the basic techniques you will need for handling your cards. Now we come to examining them more closely as they apply to complete hands and particularly No Trump contracts.

The first thing you must always do as declarer when the dummy hand goes down is to *count your certain tricks*, compare this with the number you need for your contract, and decide what risks, if any, you will have to take to establish any additional winners you require. It may be a matter of knocking out one or more adverse high cards, of "ducking", "finessing", or "holding up". Finesses may have to be taken for which you will require entries either in your own hand or dummy, or you may need to safeguard or even create an entry to an established suit, and right at the start you should make a plan. You may have to modify this as the play develops, but at least *make* a plan. The fundamental points of this are likely to be which suit to try to establish first, and the provision of entries to enjoy it once established. Remember that a suit, once established, and whether at No Trumps or a trump contract, may be used simply for running off extra tricks or for throwing away—discarding—losing cards of another suit once your own cards in the established suit are exhausted.

Establishing Your Suit:

Beginners have a very strong tendency to play out all their Aces and Kings, even those in the suit attacked by their opponents, without realising what havoc this may cause later. Your holdings of top cards in a suit are your "guards", the only cards which, at No Trumps particularly, can prevent the enemy from running off winners against you, and they should be preserved carefully until parting with them is unavoidable. Here is a wonderful example, an actual deal from a beginners' class, where declarer failed to make his contract of 6 N.T. If you look at the two hands together you will see that they contain between them every vital card in the pack except the ♡A. South was declarer and West led the ♣Q, a card which later you will learn to recognise as probably being from the top of a sequence such as ♣ Q–J–10. South won this trick with his ♣K and then won the next seven tricks with his remaining ♣A, his two top diamonds, and his four top spades. This left him with his five hearts, tailor-made for four tricks once the ♡A had been knocked out **but** South had done what we call lost control of the hand. Here are the remaining cards so that you can see what had happened:—

♠ K Q x x
♡ x x
◇ x x x
♣ x x x x

N
W E
S

♠ A J x x
♡ K Q J 10 9
◇ A K
♣ A K

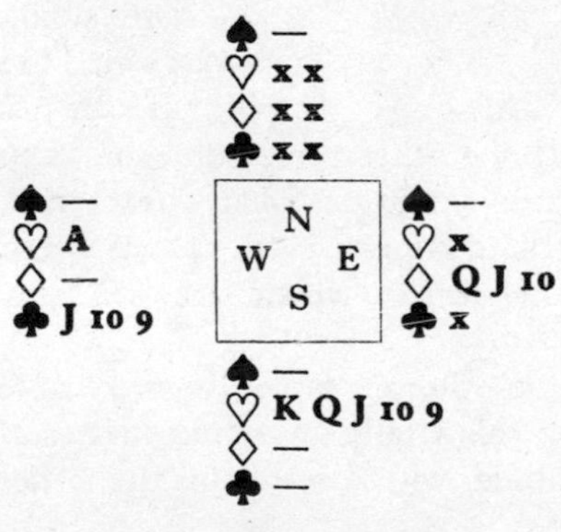

At this point, with nothing else left, South had to lead a heart and West won with the ♡A. This left South's hearts " established ", but so were West's clubs !

He happily won the last three tricks with his ♣J 10 and 9 leaving South three down instead of making his contract.

If you can get this matter of *control* into your head once and for all at this stage it will save you hundreds of tricks later on, so be sure you understand that, had South kept his second top club instead of playing it, West's clubs would not have been established. West could have won with the ♡A when South led the suit, but *South* would have won the club return and would then have been able to play out all his own established hearts. Here is the full deal. Go over this play again and again until you are sure you have it clear in your mind.

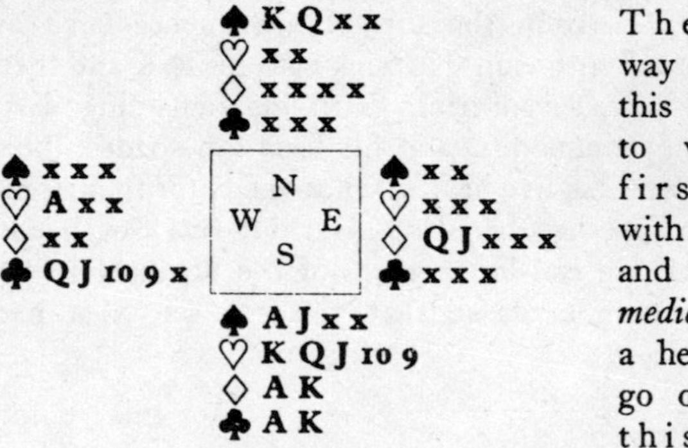

The right way to play this hand is to win the first lead with the ♣K and then *immediately* lead a heart—and go on doing this until West parts with the ♡A. At this point South has complete control of all the other three suits so, when the ♡A wins it doesn't matter what West tries, South has the first round control card, can win, and play out all his other cards which are *all* now established winners.

Let's have one or two other examples, to make sure you clearly understand this vitally important matter of *suit establishment* coupled with *control* of the other suits. Establishing a suit will provide the tricks you need, but you must be able to control the other suits so that your opponents can't sweep in and clear the board with their own established suit.

In the previous hand you only had one adverse high card to knock out, the ♡A and once it had gone you had nothing to fear. You won't, however, always be so lucky with your cards and will have to take positive decisions as to what to do for the best—in other words, to plan. Here you are South again, playing in 3 N.T. against which West leads a spade. First essential, count your certain tricks. You have the ♠ A K, the ♡ A K Q, all the top diamonds once the ◇A has gone, that is four tricks, and all the top clubs missing the Ace, so three more tricks there once the Ace has gone. On the face of it this is ample but it is still vitally important to plan correctly. You know too much now, of course, to play out your other winning spade and your top hearts before establishing your suit, but which one should you tackle first? Remember that one of your spade controls has gone to the first trick so you only have one left. West, who led the suit, may have five or even six and the two missing Aces. If you tackle clubs, West will win with the ♣A and lead another spade. Now you will have no spade guard left and your established tricks will total two spades, three hearts and three clubs, which is one short of your contract. You will need to establish at least one diamond but, if West wins with the ◇A when you try this, his spades are now established and ready to win tricks for his side. **But**—if you choose to tackle the diamonds first, you will establish *four* tricks for yourself whilst losing the lead only once, enough for your contract. West can get in and do his worst *after* you have made your nine tricks but what do you care?

So you win the first trick with the ♠K and immediately lead a diamond, not a club. It will not be luck that you make this contract, but *planning*. Notice too, that you should apply your correct technique for unblocking in the process—get rid of the ♢K from the "short" hand, and be sure to end up in the right hand, South, when it comes to playing out the established diamonds.

Now here's a slightly more difficult one for you though you will see that it is very little different from the one above. Can you work out what difference, if any, the changes make to your plan for the play of the hand?

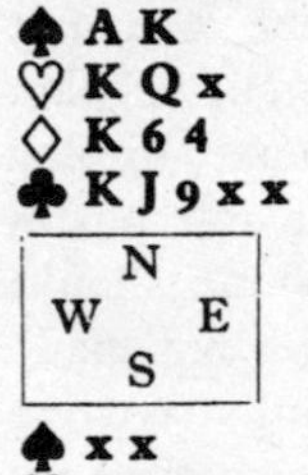

Again West leads a spade, won in dummy, but this time you must tackle the clubs, not the diamonds. The reason is that West might well have started with ♢A 10 9 x so that, to establish this suit you would have to lose the lead twice, just as dangerous as losing it to an Ace, but the club suit is missing only the Ace so that, to establish this, you need lose the lead only once. You would then win two spades, three hearts and four clubs for certain.

Now let's take this same hand exactly and play it against a heart instead of a spade lead from West. Does it seem to you that, with the same cards, you should have the same potential number of tricks? Well you are wrong. The important difference is that, against a heart lead, you hold three heart stops, the Ace, King and Queen. You can, therefore, afford to lose the lead twice before West's hearts will be established. You win the first lead in dummy and immediately tackle the clubs as before. With only the ♣A to knock out this will, again as before, establish four tricks for you. When a defender wins with the ♣A, whether he leads another heart or a spade, you will still have a cast-iron stop in either suit. You can, therefore, *afford* to go ahead with knocking out the ♢A as well. Thus you will find, if you look at the cards carefully, that against a heart lead you can make eleven tricks, losing to only the two minor suit Aces. If you cash the winning spades, hearts and clubs before knocking out the ♢**A** you'll establish their hearts for them and they'll come in with winners when you eventually have to lead a diamond.

♠ A Q x x
♡ x x
♢ A x x x
♣ Q x x

N
W E
S

♠ K J x
♡ A K x x x
♢ x x
♣ K J x

Sometimes things won't be quite as easy for you as in these two examples. Here's another one, a very ordinary sort of hand such as you will meet time and again. You are South playing in 3 N.T. against which West leads the ♢4, which is probably the fourth best of a four- or five-card suit. Count your tricks and make your plan. You have four certain spade winners, though you'll have to be sure that you play them in the right order, not "blocking" them by failing to play the ♠K and ♠J from your own hand first, once the only certain entry, the ♢A, has gone from dummy. You have two heart winners, making six, and one in diamonds, a total of seven. Where should you look for the eighth and ninth ? You could try the hearts, playing off the ♡A-K-x and hoping for a 3–3 break, but if you discovered a 4–2 break you would be faced with losing the lead twice to establish only one extra trick. This would be a poor exchange for the two *certain* tricks you can establish by knocking out the ♣A, so clubs it must be. There is, however, another lurking danger. West attacked in diamonds and you have only the one guard, the ◇A. Once this has been played you will be helpless to prevent him from playing out his established suit if he can get in again. Your clue lies in what you have learned about *holding up*. If *East* has the ♣A which, after all, is no worse than a 50–50 chance, and if you can *exhaust* his diamonds before he wins with the ♣A, you will make your contract. Here is the full deal:—

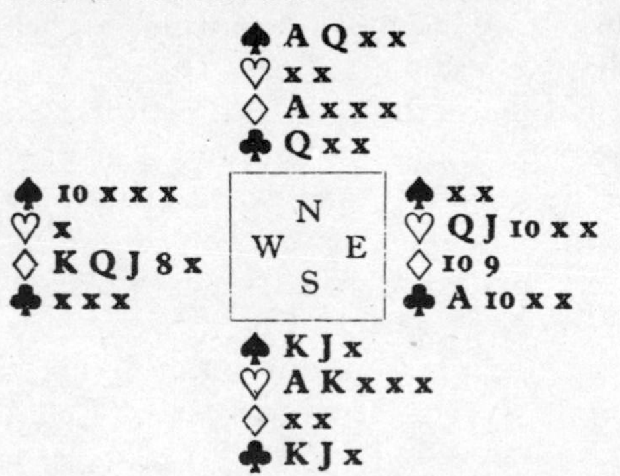

If you play North's ◇A at Trick 1, when East wins with the ♣A he will have a diamond left to lead to his partner, who will then make four tricks in the suit. These, plus the ♣A, defeat your contract. If you *hold up* the ◇A until East has none left, he will be unable to find a return lead to hurt you and, instead of going down, you will make your contract. So first you *hold up* the ◇A and then, when you are satisfied that East cannot harm you, you win with it *and lead a club*. You do *not* touch the hearts which might create an entry for West, but establish your own winners first. Change the ♣A to West's hand, though, and you could not have avoided defeat. Even if you had chosen to tackle hearts, East would have been able to lead a club for his partner to win and play off his diamond winners.

So counting your winners and deciding which suit to try to establish is the first priority when you see your own and dummy's hands together. A very close second to this problem comes entries which may either be ready-made or may have to be contrived.

The contract is 3 N.T. and West leads a small club. This time you can't even think of holding up, so you win with the ♣K. Which of our important techniques are you going to need here? Before you can decide that, you must have counted your winners, four top spades, two clubs and *four hearts if you can get the ♡A out.* You have no possible means of creating an entry in dummy other than by way of the hearts, so your only chance is to get one opponent to play the ♡A *while you still have a small heart to lead to dummy.* You must not block the suit by playing high ones from dummy and hanging onto your ♡Q. *Lead it first.* Now whichever opponent wins, you cannot be harmed. Another club you can win with your ♣A. A spade clearly would cause you no pain, and if they tried a diamond you have the suit well stopped.

Same contract, same lead. Counting winners presents no problems here and the only important thing is your plan. How do you play this hand?

The answer is very simple. Every suit is guarded and the hearts provide six certain tricks on their own as long as you don't block them. Win the first club lead, play your ♡K and overtake it in dummy with the ♡A. If this seems to you a scandalous and extravagant waste of two top cards, think what a much greater waste all those lovely established hearts in dummy would be, with you unable to get to them!

♠ A x x x
♡ A J 10
◇ Q x
♣ A x x x

N
W E
S

♠ x
♡ K x x
◇ A J 10 9 8 x
♣ Q x x

Preserving and creating entries are only different aspects of the same thing. In the hand above you *created* an entry by overtaking the ♡K with the ♡A. On this hand you have got to plan to preserve an entry. The first count of winners is not highly productive. One spade, two hearts, one diamond and one club, a total of five, but clearly the diamond suit can be a fruitful source of the extra ones needed as only the ◇K is missing. West leads a low heart which appears to establish an extra trick. If dummy's ♡10 is played and East produces only a low one, we shall have three ready-made heart tricks. If he produces the ♡Q we should still have three heart tricks because the ♡Q will be taken by the ♡K leaving ♡A–J good in dummy.

This is very dangerous thinking because this one extra heart trick is not enough for the contract, and it is vital to preserve the ♡K in the South hand in case it is needed as an entry to the long diamonds. Here is the full deal. A low heart is led from West

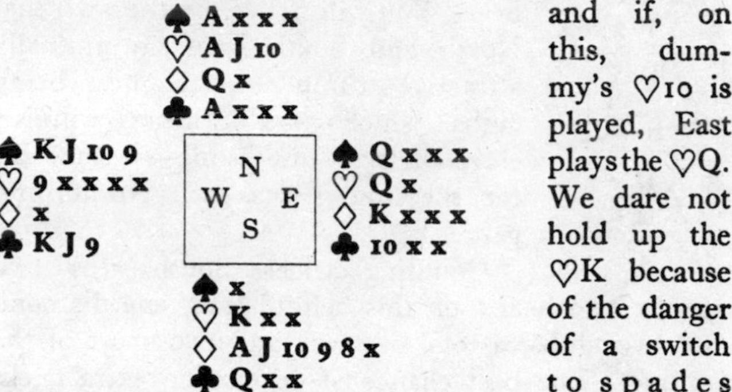

and if, on this, dummy's ♡10 is played, East plays the ♡Q. We dare not hold up the ♡K because of the danger of a switch to spades which would spell curtains to 3 N.T., so we win this trick. We want to finesse the ◇K so enter dummy with a heart to the ♡J, and lead the ◇Q. East plays low, so dummy's second diamond is led and won with the ◇8. There are no more diamonds in dummy for another finesse so the ◇A must be cashed and a low diamond given up to East's ◇K before the rest of the suit is established. At this point there is no possible entry back to the South hand.

The way to play this hand is to go up with dummy's ♡A at Trick 1, take the diamond finesse as before and then, having had to let East win the fourth round of diamonds with his ◇K, he will be unable to prevent you regaining entry to your hand. You have first round control of both spades and clubs *and the ♡K* for an entry card.

Here the contract again is 3 N.T. by South against which West leads a heart. You will notice, by the way, that North and South have no mutually attractive trump suit, the best being clubs which would mean winning eleven tricks—impossible—so they try for the nine tricks of a No Trump game.

Counting tricks South sees two spades, two hearts on this helpful lead, one diamond and two clubs, a total of seven and two short of the contract. The best chance of developing extra tricks comes from the club suit so, hoping for a 3–2 break, South plays off the ♣A and ♣K and, when East and West both follow, a third club. Now his own last two in dummy are established and he's let one opponent win a trick which he had to win anyway while he, South, was still in control of the other suits. He can win any return, enter dummy with the ◇A, and play off his two precious little clubs. After that he can make his other remaining top winners, scoring nine tricks for 3 N.T. bid and made.

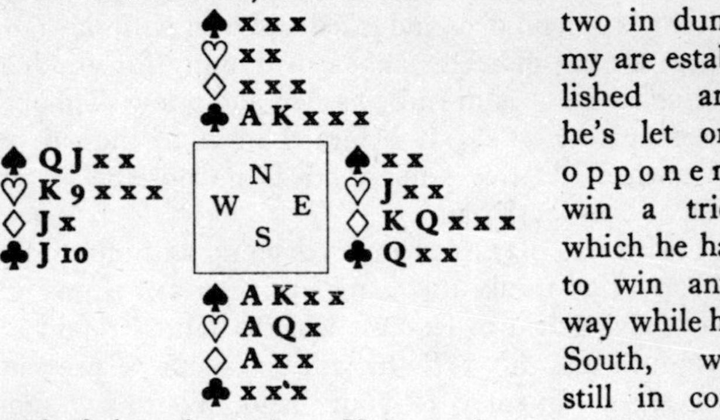

This was all quite easy, but suppose dummy hasn't got that ◇A for an entry card to the established clubs.

When South gives up that third round of clubs the two last will be established but he will have no way of getting to them. Look at the full deal on the previous page. The ♢A has changed places but what a world of difference this makes to the play ! South still needs four club tricks for his contract but, as you know, it takes three rounds to establish the suit, by which time he won't have a club left himself. Against the same lead, South wins with the ♡Q and leads a club, but instead of winning this in dummy he **ducks,** playing a little one. East wins and returns a heart which South takes with the ♡A and his two remaining clubs to dummy's ♣A-K clear the suit leaving him in dummy to play his last two little x's. He will have created, as it were, an entry card out of thin air. It has cost him nothing because he's only lost one club trick that he always had to lose, but he chose to lose it while he was not only still in control of the other suits as before, but in control of the entry problem.

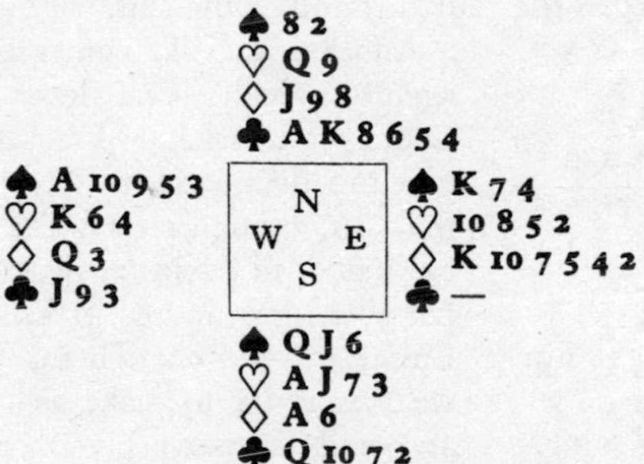

Again South is in 3 N.T. and West leads the ♠5. East wins with the ♠K and returns the ♠7. West wins South's ♠J with his ♠A and returns a third spade which South wins with the ♠Q. South has already counted his winners—one spade, one heart, one diamond and six clubs, enough for his contract, but care and foresight is needed in the handling of the clubs as there is no other entry to dummy without giving up a trick to the opponents who hold two established spades. South, therefore, must ensure making his nine tricks before letting them regain the lead. Work out how to play the clubs for yourself. Got it? Yes, this is an exercise in "unblocking". Lead the ♣Q playing dummy's ♣4. Next lead the ♣10 and overtake it with dummy's ♣K. Now the suit is unblocked and you can play your ♣7-2 on dummy's ♣A-8 and will not be forced to win a club trick in your own hand, leaving yourself with no other entry to the established suit. This, of course, was a case of not only playing the high card from the short hand first, but of getting rid of the second high card which could do you just as much harm. Try out what happens if you leave yourself with either the ♣Q or ♣10 on the fourth round of the suit.

♠ K Q x x
♡ x x x
◇ A K
♣ A x x x

N
W E
S

♠ A x
♡ A Q J x
◇ x x x x
♣ K x x

Another 3 N.T. contract by South against which West leads the ♣Q. Count your tricks—three top spades, two top diamonds, two top clubs and the ♡A, though clearly the hearts can be made to yield at least one, and possibly two more tricks than this. Either will be enough for 3 N.T. but we always try to make as many tricks as possible on any given hand. There is no need to duck the lead, though we do want to win the trick in dummy for the heart finesse. So up goes the ♣A and a heart is led. South plays his ♡J which wins, marking East with the ♡K but South is not content to play off his ♡A as East may have more than one " x " to guard his ♡K. Returning to dummy via a diamond, declarer leads a second heart, finessing the ♡Q. This too wins and now, with no further finesse available, he plays off his ♡A. On this West plays a little heart and East drops his ♡K. Can you see what has happened ? In addition to finessing twice and catching the ♡K without the loss of a trick, the suit has " broken " like this. South's last " little x " is the thirteenth and, therefore, the best and only heart left, good for another trick. So by playing the heart suit carefully and making the most of the fortunate distribution, South was able to convert it from its original trick value into four! For the mathematicians amongst you he had, in fact, a 50 per cent. chance of finding the ♡K with East and a 36 per cent. chance of a 3—3 break. As the effort could cost him nothing, it was well worth making it.

♡ x x x

♡ x x x   N / W E / S   ♡ K x x

♡ A Q J x

Now here's another problem for you and, as usual, South is playing in 3 N.T. If you wonder how he reached this contract, he undoubtedly opened the bidding with 2♣, North gave the negative response of 2◇ and South rebid 2 N.T. With four points North, of course, raised to 3 N.T. Against this West leads a spade. South, counting his tricks, sees that the lead has given him a " free " finesse because he is now certain of two spade winners. Although he has the four top hearts he has only three heart winners as they overlap. He has two diamonds and sees that to be successful he must rely on a fortunate club distribution. Clearly also it is a matter for finessing—both the ♣A and ♣Q are missing, so entries will be needed in dummy. South wins the first lead in his own hand, playing his ♠A on the ♠K from East, and leads his low heart, winning in dummy with the ♡J. He then leads a club and, silently putting up a prayer when East produces a little one, he plays his ♣8. (You will notice that he has the full sequence from the ♣J downwards, so that the ♣8 is equal in value to any of the higher ones.) On the ♣8 West plays the ♣A. What does this suggest to you? That East has the ♣Q, of course. If West had had it he could have won the trick with it without using his ♣A. West leads a second spade, won by South and now comes the key play to success on this hand. South leads his ♡Q and *overtakes it* with dummy's ♡K. This gives him the second vital entry to dummy and he can now lead another club to finesse again. Here is the distribution for which he was hoping, and had the good fortune to find. Winning this second finesse with the ♣9, South drops East's ♣Q with his ♣K, and the rest of the suit is now established.

You have now had a number of exercises in establishing suits and gaining extra tricks by various means. One could, of course, go on almost to infinity with examples, but what you need now is practice to help you to become familiar with the different situations so that you can recognise them, and judge which one or more of the techniques to apply to any given hand. Before we leave this chapter though, there are two further points to be explained, the first of which is the time factor—what is generally known as timing or gaining a tempo.

The Time Factor:

You have already learned something about this without actually naming it. In the very first hand of this chapter it was essential for the timing to be correct, to the extent that the earlier the ♡A was forced out from the opposition, the better. But the time factor can come into things in a very different way, as in the second hand we looked at. You had to select *which* suit to establish, the reason for your choice being that the alternative did not ensure you the *time* to make your contract before your opponents caused trouble with their long suit. Look at this hand:—

Playing 3 N.T. against a spade lead from West, you clearly have *time* to establish the club suit. It is missing only the ♣A and you have a second guard in spades, the suit attacked. Further than this, you also have first round control of both diamonds and hearts. So immediately, winning Trick 1, you lead a club. No harm can come to you. You are certain of two spades, three hearts (and possibly a fourth if they obligingly break 3—3) plus five club tricks once the ♣A has gone.

♠ x x
♡ Q x x
◇ A x
♣ Q J 10 9 8 x

	N	
W		E
	S	

♠ A K
♡ A K x x
◇ K Q x x
♣ x x x

Remove the ♣K from the North hand, substituting a small one, and see the difference. The ♣A and ♣K are now both missing. You win the spade lead and one of your guards has vanished. If you now try to establish your club suit back will come a spade taking your last guard and the enemy's suit will be established while your own is not. They will have gained the tempo and if you let them get the lead again before you have made your nine tricks you can say goodbye to your contract. Is there any way out of this difficulty? Have you carefully counted your possible tricks yet except to realise that the clubs won't help? Let's see. The ♠A-K, three top hearts and three top diamonds, and there is one chance of making the ninth trick in time. As you learned from a previous hand, there is a 36 per cent chance of a 3—3 break of the six outstanding hearts which is certainly a better hope than playing on clubs which you *know* can't help you.

Take exactly the same cards as these and play against a heart lead from West. Now *you* have the tempo because you have three stops in hearts only one of which falls to the opening lead, so you can afford to lose the lead twice while you knock out the opposing high clubs.

So you see what a difference the time factor makes. On the first hand, with a spade lead, you can afford the time to establish the clubs and on the second you can't so you take your only possible alternative of hoping for the heart break. On the same cards and a different lead, time is on your side and, even missing the two top clubs, you can afford to establish them.

As already pointed out, you have met this time factor but knowing, understanding about it, and recognising its importance, is another thing again. When you are deciding how to play a hand, whether to duck, finesse, or anything else, you must now consciously add "Have I got *time* to do this?" If you find the answer is "yes", go ahead and do it. If it is "no", search for any possible safer way of playing, and if you find it is "maybe", then do it unless you can see a line of play which is safer for certain.

It is possible that you will find you have a choice of two lines of play and here, unless one offers you better odds than the other, you may just have to guess. This brings us to the second of our two final points, making use of inferences which may change a blind guess into something near a certainty.

Gaining Inferences from the Bidding:

♠ A Q 10
♡ x x
◇ A Q 10 x x
♣ J x x

N
W E
S

♠ J x x
♡ A Q 10 x x
◇ x x
♣ A Q 10

Playing in 3 N.T. against a club lead and with no opposition bidding, you would be faced with two identical red suits and two identical black suits. Clearly your extra tricks must come from one or other red suit but *which* is nothing more than a guess. One declarer might be lucky and make the right guess whilst another would not. Suppose, however, that West had been the dealer and had opened the bidding with 1♡—would you still have nothing but a guess to guide you? No, far from it. To have opened the bidding West must hold very nearly every missing picture card. He's far more likely than not to hold the ♡K-J as well as length in the suit and he probably has the ◇K if not the ◇J too. The original club lead will have told you whether or not he started with the ♣K which (counting up his points for his opening bid) will give you a very good idea of whether he has the ♠K. At any rate, even if he's missing one of these cards, the clear inference for you is that the red light shines against any attempt on your part to establish your hearts so your choice must go to the diamonds. If, instead of bidding 1♡, West had bid 1◇, would this put you off trying to make extra tricks in this suit? No, for this time North's diamonds are *over* West's, and whilst West very probably holds at least one of the missing heart honours, he almost certainly has the ◇K-J. So though you could not hope to establish five, or even four diamond tricks, you would certainly hope for three.

Your opponents' bidding, then, can often give you a clue as to how to plan your play of a hand. Not only will it indicate where probable length and strength in a particular suit lie but you may be able, as your skill progresses, to count and place practically every card in the pack.

QUIZ ON CHAPTER 14

1.

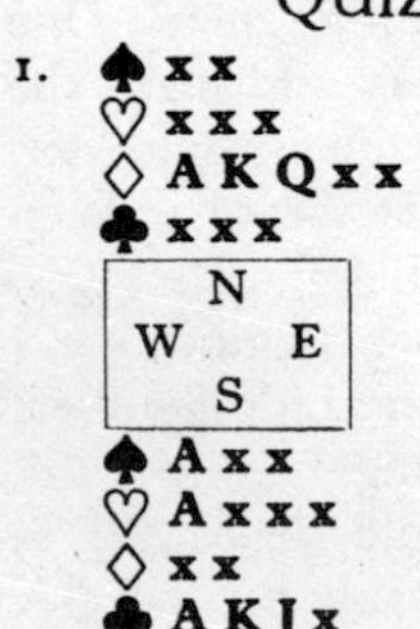

You are South playing in 3 N.T. against which West leads a low club. East plays the ♣Q.

(a) What card do you play to Trick 1 from your own hand?

(b) What cards do you play to the second trick, both from your own hand and dummy, and why?

(c) Instead of a club West leads the ♠K. Without even giving yourself time to think about it, you win with the ♠A. What card do you play from your own hand at Trick 2, and what from dummy? Why?

2. ♠ x x
♡ x x x
◇ A K Q x x
♣ A x x

♠ A x x x
♡ A x x x
◇ x x
♣ K J x

You are South playing in 3 N.T. against which West leads a low club.

(a) Which card do you play from dummy and why?
(b) What cards do you play at Trick 2, both from your own hand and dummy, and why?

3. ♠ x x x
♡ x
◇ K Q J 10 9 x
♣ K x x

N
W E
S

♠ A x x x x
♡ A J x x x
◇ x
♣ A Q

You are South playing in 3 N.T. against which West leads a low club.

(a) Which card do you play from dummy and which from your own hand, and why?
(b) What do you lead at Trick 2?
(c) If the opponent who holds it decides to *hold up* the ◇A how would you proceed?

4. ♠ A Q 9 x
♡ K 9 x
◇ x x x
♣ A K x

♠ J 10 x
♡ Q 10 x x
◇ A Q J x
♣ x x

You are South playing in 3 N.T. against which West leads a low heart. You play low from dummy and East produces the ♡8 which you win with the ♡10.

(a) What card do you lead from your own hand at Trick 2?
(b) If the card you led wins, what do you lead next?
(c) What do you lead from dummy when you are in that hand and if this proves successful what do you do next?

5.

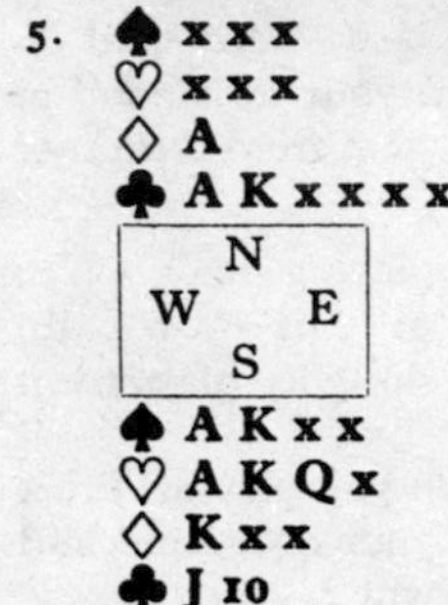

You are South playing in 6 N.T. which means you may lose one trick only. West leads a low diamond which you obviously can't avoid winning in dummy.

(a) What is your only hope of making your contract?

(b) What card do you lead from dummy at Trick 2 and why?

QUIZ ON CHAPTER 14—ANSWERS

1. (a) You win the trick with either the ♣A or ♣K—it doesn't matter which as they are of the same value to you.
   (b) You lead a low diamond and *duck it* in dummy, i.e., play a low one. You can count three club tricks, one spade and one heart, so you need four diamond tricks for your contract. Ducking the first guards against a 4—2 break in one of the opposing hands.
   (c) You play a low diamond and win it in dummy with one of the top cards. You can count only seven sure tricks, you have no guard left in spades, and you dare not let your opponents win a trick. Your only hope is that the diamonds will break 3—3 because if they don't you're sunk anyway.

2. (a) You play low from dummy, allowing the lead to come up to your hand. The lead has presented you with a "free" finesse up to your ♣K-J, so you are now sure of three club tricks.
   (b) A low diamond from your hand and a winner from dummy. You have the ♣A for an entry to dummy if the diamonds fail to break 3—3 so you can afford to cash the ♢A-K-Q in hopes. If they break 4—2 you can give up the fourth trick without fear.

3. (a) You play low from dummy and *the ♣A* from your own hand, the reason being that the ♣K is your only entry to dummy, which you must preserve in case the ♢A does not appear on the first round of the suit.
   (b) At Trick 2 you lead your singleton diamond.
   (c) If the ♢A is not played you will be in dummy. You go on leading out high diamonds until someone *does* come up with the ♢A. You can win either a heart or spade return with your Ace of that suit and then lead the ♣Q and overtake it with the ♣K. Thus you will come to one spade, one heart, five diamonds and two clubs.

4. (a) The ♠J.
   (b) If the ♠J wins, i.e., if the finesse wins, you lead the ♠10.
   (c) If the ♠10 also wins you lead your third spade, win in dummy with the ♠Q if the ♠K hasn't appeared and switch to a diamond, finessing the ♢J against the ♢K. If successful, repeat the dose by re-entering dummy with a club to the ♣K and finesse the ♢Q. You can then return the dummy via the ♣A, play off the last top spade, and throw a heart. You still have a diamond left to lead to the ♢A-x for, possibly, two tricks.

5. (a) Your only hope of making this contract is to find the five outstanding clubs breaking no worse than 3—2.
   (b) At Trick 2 you lead a *low* club from dummy. This is just another way of ducking. You know that you will have to lose one trick to establish the suit, and the sooner you do it the better. If you can't establish it you aren't going to make the contract, and you need a 3—2 break as you have no other entry in dummy. Someone will make the ♣Q but, provided you get the break, you will have a club left to lead to dummy where the ♣A-K will drop the outstanding clubs.

CHAPTER 15

Planning Trump Suit Contracts

♠♡♣◇♠♡♣◇♠♡♣◇♠♡♣◇♠♡♣◇♠♡♣◇♠♡♣◇

YOU will have noticed when you were studying the bidding that we have set great store by finding a good partnership fit for trumps, and that normally this means a minimum of eight cards between the two hands. This blissful state of affairs doesn't always materialise but at least it is what we aim for because, with eight out of the thirteen, declarer will have the balance of power in the suit. This, of course, is the reason why we hesitate to give direct trump support with less than a 4-card fit—if partner has opened on only four, responder needs four as well, to be sure of the eight-card total. Only if partner *rebids* the suit which, you will remember, promises at least five, should you offer support with three cards. As with most rules this has its exceptions as has been previously explained, but this need not trouble us for the moment. More often, without a trump fit, you will have agreed to play in No Trumps, to which the whole of the last chapter was devoted, so now we turn our attention to the planning and play of trump contracts.

Firstly, you are likely to have an agreed trump suit—a suit with added power—the teeth which have the ability to bite off your opponent's winning cards in their prime—chosen because you and your partner like it best. By the same token their trumps, if you fail to extract them, will have the ability to bite off your winning cards, and the main difference between playing a Trump and a No Trump contract is the handling of the trump suit itself. You must learn to distinguish between the hands where you should *draw* trumps immediately, and those where some of them can be put to a more useful purpose first.

The techniques you have learned already will stand you in good stead as they all come into the play of trump contracts. Once you have mastered the handling of your trumps you may even find your entry problems simplified, as you will be able to do what we call "ruff", that is, win a trick with a trump when one hand has none of the suit led.

Let us suppose that we are playing these examples with spades as trumps:—

♠ x x x

N

S

♠ A K Q J 10

You have eight between the two hands and if, as you would do in No Trumps, you played them out, you would have five solid established tricks. If, playing in a spade contract instead, you decided to draw the opponents' trumps, you would lead out your top cards and, as the outstanding spades can't be divided *better* than 3—2, you would have drawn all dummy's trumps—all dummy's teeth—too. Similarly, if you reduce your trumps to an original holding of ♠A K Q x x opposite to three in dummy, your ♠ A K Q are likely to draw all the outstanding ones from your opponents, leaving none in dummy either, but also leaving you with two "little x's" which are good for tricks anyway.

Now let's add a second suit to the hand:—

♠ x x x
♡ x x

♠ A K Q J 10
♡ —

If, being void in hearts, you use one of your big trumps to ruff one of dummy's hearts you are gaining nothing. Your big spade was a trick anyway. Similarly, holding the second selection, ♠ A K Q x x, the "x's" were likely to be tricks anyway, so you *gain* nothing by using one for ruffing. In either case you had a probable five spade tricks. It is a very different story, however, if you transfer the heart void to dummy's hand:—

♠ x x x
♡ —
N
S
♠ A K Q J 10
♡ x x

Now if you can contrive to "ruff" your own two losing hearts *before* dummy's trumps are extracted, you will *gain* two tricks. You will have your own five winners as before, but will have utilised two of dummy's little trumps to very good purpose. Here, of course, our old friend "timing" would come in, because you would be unable to draw your opponents' trumps before you did your ruffing as this would leave you without trumps in dummy. Notice, too, that this ruffing gave you two entries to dummy which might be very useful. Perhaps you have a holding you want to finesse, or perhaps dummy has a holding on which you can make useful discards. Remember, though, that if your opponents still have trumps they may be able to use them to good effect just as you can, so your planning of trump contracts will revolve round whether or not to draw trumps immediately.

If, in this example, you draw trumps, you will exhaust everybody's including your own. Your four in the South hand are the four top winner, so would it not be a good idea to look for a way of using some of dummy's trumps to better advantage than just following suit to your winners? We'll add a second suit to our example, and you will then see the reason for the value of a short "side suit" in dummy. If you draw

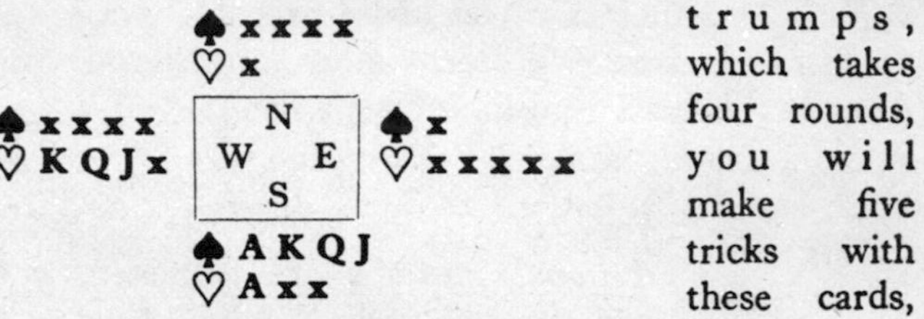

trumps, which takes four rounds, you will make five tricks with these cards, your four winning spades and the ♡A, and you will be left with two miserable little hearts which cannot possibly win. Suppose, however, that you can manage to ruff the two losing hearts while you still have trumps in dummy, can you see that you will convert your original five winners into seven?

The moral of all this is that trumping in the long hand will gain you nothing—such a trick will be a trick made, not gained, as it was going to make anyway; but trumping in the short hand will gain tricks, because you will win with trumps which would not themselves have won otherwise.

Learning to recognise the different situations is not as difficult as it sounds. Basically, if you have a shortage in a side-suit in dummy you should try to use dummy's trumps for ruffing and should only draw trumps before doing this if an obvious danger looms or if your contract is safe whatever you do. Similarly, if you have plenty of trumps to spare, draw the opponents' in case they can do you damage. Remember that what you have to decide from the outset of the hand is whether to draw your opponents' trumps immediately, or whether to attempt to use one or more from the "short" hand before you do this.

This preoccupation with whether to draw the

opposing trumps or not is because of the danger undrawn trumps can be to declarer. Playing in No Trumps, a suit headed by the A–K–Q–J is always good for four tricks because it is four solid top winners with nothing to threaten it. Playing at a trump contract, however, the situation is quite different. Declarer is not the only player at the table with a trump holding and nor has he any exclusive right to a void, singleton, or doubleton in a side suit. If you try to play out these four cards while the opponents still have little trumps knocking around they will step in smartly and cut off your winners in the prime of life. Here's a complete deal which illustrates the point very clearly.

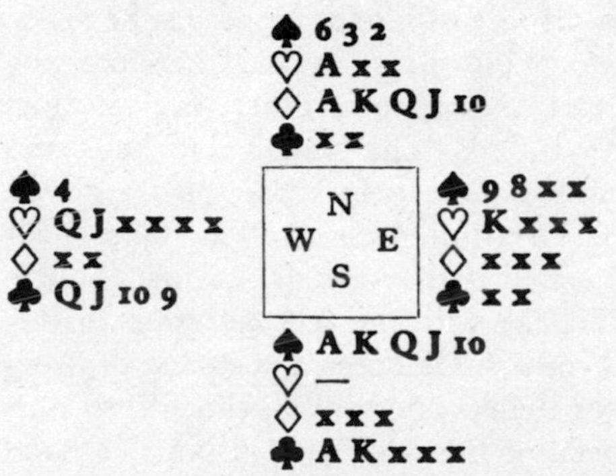

South is playing in 7♠ against which West leads the ♣Q. The contract is a very easy one as long as South is careful. If he feels tempted to ruff any of his losing clubs in dummy he must resist the temptation. If he tries to do this, he must take two rounds of clubs first to exhaust dummy's and then lead a third round. At this point East also is clear of clubs and, which is worse, he has trumps higher than any of dummy's. He will, therefore, happily over-ruff to defeat the contract. Ruffing clubs, then, is highly dangerous. It is also unnecessary, because North has the ♡A and five top diamonds, which between them will provide South with the three discards he needs for his losing clubs. Note also, by the way, that if South tries to discard his losing clubs before drawing trumps West, who has only a doubleton diamond, would have the pleasure of winning the third diamond with his little singleton 4♠!

This, then, is a clear case for drawing trumps with all possible speed, but what about this variation? Again South is in 7♠ and West leads the ♣Q. Can

♠ x x x
♡ —
◊ A K Q J x
♣ K x x x x

N
W E
S

♠ A K Q J 10
♡ x x
◊ x x x x
♣ A x

you see the vital difference? It is that the four diamonds in South's hand allow declarer one discard only, on the fifth diamond in North's hand whereas, to dispose of his losing hearts, he needs two. One heart must, therefore, be dealt with in some other way—it must be ruffed. The ruff must be taken immediately, before trumps are drawn because dummy, as well as the opposition, will be exhausted if they are drawn first. South, therefore, wins the lead with the ♣A and immediately leads a heart and ruffs it. He doesn't postpone drawing trumps any longer than was essential, though, so now that he has no need of the other two in North's hand he leads a trump, draws his opponents' teeth, and then runs off his other winners for thirteen tricks, the last of which will be his second losing heart on North's fifth diamond.

You won't, of course, always be playing in a Grand Slam contract when these occasions arise, and here are a few more examples of less exalted contracts, which will help to get your mind working along the right lines.

♠ A Q x x x
♡ K x x
◇ x
♣ x x x x

N

S

♠ K J 10 x x
♡ A x x
◇ x x x
♣ A x

West leads the ♡Q against South's 4♠ contract. It is clear that South will end up with a losing heart, a losing diamond, and a losing club, and also that he must ruff two diamonds in dummy to ensure that these are not losers too. South has, however, plenty of trumps for all possible purposes and can well afford to draw the enemy's three outstanding ones so as to take no risks. Even if they break 3—0 he will have two left in dummy—all he needs. So this is a moment to draw trumps.

♠ A K Q J 10
♡ x x x
◇ x
♣ x x x x

N
W E
S

♠ x x
♡ A K Q J 10
◇ x x x x
♣ K x

West leads a low spade to your 4♡ contract. To draw or not to draw? You can see that it would be nice to ruff losing diamonds first, but to do this you would have to give up a diamond trick—you haven't got the ◇A. If West won and led another spade you would have no entry back to dummy, and the spades, once trumps are drawn, will give you three discards of losers. So this is a moment to *draw*, because you can see your ten tricks for certain, five top trumps and five top spades. Give South the ◇A and an overtrick can be made. The first spade would be won as before, a diamond led to South's ◇A and a low diamond ruffed. A trump is then led and used as an entry to South who must then draw the outstanding trumps. If he tries to get a second diamond ruff he'll find he's back in trouble for entries. Work it out and see.

West leads the ♣K against South's 4♡ contract. How do you plan this hand ? It takes a little extra thought because it is a situation you haven't quite met before.

Note that, if you draw trumps, you can make four tricks in the suit plus three other Aces if the trumps break 4–1, but you have all the tops in sequence even if they are divided between North and South. Your plan for this hand, then, is a complete cross-ruff. You have the ♣A opposite North's singleton and the ♠A opposite your own singleton. **A golden rule** for playing a cross-ruff is to cash "side winners" first. So you win with your ♣A, cash your ♢A and then play low to dummy's ♠A. After that you play a spade from dummy and ruff in South, a club from South and ruff in dummy, and so on until your clubs and North's spades are exhausted. You'll find you're left with one winning trump in either hand—your tenth trick—and three losing diamonds which you can afford to give up.

Having given you the golden rule of cashing side winners one must, at this point, explain why. You need, in this instance, the ♢A to make up your ten tricks but you have decided *not* to draw trumps. This means that, by the end of your cross-ruff, the opponents will have more trumps than yourself or dummy. Furthermore they may have been able to discard diamonds and then, when you try to win with your ♢A, trump it.

Here's the full deal as it very well might be. Lay out the cards from a pack and see how it goes when you cash the ♢A, and then if you fail to do this. You will find that on the second and third club ruffs

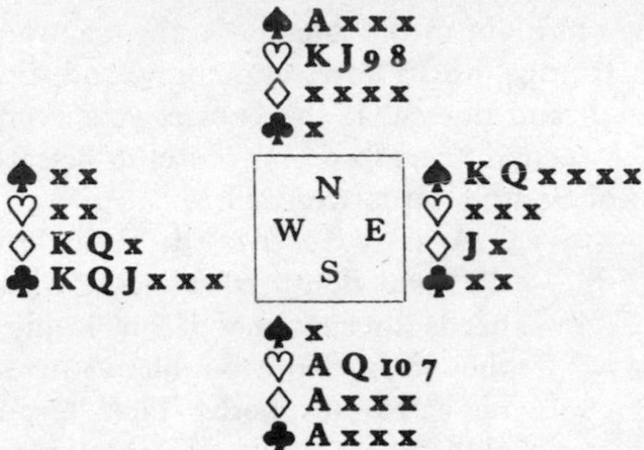

East will have been able to discard his two diamonds. You, having used up your hearts for ruffing, will be unable to draw more than one of his three, and he will trump your ♦A. If, on the other hand, you had cashed it before he could get his discards, it would have made a trick for you once and for all.

Let's now return to some other examples which will give you practice in this decision as to whether to draw trumps or not as well as showing you how the techniques you have already learned are still of vital importance.

♠ K 9 x x
♥ A K Q
♦ x x x
♣ x x x

N
W E
S

♠ A Q J x x
♥ x x
♦ x x x
♣ A Q J

Against South's 4♠ contract West starts off with three top diamonds and then switches to a trump. South has already lost all the tricks he can afford if he is to make his contract. Can you see what the contract depends on, and what he should do next ?

The answer is that it depends solely on the club finesse. South has ample trumps to draw the opponents' even if they break 4–0. He can throw away one club on the third top heart once the trumps are drawn but that won't get him out of the finesse. So the way to play is to draw trumps, lead a heart to dummy, and then play a low club and finesse. If the finesse wins everything is fine. A second heart to dummy, a club discard, and the rest of South's cards are good.

Against South's 4♠ West leads the ♣Q and South takes stock. Clearly he needs to ruff one of his losing clubs though having a doubleton in dummy he can't ruff both. That means one club loser only. He has plenty of trumps and, unless the outstanding four break 4–0, he can extract the opponents' before taking the ruff. He has no losing hearts and, depending on the lie of the diamonds, one loser or two.

So South wins with the ♣A and tests the trumps. Both East and West follow, so he draws the rest which, as it happens, fall 2–2. Then he leads a low club, deliberately losing this trick. West wins and switches to the ♡J. South wins, leads his last club and ruffs it in dummy and now the time has come to tackle diamonds. He leads a low one from dummy and has no way of knowing what to do except on a guess. He decides on a finesse, so plays his ♢10 which West wins with the ♢A. This, of course, means that South has successfully finessed the ♢J, his ♢K and dummy's ♢Q are now winners, and he makes 4♠ +1 instead of only 4♠.

Lest you should feel that spades are always trumps, we'll play this hand in 6♢, against which West leads the ♡K. Now nothing could be clearer to South than that he must lose a trick to the ♢A but the lead has taken his only heart stop and he still has a heart loser in dummy. With ample trumps he can ruff his own other two hearts, but as soon as East or West gain the lead with the ♢A they are going to cash a heart winner with all speed. This is a case of our old friend *timing* coming to the rescue. Can you see what South must do?

South wins with the ♡A and, instead of touching trumps, he leads a spade to dummy's ♠K. He then leads dummy's last spade to his own ♠A and *plays his ♠Q on which he discards dummy's other heart.* Having done this he can afford to clear trumps because, whoever wins with the ♢A will get no joy from trying to cash a winning heart—dummy will be able to ruff it.

This next hand is played in 4♡ against which West leads the ♣Q. Take a good look because once again, this is a slightly different situation from those you have met before.

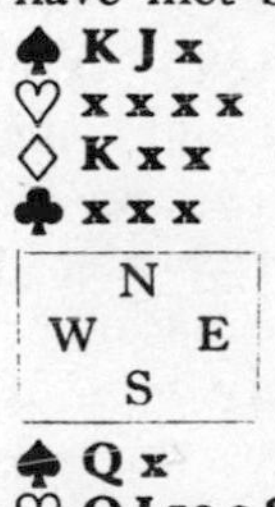

South sees that he is missing both the ♡A and ♡K—two losers—the ♠A is missing and, as things are at the moment, with three clubs in either hand he also has a club loser. If he tries to clear trumps *before* he solves this situation his second top club will be knocked out and he won't be able to avoid the four losers. In other words, timing again, though also plus our old friend "suit establishment". It's only a little suit, the ♠K J x opposite to the ♠Q x, but one of these can be *established* for a discard. South wins the club lead and immediately plays his ♠Q. East wins this with the ♠A and returns a club but South still has the ♣A. He wins, leads his last spade to dummy's ♠K and plays out his established ♠J *on which he throws his losing club*. Only then, with this danger averted, does he tackle the trumps.

Let's take a hand, vary it by one card several times, and examine the difference this one card makes to the line of play. In each case you are South, playing in 4♠ against a heart lead from West.

Here, with ample trumps and time, South wins the lead with the ♡A, draws trumps, then enters dummy with a club and discards his two heart losers on dummy's other high clubs. With at least one trump (depending on the break) left in dummy, he can only lose two diamond tricks because he will be able to ruff his own last card in the suit. In this way South makes an overtrick—and it is always declarer's duty to make as many tricks as he safely can.

This time South is missing the ♠A. You might think that as he could make an overtrick on the previous deal he would be safe for his contract, losing only the ♠A in addition to his other losers, but here *time* is against him. If East or West gain the lead with the ♠A they can "cash" two top hearts and two top diamonds which, added to the ♠A, means two down. So winning with the

♡A South must immediately lead a club and discard his two losing hearts on dummy's other two high clubs, only after that attacking trumps.

♠ 10 x x x
♡ K x x
◇ x x
♣ A Q x x

	N	
W		E
	S	

♠ K Q J x x x
♡ A x x
◇ x x x
♣ x

Now North has the ♡K instead of the ♣K, which means that the heart lead does not leave declarer defenceless in the suit. What, however, is the situation ? One certain spade loser, one in hearts and two in diamonds unless . . . ? South wins with the ♡A in his own hand and immediately leads his singleton club, finessing the ♣Q. If this holds he will play the ♣A and discard his own losing heart on it. He will then have three losers only, the ♠A and two diamonds. Note that if the club finesse fails he will be no worse off than he was before, which was facing one down on his contract. He'll still be able to get one discard on the ♣A and he will merely have exchanged one loser for another whilst giving himself the chance of success.

♠ 10 9 x
♡ x x x
◇ x x x
♣ A K Q x

	N	
W		E
	S	

♠ A Q J x x x
♡ A x x
◇ x x x
♣ x

Sometimes it's the trump suit itself that has to be finessed. So far our examples have shown nice solid trumps missing only one or both of the "tops", but life's not like that, and far more often you will be trying to avoid losing to missing trump honours just as you have learned to do with the other suits. Here South is in 4♠ and West starts off with three winning diamonds—all South can afford to lose—and then switches to a heart. On what does this contract now depend ? Yes, on the *trump finesse*, but it is also vitally necessary to get rid of the two losing hearts in the South hand. South wins the heart switch with his ♡A and immediately plays his singleton club to dummy's ♣Q. He would prefer to run no risks by drawing trumps at once, but he is short of entries to dummy so *first* he plays off the two remaining top clubs, discarding his two losing hearts. He then leads the ♠10 and, if East plays low, he finesses by letting it run. If the finesse holds he repeats the spade lead with the ♠9, thus catching the missing ♠K without the loss of a trick. Obviously if the spade finesse is wrong he will go down one, but he won't go down three because, by correct "timing", he has ensured having no heart losers.

Here's quite a different set-up with South again in 4♠. West leads out three rounds of top diamonds and South ruffs the third of these. He started with nine trumps between the two hands so there are four outstanding and if these break 2–2 he will have no trump loser so won't have to rely on the club finesse for his contract. Hoping for the best he plays the ♠A, both East and West following suit. He then leads a low spade and West discards a small heart. This means that East has the ♠Q–J left, one of which *must* win a trick, so whether he likes it or not, South must fall back on the club finesse. He wins in dummy with the ♠K and—here's the important new point for you to note—he does NOT draw East's remaining trump. It is the master, and nothing will prevent it from winning sooner or later, but to draw it would take two of his own trumps, one from either hand. So leaving it where it is, South takes the club finesse. When this holds he re-enters dummy via a heart and finesses the clubs a

second time. If East's ♣K appears South takes it with the ♣A and plays his remaining ♣Q. East can please himself whether he uses his ♠Q on this—it doesn't make any difference to South.

Such play can, in fact, provide a cheap and easy way of drawing a trump which cannot avoid winning.

With this next combination, South must lose one trump trick as even if they break 3–2 one opponent will be left with a winner. So after the ♠A–K have been played out, drawing eight trumps in all, declarer and dummy will each have two little ones and either East or West the "boss". If South needed to draw it, as he might, it would cost him a trump from both his own hand and dummy. If it is not vital to draw it he may well get rid of it much more cheaply. Here's the full deal:—

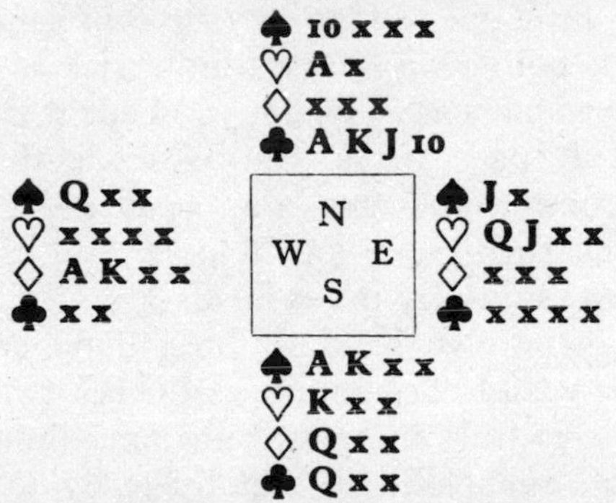

South is in 4♠ and West starts off by winning with his ◇A–K and leading a third diamond which South wins with the ◇Q. He then plays off the ♠A–K which leaves West with the ♠Q. With no way of avoiding this loser, South leaves it where it is. He cashes his ♣Q (unblocking it) and leads a second club to dummy.

Next comes dummy's third high club and whether West plays his ♠Q or not makes no difference—it is the only other trick South will lose.

We can't leave this chapter on planning trump suit contracts without learning to establish a side suit by ruffing.

♠ AKxxxx
♡ Ax
◇ xx
♣ Axx

	N	
W		E
	S	

♠ x
♡ xxx
◇ AKQJ109
♣ xxx

You are South playing in 6◇ against which West leads a heart. You can see two losing clubs and a losing heart because one loser can go on dummy's second spade, but you can only afford to lose one trick, not three. Have you any hope at all of making this contract? Yes—if the outstanding spades break 3–3, which will mean you can establish the side-suit by ruffing. So winning with the ♡A in dummy you lead the ♠A and follow this with a little one, ruffing in your own hand. This, of course, is not *gaining* you a trump trick as all your trumps are winners anyway, but you hope it is gaining you a lot of spade tricks. Having made the ruff—to which both opponents play spades—you draw trumps. You then cross your fingers, lead a club to dummy's ♣A and play the ♠K, discarding a heart or club from your own hand. If both opponents play spades your wish has come true as the last two spades will fall to this trick and your remaining three "little x's" will be established in dummy ready to receive your other losers. Thus you will make all thirteen tricks, let alone your contract of 6◇.

Change the two hands just very slightly, by putting one of your trump winners in the North hand. This would mean that you owned an extra entry card to dummy and this, in turn, would mean that you could

♠ A K x x x x
♡ A x
◇ Q x
♣ A x x

	N	
W		E
	S	

♠ x
♡ x x x
◇ A K J 10 9 x
♣ x x x

make your contract even against a 4–2 break of the outstanding spades. Look . . .

Winning the heart lead in dummy, you should play the ♠A and then a low spade trumping in the South hand. Next lead the low diamond to dummy's ◇Q and lead a second spade trumping again. Next draw trumps and finally, re-enter dummy with a club to the ♣A, play the ♠K and the other two established spades, taking three discards in your own hand. Only an extremely unlucky 5–1 break in spades will defeat this line of play.

When you were playing in No Trumps you had to establish your long suits such as this simply by giving up a trick or tricks to the opponents. Playing in a trump contract, as you can see, you may be able to do it by this additional means of "ruffing out" and, if you are wondering how to recognise the possibility of this situation, your clues are a long suit in dummy, ample trumps because, remember, you will be shortening your own trump suit in the process, and enough entries to dummy both to establish the suit and enjoy the fruits of your efforts when you've done it. It won't avail you anything at all to establish the spades if you haven't an entry card left to get to them.

Finally, on p. 196 of this chapter we said that ruffing in the long hand would not gain you a trick, and being a thoughtful reader you will doubtless have noticed that this establishing by ruffing does involve ruffing in the long hand. To this dictum, then, let us add that ruffing in the long hand will not gain you a *trump* trick though, if it is done with some specific purpose, it may well gain you tricks in other suits. So don't run away with the idea that it is forbidden to ruff in the long hand. You may do so happily either to bite off the head of an opposition winner, to establish a side suit for yourself, or even as a convenient method of regaining entry to your own hand. As your skill and experience progress you will learn many other occasions when it is not only the safest, but the only line of play.

QUIZ ON CHAPTER 15

1. 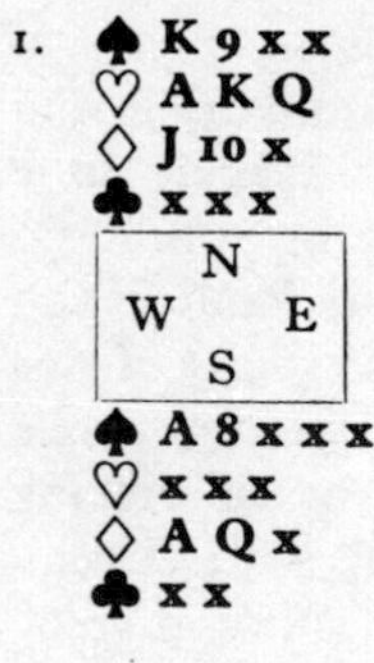

The contract is 4♠ by South against which West leads first the ♣A, then the ♣K and thirdly, the ♣Q.

(a) What should South play at Trick 3?
(b) What should he play at Tricks 4 and 5?
(c) If West plays a low heart at Trick 5 what does the contract now depend on?
(d) How should South plan the rest of the play?

2. 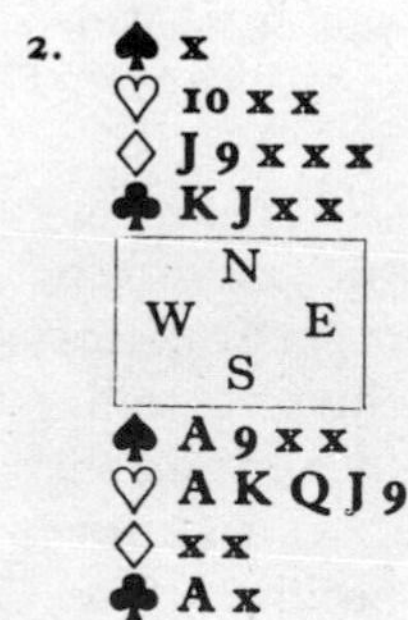

The contract is 4♡ by South. West leads the ◇A which wins and then switches to a low trump.

(a) How must South decide to play this hand?
(b) Having won the trump lead, what does he play to Trick 3?
(c) In what order does he play the rest of the tricks?

3. ♠ x x
♡ K 10 x x
◇ x x x
♣ A Q x x

N
W E
S

♠ A x x
♡ Q J 9 8 x
◇ A x x
♣ K x

The contract is 4♡ by South against which West leads the ◇K. South wins with the ◇A.

(a) What apparent losers has South got at this point?
(b) How can he hope to circumvent at least one of these?

4. ♠ x x x
♡ J 10 x x
◇ x
♣ A K x x x

N
W E
S

♠ A x x
♡ A K Q 9 x
◇ A x x
♣ x x

The contract is 6♡ by South against which West leads the ♠K. South wins this with his ♠A, at which point he has two losing spades in either hand.

(a) Can South hope to make his contract and if so how?
(b) What should South lead at Tricks 3 and 4?
(c) Assuming that the outstanding trumps break 2—2 what should South lead at Trick 5 and how should he play the rest of the hand?

5. ♠ 8 7 6 5 4 3
♡ —
◇ 7 6 5 4 3 2
♣ 2

N
W E
S

♠ A K Q J 10 9
♡ 7 6 5 4 3 2
◇ —
♣ 3

Spades are trumps and West leads the ♣A which wins the trick. He then switches to the ◇A. There is one outstanding trump, the ♠2, with either East or West.

(a) When declarer gains the lead, should he draw this trump or not?
(b) When West leads the ◇A at Trick 2, what is the maximum number of tricks Declarer can make, and how should he go about it?

QUIZ ON CHAPTER 15—ANSWERS

1. (a) At Trick 3 South uses a small trump to ruff the club.
   (b) At Tricks 4 and 5 he plays the ♠A and a low one to the ♠K, hoping for a 2—2 break in the outstanding trumps.
   (c) West's heart at trick 5 shows that East has an unavoidable trump winner so the contract now depends on the diamond finesse.
   (d) As East's trump is a winner anyway, South plans to leave it where it is and to lead the ♢J. If this wins he will lead another diamond and finesse again.

2. (a) South decides that he must ruff two losing spades before he draws any more trumps—already West's switch has cleared one off the table.
   (b) At Trick 3 South plays the ♠A.
   (c) Trick 4, South ruffs a low spade.
   Trick 5, South returns to hand with a club to his ♣A.
   Trick 6, South ruffs a second spade.
   Trick 7, South cashes dummy's ♣K.
   Trick 8, South returns to hand by ruffing a club.
   Trick 9-10-11, South cashes his top trumps and gives up his losing spade and diamond for the last two tricks to the defence.

3. (a) South appears to have one spade loser, one heart, and two more diamonds—too many for his contract.
   (b) Provided both East and West each have three clubs (more likely than not) he can get rid of one of his losers on the third high club. He must do this immediately, before he loses a trick to the trump Ace, otherwise he will find himself losing two diamonds and will be unable later to avoid losing one spade.

4. (a) Yes, South can hope to make if he is able to establish dummy's club suit for discards.
   (b) With such a good supply of trumps South can afford to try to safeguard himself against accidents so at tricks 3 and 4 he leads two rounds of trumps.

(c) When they break 2—2 all is easy. Next he plays out the ♣A-K and ruffs a third club. If both, opponents follow to this, the last two in dummy are established. Dummy is re-entered by ruffing a diamond and two spades discarded on the two clubs, South thus coming to 13 tricks. If only one opponent follows, dummy is re-entered via a diamond ruff as before and another club ruffed. The last diamond is ruffed in dummy for another entry and the now established thirteenth club led for one spade discard. One losing spade has to be given up, but declarer makes 12 tricks and his contract.

5. (a) No, South should not draw this trump. Even though he and dummy have twelve between them, he should leave it wherever it is.

(b) South can make twelve tricks, that is, all the rest, on a complete cross-ruff. His trumps are in unbroken sequence and at no time, therefore, will an opponent be able to over-trump with the ♠2. South ruffs the ◇A in his own hand, ruffs a heart in dummy, and so on, for all the remaining tricks.

CHAPTER 16

SECTION IV
The Play of the Cards in Defence

Opening Leads

♠♡♣◇♠♡♣◇♠♡♣◇♠♡♣◇♠♡♣◇♠♡♣◇♠♡♣◇

SO far the only angle we have considered has been declarer's who, having won the auction, is doing his best to make his contract. Bridge, however, is not a kindly game where the defending pair sits meekly back following suit and allowing declarer to have it all his own way without active opposition. Indeed good defence requires as much skill, if not more than, good declarer play.

The reason for this is that declarer has the initial advantage of being able to see both his own hand and dummy's and, therefore, to plan them as one unit. Both defenders can, of course, see their own hand and dummy's, and will also have heard the bidding from which valuable information can often be gleaned, but they cannot see their partner's cards. It follows, then, that if their defence is to be an intelligent combined operation aimed at defeating the contract if humanly possible, the defenders must employ positive means of passing information between them. One such means is the opening lead which can frequently be made to carry vital information. The card partner plays to the lead can also be vitally important, as can either defender's subsequent discards.

The opening lead is always the first defensive play in every hand so it is, perhaps, only logical to consider it first. It is the first message passed between the partners and it is extremely important that the partner of the opening leader should understand it. It is also most important that it should be designed to harry declarer rather than to help him.

Many opening leads are standardised, and you will find a table of them on page 274. If your hand contains one of them you can make it knowing that your partner will understand the message. At other times you will have to find a lead for yourself. When doing this bear in mind that your primary considerations must be not to confuse your partner and not to help declarer.

Leading Partner's Bid Suit:

If your partner has bid a suit during the course of the auction your choice is made easier because it is almost always best to lead his suit. Exceptions do arise occasionally, but rarely enough for you to ignore them at this stage so, knowing which suit to lead leaves you only to learn which card in it to select. The standard rules are:

(*a*) Holding four or more cards headed by any honour *except* the Ace, lead the fourth best (*i.e.*, the fourth from the top—J 9 6 2, lead the 2, Q 8 7 5 3, lead the 5.)

(*b*) With three cards headed by any honour *except* the Ace, lead the lowest, (i.e., from K 7 4 lead the 4, from Q 9 2 lead the 2 and so on.)

(*c*) Holding the Ace of your partner's suit, lead it *first* if defending a suit contract. This guards against the risk that either declarer or dummy holds the King opposite to a singleton. You may *underlead* the Ace, that is, lead the 4 from A 6 4, if defending a No Trump contract.

(*d*) With two touching honours or from a sequence of touching cards, lead the top.

(*e*) With three small cards lead the top first, and be sure to follow with the *middle* one on the second round of the suit (i.e., from 7 5 3 lead the 7 and play the 5, not the 3, next time).

(*f*) With any doubleton, whether headed by an honour or not, lead the higher of the two first. (K–x or Q–x, lead the honour, and 8–3, lead the 8.)

(*g*) With a singleton you have, of course, no choice of card. Lead it anyway.

You will see from the above that the lead of a small card in your partner's suit immediately suggests that you hold either four or more or three headed by an honour. If, for example, you lead the 2, this could be your fourth best, or your lowest from the King, Queen or Jack, or it could be a singleton. Your partner will very likely be able to judge which it is from a combination of his own hand, what he sees in dummy, and the bidding he has heard. He will already know for certain that you haven't got the Ace, three worthless cards, or a doubleton. If your lead is a higher card such as the 8 or 9, this is most unlikely to be the bottom of three to an honour, so is probably top of three, of a doubleton, or a singleton. Already, you see, some positive information as to the contents of your hand will be building up for your partner.

Leading Against Suit Contracts:

If your partner has not bid during the auction you have no guidance from him as to his preference, so will have to select a suit of your own. The top card of a suit headed by a sequence (K–Q–J, Q–J–10, J–10–9, etc.) is usually a sound choice, as it is unlikely to aid declarer even if it doesn't actively harass him. Furthermore, such a lead will pass to your partner the information that you hold this sequence, so that he will immediately be able to place certain cards in your hand. Another reason for leading from the top of a sequence will become apparent if you think back to what you have learned about finessing, which in turn emphasises the reasons why you should always *avoid* leading *from*, or away from, a tenace or unsupported honour. You will remember that declarer, with a holding such as A–Q or A–K–J, will probably have to fall back on a finesse in the hope of avoiding losing a trick to the missing honour. If you lead *away* from that particular honour you will virtually be taking his finesse for him and ensuring that it wins. Here, if you lead either the King itself or a low card away from it, South will win two tricks in the suit without further effort whereas, left to himself, he will probably finesse the Queen into your hand and you will make the King.

	N	
K x x	W E	
	S	
	A Q x	

Similarly, if you lead away from a tenace such as this Ace-Queen you present South, if he holds the King, with a certain trick, but if you wait for him to tackle the suit or for your partner to lead it, both your honour cards are in a position to kill his. Leading from a sequence this doesn't happen. You run no risk of leading into a tenace and instead will, with any luck, be driving out declarer's stops and establishing tricks of your own. At a trump contract where declarer is in control of the trump suit you can't expect to make many tricks in a side suit, but you may establish one or two high cards before the rats get at them.

	N	
A Q x	W E	
	S	
	K J x	

Add the Knave to your Ace-King combination, making it A–K–J and, against a suit contract, you can hope to take two tricks and possibly even three if you handle it correctly. Suppose the suit is divided like this and you play out your Ace and King, South's Queen becomes good. If instead you play first the Ace and then switch to some other suit, when your partner gains the lead he will send your original suit back to you, at which time you will hold the K–J tenace over South's Q–x.

	North	
	x x x	
A K J x	N / W E / S	**x x x**
	Q x x	

There is one exception to the rule about leading the Ace first from A–K suits and that is if your Ace and King are your only two cards in the suit. In this case you lead the King first and then the Ace, the specific message of which is that you have no more and would, therefore, welcome a chance to ruff a third round if partner can get in and lead it to you.

♠ **K x x**
♡ **A Q x**
♢ **Q x x x**
♣ **K J x**

You could, of course, find yourself on lead from a hand like this, with every suit headed by a tenace or unsupported honour. Unfortunately you can't ask to be excused from leading but take heart—it would be difficult for anyone and you'll choose right if it is your lucky day!

♠ **K x x**
♡ **A Q x**
♢ **Q x x x**
♣ **x x x**

If you have one suit composed of worthless cards only this can get you out of your difficulty, but you still must know the right card to lead. From three worthless cards lead the top—this is known as leading 'top of nothing'—and play the *middle* card, not the lowest one, on the second round of the suit. This is just as you did holding three worthless cards of your partner's bid suit, so it should not be difficult to remember. From a worthless doubleton lead the top card. You may strike lucky and get in a ruff later. Similarly the lead of a singleton can often produce a ruff for you if your partner can get in and lead it back to you before declarer has had time to draw all your trumps. Note, however, that a singleton honour is unlikely to be a good choice. Declarer, not knowing that it is unguarded, may well finesse it into your hand and allow you to win with it if he is left to play the suit himself.

In general, against suit contracts where declarer has the added power of the trump suit on his side, it is better to attack with good honour holdings in an effort to drive out his stops and set up tricks for your side. You will seldom be able to make tricks with little cards because, by the time you get to them, declarer or dummy will be able to ruff. You've seen this happening, and also being deliberately planned by declarer, in the examples in the previous chapter. The situation is, however, very different if you are defending a No Trump contract.

Leading Against a No Trump Contract:

As against suit contracts, if your partner has bid a suit during the course of the auction, you should lose no time in trying to help him to establish it, even though he has been over-bid in No Trumps, and only in exceptional circumstances should you take it upon yourself to refuse to lead your partner's bid suit. The card to select, if you have a choice, is as listed on page 274, always remembering that if defending a No Trump contract, you may lead your lowest one from A x x. If you decide *against* leading his suit you had better have a pretty good alibi ready, especially if the lead would have defeated the contract and your choice knocks out your partner's only entry card to what he had hoped would become an established suit.

Without a bid from your partner to direct you, you will be back on your own resources and quite different principles apply against a declarer without the added teeth of a trump suit. You are no longer in a hurry to win with your top cards before declarer can trump them, and are far more anxious to try to establish a long suit of your own, if you have one, while you still have your high cards for entries. In this situation the customary lead is the fourth best—the fourth highest from the *top*—of your longest and strongest suit. The object of this is to drive out declarer's stops in the suit while you still have a hope of getting in to make the "long" cards in it when established.

You will have noticed in several of the examples in Chapter 14 that West led an honour such as the Queen. This you are now able to recognise as the top of a sequence which will give nothing away to declarer.

65
QJ1083 W N E S 742
AK9

Suppose the suit were divided like this. A lead of West's fourth best, the 8, would allow declarer to win with his 9 for three tricks in the suit, while a lead of the Queen, the top of a sequence, avoids this risk. Note, by the way, that a lead of either the Knave or 10 would have the same effect as far as declarer is concerned but would not pass the information of the sequence from the Queen downwards to East.

Failing an honour sequence such as this, select the fourth best of your longest and strongest suit as your best attack against a No Trump contract.

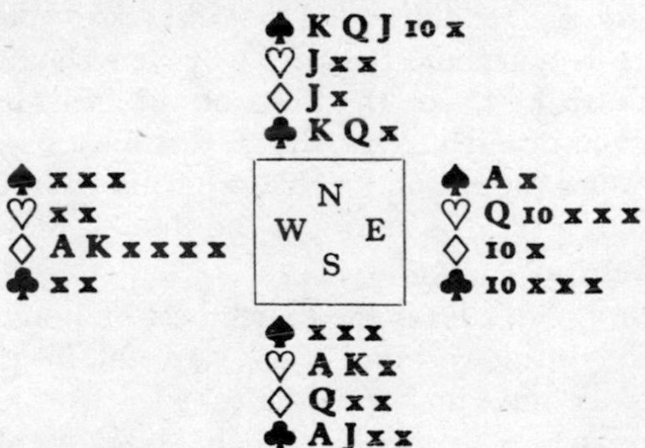

Against a suit contract by South you would lead out, or "cash", your ◇A–K while the going was good, afraid that declarer might have a means of disposing of his own or dummy's cards in the suit thus enabling him to ruff. You can see for yourself that, played in a suit, a lead of your fourth best would give declarer a free trick. Either dummy's ◇J or his own ◇Q would win and he would then have only one losing diamond and would be able to trump your second winner. However this isn't a suit hand and South is playing in No Trumps. In this case, if you lead out your ♢A–K what happens is that declarer's ♢Q will be good to win the third trick in the suit and you will never be able to gain the lead to win with your three remaining established "little x's", so declarer will make his contract not only with ease but with overtricks. If you lead a little one, however, relying on partner to be able to assist you in some way, it is very different. East can only produce the ♢10 but South dare not duck this as, if he does, he'll never win a diamond trick at all. So he wins and, if you count up his tricks you'll see that he can't make his contract without clearing the spades. East has the Ace and, far more important, a second diamond to lead back to you.

There is a technical reason why you should lead your fourth best, not the third or the fifth, but the fourth, and experience has shown that most beginners like to know the reason for this, which is the information it can give. It is known as the Rule of Eleven.

The Rule of Eleven:

When a player leads the fourth best of a suit, even if it is only the lowest card of a 4-card suit, his partner deducts the pip number of the card led from eleven, and the answer to this sum is the exact number of cards *higher than the card led*, divided between the *other* three hands.

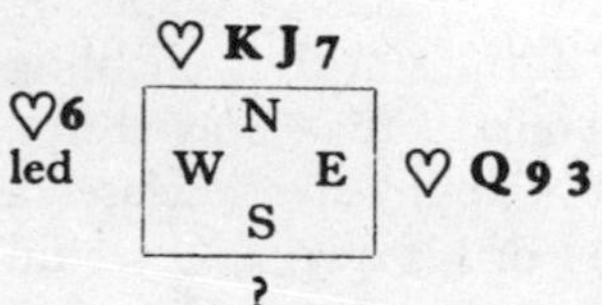

This can often give a very accurate knowledge of declarer's cards. West leads the ♡6 and you, East, immediately deduct 6 from 11. The answer is 5 so you know that there are five cards higher than the ♡6 divided between dummy, yourself and declarer. Dummy has three of these and you have two, total, five visible. South, therefore, has no card higher than the ♡6. If he plays dummy's ♡7 your ♡9 will win the trick.

One must, of course, point out that declarer too can use this Rule. Unable to see the East cards, he would deduct the 6 from 11 himself, and seeing three of the five cards in dummy, would arrive at the unerring conclusion that you held two higher than the ♡6. It is, however, generally much more important to keep the defending partners properly in the picture. Remember they have to find out about each other's cards while declarer already knows what he and dummy have got.

There is a reason why the Rule of Eleven operates in this way, of course, but it is quite unnecessary for you to bother yourself with it at this stage. It is not why it works, but how it works and how to use it that are important. For any of you, however, who feel an urgent need to know why, you can find a full explanation in an earlier book, "Your Lead, Partner", by the same authors.

It may be that your longest and strongest suit is the one which has been bid earlier in the auction by declarer. In this case, unless your own holding in it is clearly worth while, you should think very seriously before leading *into* declarer's suit and, thereby, helping him to establish it. Suppose the final contract is 3 N.T. declarer having opened the bidding with 1 ◇ and you hold a hand like this:

♠ K x x
♡ 9 6
◇ K J 8 6 5
♣ 5 3 2

Your longest and strongest suit has been bid on your right and, if you lead your fourth best, the ◇6, it's odds on you'll be helping declarer to a free trick. You must, therefore, refrain from leading diamonds. Spades you eliminate automatically as you don't want to lead away from the unsupported King, which leaves you with hearts and diamonds. You have a choice between the ♡9, top of the doubleton and the ♣5, the "top of nothing". Which do you choose, or is it a matter of guessing? Early in this chapter it was pointed out that it was important for your partner to understand your lead which, conversely, means that you must try to avoid a lead which he could misunderstand. There is just such a danger if you select the ♣5, which might very easily be mistaken for a fourth best and confuse his defence for the rest of the hand. So your choice falls on the ♡9 which could not be a fourth best because, with three higher cards in hearts you would have three honours, one of which you would have led. Your partner will know that you have thought it best to make a purely defensive lead, not attacking any particular suit, and from this alone he may be able to draw helpful conclusions.

If none of these suggestions helps at all, whether your lead is against a trump or No Trump contract, it is generally safer to choose a lead *through* strength rather than *up to* strength. That is to say, if a suit has been bid on your left you could reasonably expect the strength in it to be on your left and might elect to lead *through* this to any strength your partner may hold in it, rather than up to the strength of a suit bid on your right.

The very reasonable bidding has been 1◇ from

South, 1♠ from North, 2 N.T. from South raised to

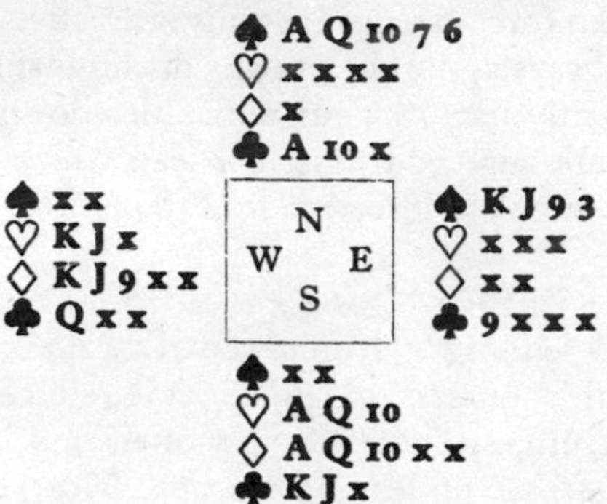

3 N.T. by North. For declarer, however, it is one of the nightmare hands that crop up from time to time where every card lies wrongly for him. He can never make his contract, but thoughtless defence can help him to make more tricks than he could on his own. West's long suit has been bid by declarer, on the right, and is, moreover, headed by a valuable tenace, so this lead up to strength should be avoided. A lead from the heart tenace is unthinkable and the possible alternative of a club might—and as you can see would, give declarer a certain three tricks in the suit when, left to himself, he could "guess" the club finesse either way and be wrong as often as he would be right. This only leaves spades, the suit bid on West's left, so he chooses to lead this suit *through* the strength and, as it happens, strikes lucky as East holds all the important cards over North's tenace.

Leading *through* strength and *up to* weakness is a principle which may be followed whatever the contract, and your conclusion that you must make such a lead is usually reached by a process of elimination. On the hand above, for instance, hearts, diamonds and clubs were eliminated as dangerous, leaving only spades. When, therefore, no lead seems attractive or even possible, always apply the process of elimination which will frequently narrow your difficulties down to three suits you are sure you must *not* lead which, in turn, leaves you virtually forced to lead the fourth.

Leading Trumps:

When defending a trump contract, don't be surprised if this process of elimination reduces you to leading a trump, as you will very often find it will do. Don't be *afraid* of leading trumps. Most beginners find this extremely difficult to accept, but frequently a trump lead, even when not forced on you by the process of elimination, is the best from the defence point of view. Apart from possibly getting you out of trouble when all other leads seem dangerous, it can be the one lead to defeat the contract.

You will remember that quite often declarer will be wanting to use up one or more of dummy's little trumps before he draws the opponent's.

Here South is playing in 4♠ and you, West, have to lead. Your process of elimination cuts out hearts and diamonds and while you might select a "top of nothing" club, this would, like either of the other two suits, allow South to make his contract. If, however, you lead a trump declarer is helpless. If he tries to get a heart ruff you can foil him by winning and leading a second trump and, even worse for him, he will never be able to get into dummy to make use of the clubs for discards.

There is one other point which has not yet been stressed and that is leading from a suit headed by the unsupported Ace, which at times may be necessary. As with all suits headed by an unsupported honour you avoid the lead if you can, hoping not to aid declarer by leading up to his holding and also hoping that your own big cards can be used to kill his later rather than being expended on "little x's". If, for want of anything more promising, you have to lead from a suit such as A x x or A x x x at a suit contract, never *under-lead* the Ace, that is, never lead a low card away from the Ace—play the Ace itself. Too often the under-lead will find declarer or dummy with the King opposite to a singleton and you will make no trick at all in the suit, whereas the lead of the Ace would at least have given you one.

* * *

Finally, as with so many things, there are fashions in leading. Many players, for instance, still lead the King from suits headed by the Ace–King. This is rather old fashioned and if you stick to the standard leads, and make sure your partner is doing the same, you won't go far wrong.

QUIZ ON CHAPTER 16

On each of the hands below you are West, on lead against the bidding shown. What card would you lead?

	Hand	*S.*	*W.*	*N.*	*E.*
1.	♠ 8 5 4	1♠	—	2♦	—
	♥ A K 2	2 N.T.	—	3 N.T.	—
	♦ 8 6 4	—	—		
	♣ J 10 9 8				
2.	♠ 7 5 4	1 N.T.	—	3 N.T.	—
	♥ A K 7 5 4	—	—		
	♦ J 6				
	♣ Q 9 6				
3.	♠ J 10 9	1♠	—	2♠	—
	♥ A 6 4	—	—		
	♦ Q 6 3				
	♣ K 9 7 4				
4.	♠ 8 6 5	1 N.T.	—	2 N.T.	—
	♥ K J	3 N.T.	—	—	—
	♦ A 9 3				
	♣ 9 8 5 3 2				
5.	♠ Q 7 6 3 2	1♥	—	2♣	—
	♥ J 9 7 5	2♥	—	4♥	—
	♦ 7	—	—		
	♣ 9 4 2				
6.	♠ 7 5 4	1♠	—	3♠	—
	♥ A K 7 5 4	4♠	—	—	—
	♦ J 6				
	♣ Q 9 6				
7.	♠ 8 6 5				1♠
	♥ K J	1 N.T.	—	3 N.T.	—
	♦ A 9 3	—	—		
	♣ 9 8 5 3 2				
8.	♠ Q 9 3	1♥	—	2♣	2♠
	♥ 8 7 6 2	—	—	4♥	—
	♦ 8 5 4 2	—	—		
	♣ 10 9				

		S.	*W.*	*N.*	*E.*
9.	♠ K Q J 7				1♢
	♡ K Q 8 3	2♣	Dbl.	—	—
	♢ 7	—			
	♣ A J 10 6				
10.	♠ 8 6 3	1♡	—	2♣	2♠
	♡ 8 7 6 2	—	—	4♡	—
	♢ 8 5 4 2	—	—		
	♣ 10 9				
11.	♠ Q J 10 6 2	1♡	—	2♣	—
	♡ 7 5 4	3♢	—	3♡	—
	♢ A 7	3 N.T.	—	—	—
	♣ 9 4 2				
12.	♠ K 9 3			1♣	—
	♡ A Q 7 6	1♡	—	2♣	—
	♢ 9 6 2	2 N.T.	—	3 N.T.	—
	♣ Q 8 5	—	—		
13.	♠ K 8 3			1♠	—
	♡ 8 5 3	2♡	—	4♡	—
	♢ A K	—	—		
	♣ K 6 4 3				
14.	♠ 8 7			1♣	—
	♡ K J 7 5	1♠	—	4♠	—
	♢ A Q 3	—	—		
	♣ Q 9 4 3				

QUIZ ON CHAPTER 16—ANSWERS

1. ♣J, the top of a sequence which, even if it isn't a very long one, may set up a trick for you.

2. ♡5, the fourth best of your longest and strongest suit, which may well develop tricks for you if you can get it established.

3. ♠J. The trump lead here is because no other looks promising and you don't want to risk giving anything at all away.

4. ♣3, the fourth best of your longest suit. You have two possible entry cards, the ◇A and the ♡K, so might be able to establish and then use, long clubs.

5. ◇7. You might strike lucky and find East able to give you one or even more ruffs. Anyway you have no other obviously profitable line of defence.

6. ♡A. This is exactly the same hand as No. 2 above where, defending a No Trump contract, you led fourth best. Against a trump contract you must try to make two tricks with your tops before it is too late.

7. ♠8. This is axactly the same hand as No. 4 above where, without guidance from your partner, you tried an attack in your own long suit. Now partner has bid 1♠ and, even though he has been overcalled in No Trumps which shows that South has a spade guard, you must try to help East establish his suit before it is too late.

8. ♠3, leading the lowest card of your partner's bid suit when your holding is headed by an honour other than the Ace.

9. ♠K. You, West, have made a business double of South's 2♣ and, moreover, you have a singleton of your partner's bid suit. However your trumps are too good and damaging to waste on ruffing at this stage and it is far better to try to set up tricks in the spade side suit for yourself. Ruffs can come later if you can't do even more damage by conserving your trumps to harass declarer.

10. ♠8, the highest of three worthless cards in your partner's suit.

11. ♠Q, the top of your sequence. This will not give anything away as it can't be leading into a tenace, and it is just possible that, with the ♢A for an entry later, you will be able to clear the suit in time to do damage.

12. ♢9, the "top of nothing". The process of elimination gives you this lead, as the others are all highly unattractive on the bidding.

13. ♢K, which you propose to follow by the ♢A. This will tell your partner of your doubleton and he may be able to gain the lead to give you a ruff before your trumps are drawn, which would amount to four tricks to defeat the contract.

14. ♠8. Again the process of elimination which, this time, results in a trump lead. Hearts, diamonds and clubs are all most unattractive from your point of view.

CHAPTER 17

Defensive Measures & Counter-measures

♠♡♣◇♠♡♣◇♠♡♣◇♠♡♣◇♠♡♣◇♠♡♣◇♠♡♣◇

WE'VE looked now at opening leads and seen that, on frequent occasions, the card led will convey a definite message to the leader's partner who, for purposes of conveniences in these exercises, is East. Now we must cross the table to his seat as it is his turn to try to pass information to West and, at the same time, to assist or initiate a possibly profitable line of defence.

Third Hand Plays High:

"Third hand plays high" is, if not a golden rule, at least a good basis to work on, and "Return your partner's lead" is another, but both must be used with intelligence and discretion. Turn back to the hand on p. 225 where West led a spade *through* North's strength. Unless declarer played the ♠A East would certainly play high, *but only high enough to win the trick*, so if dummy's ♠6 is played, East would play the ♠9. Nor would he dream of returning the lead which was obviously made as a way out of trouble for West. He would, instead, choose to lead *up to* weakness in dummy, which is likely to be through declarer's strength towards whatever West has been safeguarding by his passive opening lead. He would not choose a club, towards dummy's strength, which would eliminate declarer's guess as to which way to finesse in exactly the same way as an opening club lead would have done.

Let us change the East spade holding on this same hand by just one card, giving him the ♠8 in place of the ♠3, so that his cards are the ♠K J 9 8 over dummy's ♠A Q 10 7 6. This brings us to another important aspect of passing information between the defenders because, with this second holding, East should play the ♠8, not the ♠9, on North's ♠7. In other words, contrary to the rule for leading where you start with the *top* of a sequence, when winning, or trying to win a trick, you must do so with the *lowest* available card. This, if you have two or more in sequence, means playing the lowest first.

	♠ 9 6 4	
♠ 8 5 3	N W E S	

Suppose West leads his top-of-nothing ♠8, dummy plays the ♠9 and you, East, play the ♠K on which declarer puts the ♠A. So now West has seen his cards, dummy's, your ♠K and declarer's ♠A. Has he, do you think, any idea at all of where the other missing honour cards are? If he can't rely on you to try to win this trick with your lowest available spade he will have no idea at all. You may have the ♠Q, the ♠J, or both, or declarer may have them both, and no information will have been given to West. If he can rely on you to play your lowest available card, still within the terms of "third hand plays high", if you play the ♠K he will *know* that you haven't got the ♠Q though you may possibly have the ♠J. If, however, you play the ♠Q and declarer the ♠A there is at least a reasonable hope that you have the ♠K. Declarer could be using his ♠A when he didn't need to, but there is a 50–50 chance, now known to West, that you have the ♠K. Similarly, if on the lead you play the ♠J which draws declarer's ♠A, it is a reasonable chance that you hold the missing honours, the ♠K and ♠Q.

In this example West again leads a spade and declarer puts up dummy's ♠J. If you win the trick with the ♠K your partner will have no idea whether you or South holds the ♠Q. If, however, you win with the ♠Q and declarer can only play a low one, it is more than a reasonable assumption that he was unable to win with the ♠K because he hadn't got it. Remember this because it's important. Lead from the top of a sequence, win, or try to win, from the bottom.

These are, of course, examples of third hand playing high. Let us examine the reason behind this rule, which is intended to make life as difficult as possible for declarer.

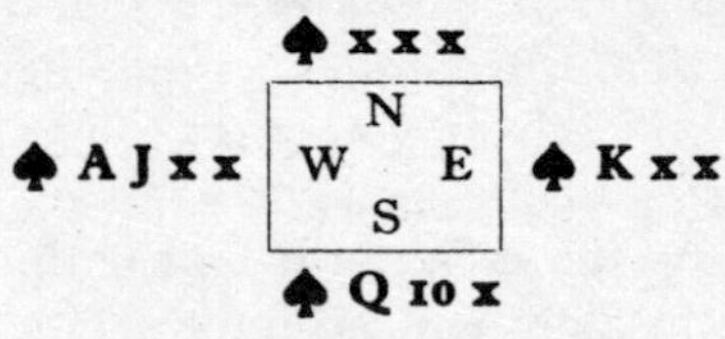

West leads his fourth best (also his lowest) spade. If, as East, you play low, South will be able to win with his ♠10. If, however, you play high, that is, the ♠K, you will win the trick and then, returning your partner's lead, you will be leading through declarer's Q-10 to your partner's A-J and declarer will be unable to win a single spade trick.

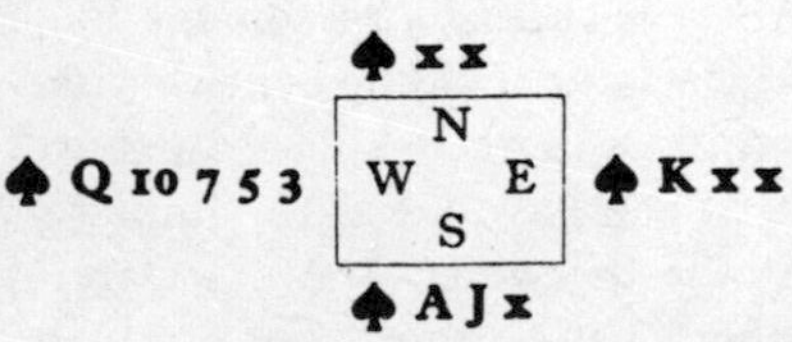

Against a No Trump contract West leads the ♠5. If you play low South will win with the ♠J and will still have the ♠A for a second stop in the suit. If you play your ♠K, either declarer will hold up, in which case your ♠K will win and you will return the lead through South's ♠A-J, giving him only one spade stop, or he will win your ♠K with his ♠A. Your King's life will not have been sacrificed in vain as, when you regain the lead, you will be able to lead through declarer's ♠J-x to your partner's ♠Q-10.

As already pointed out, this principle must be used with discretion, which brings us to the use of a finesse in defence. Against South's No Trump contract your partner, West, leads the ♠5, dummy's ♠2 is played and now comes your big moment—what to play. Should you, as third hand, play high? Applying your Rule of Eleven you can tell that South holds *two* spades higher than the one led, the ♠5. If they happen to be the ♠A-J and you play your ♠K you present declarer with three tricks in spades. If they are the ♠A-9, parting with your ♠K gives him two tricks as he will win with the ♠A and his ♠Q in dummy will be the best. If they are the ♠9-8, which means your partner started with the ♠A-J, you will give declarer one trick because, though your ♠K will win, his ♠Q is bound to win a trick later. All of this adds up to just one thing—you have nothing to lose and everything to gain by playing the ♠10 on the first round. True South may hold the ♠J-9, but this must be good for one trick while your ♠K will be intact, sitting over and ready to bite the head off his ♠Q. This sort of situation is often called finessing against your partner. It is an inaccurate description as it is, in fact, a finesse against dummy. Such a defensive finesse

is taken if you can judge that, in view of the possible combinations of cards held by West and South, you will do more damage by retaining instead of parting with your high card.

Second Hand Plays Low:

Another often-quoted dictum for defence is "second hand plays low". This means that when either declarer or dummy leads a card, the defender on the left should play low, leaving any attempt to win the trick to fourth hand. As a golden rule this is as fallacious as it could well be because there are numerous occasions when exactly the reverse applies—second hand should, and indeed must, play high.

If you understand the reason behind this dictum it should help you to apply it intelligently or ignore it when the occasion arises, so here is a little phrase which may stick in your memory—Aces were born to kill Kings and Kings were born to kill Queens. In other words, if you can conserve your high cards until you can play them on the opposition's high cards, thus "killing" a potential winner, it will be much more profitable than using up an Ace, say, on two "little x's". Here is a very ordinary sort of suit distribution,

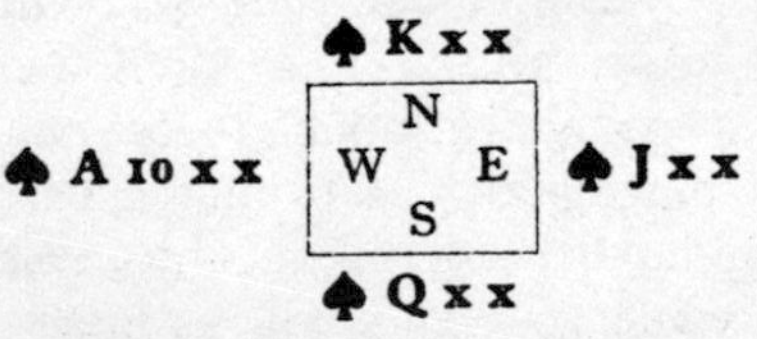

something similar to which will crop up hand after hand. If South leads a small spade and West, as second hand, plays high with his Ace, a small one will be played from North and subsequently both South's ♠Q and North's ♠K will be winners. If, however, West plays low, it is true that North's ♠K will win the trick, but

West's ♠A-10 will be left sitting as a tenace over South's ♠Q-x, for one trick only in the suit. Alternatively declarer could, not knowing the position, have led first from dummy, playing a low one towards his own hand and putting on the Queen. In this case West would be fourth hand and should play high, taking his chance to kill the ♠Q, or we should be back to the first position where declarer made two tricks in the suit.

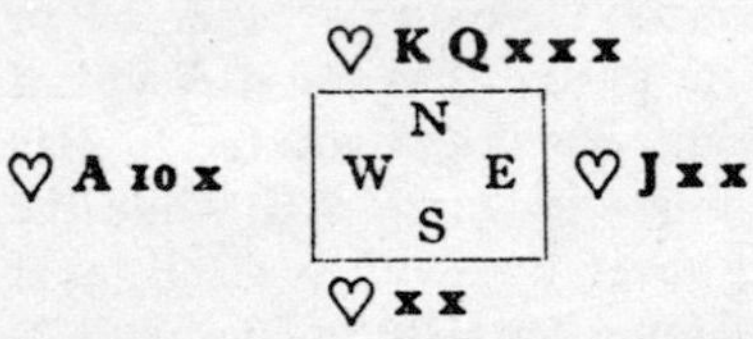

In this example, if South leads low towards dummy's ♡K-Q and West immediately plays the ♡A, North's ♡K-Q, will subsequently drop both East's ♡J and West's ♡10 and declarer will have four winners in the suit. The only way of avoiding this is for West to play low, at any rate on the first round, in the hope that South may have difficulty in re-entering his own hand to repeat the process. If you turn back to p. 163 you will find that this is the same suit distribution shown from declarer's point of view. It was pointed out that if declarer could contrive to lead twice *towards* dummy's ♡K-Q, he would lose only one trick as long as West held the ♡A. Reverse the East and West holdings, though, giving East the ♡A, and he should use it on the first round to kill one of dummy's honours. This will ultimately leave the ♡J "boss" which declarer will only be able to avoid losing if he is able to ruff.

Whatever you do, however, don't let this second-hand-plays-low become a Law of the Medes and Persians to you. If you go on playing low for too long you will often give declarer tricks he couldn't otherwise win. In the example above for instance, if West doesn't play his ♡A on the second round at a trump contract, declarer, with a trump to spare in his own hand and an entry in dummy, would ruff the third round, dropping the ♡A, and could then re-enter dummy with his outside entry to use the two established "little x's" for discards. Again, suppose declarer leads low from his own hand towards dummy's ♠Q. As you can't see his hand you don't know whether he or your partner has the ♠A and, if South has it and you fail to play high immediately, winning with your ♠K while the going is good, you will never win with it at all, as it will then be bare and will fall when South plays his ♠A.

	♠ Q x x	
♠ K x	N W E S	

From the other side of the table, there will be occasions when fourth hand must hold up rather than automatically play high and we shall be coming to some examples presently. Such decisions will often be difficult, so it should encourage you to know that even widely experienced and expert players can make errors of judgment. If, however, you are alert to the possibilities, you will already be a long way on the road towards playing the good game of bridge which can only come with time and experience.

There are other positions where, even without the use of judgment, it is absolutely essential for second hand to play high, and this takes us on to the important principle of "promotion".

Promotion:

Promotion can often be achieved by playing a high card on a high card—"covering an honour with an honour"—led either by declarer from his own hand or from dummy. It may appear to be the possible sacrifice of the card, but it is done with the hope of promoting a winner either for yourself or for your partner, later in the game.

In the section on finessing you met the situation where declarer, short of entries to one hand or the other, led a high card intending to "run" it if not covered. "If not covered" is the operative phrase, because this technique of promotion depends on covering the high card with a high card in various circumstances where it might help you or your partner.

In trouble for entries and in dummy for, perhaps, the only time, declarer wants to finesse the spades, so he leads dummy's ♠Q. If East *fails* to cover with his ♠K South will play small, running his Queen, which will obviously win. He will then lead a low one from dummy and finesse his Knave. On the third round his Ace will drop both West's last spade and East's ♠K and declarer's thirteenth spade will be established for four tricks in the suit. If, however, East covers the ♠Q with the ♠K, South will have to use his ♠A to win the trick. His Knave will take the second trick, *but East's ♠10 will be the master* and will win the third trick—three spade tricks for declarer instead of four.

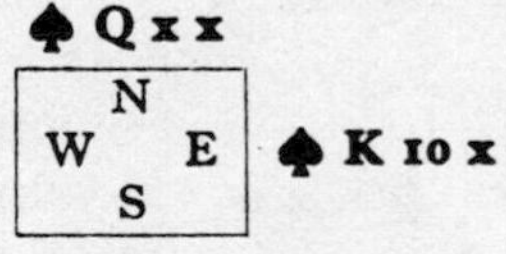

Reading this, of course, you could see all four hands, but in play you would see only

dummy's and your own, East's, and as you have seen, you would cover the lead of the ♠Q in order to promote your ♠10. Would you cover in this second example if North's ♠Q were led? Yes, most certainly you *would*. This is because your partner may have the missing ♠10 so that, instead of promoting it for yourself, you promote it for him, which is every bit as valuable as a trick.

Complete the thirteen cards of the suit as they well might be. If you don't cover the Queen with the King, South will let it run as before. He will then finesse as before, and make four spade tricks as both your ♠K and West's ♠10 will drop on the ♠A. If you *do* cover, South will have to use up his ♠A to win, his Knave will be good, but West's ♠10 will have been promoted to "boss" for the third trick. The reason why this happens is that covering forces declarer to use up two of his high cards to win one trick, instead of making a separate trick with each of them. If declarer himself held the ♠10 your play of the ♠K would have been in vain, though it won't have lost you anything you weren't going to lose anyway. You would cover the

Knave if led here in just the same way, hoping to promote something

for your partner. In fact you should cover even the 10 with the same hopes in mind.

Don't overlook the fact that, as West, you should cover in just the same way. This time, of course, you can't see the South or East hands, but there is every bit as much chance of a promotion for East as there was previously for West.

Now we come to some "don'ts" about covering, which are just as important as the "do's". The first of these is never cover if the honour you hold cannot be caught.

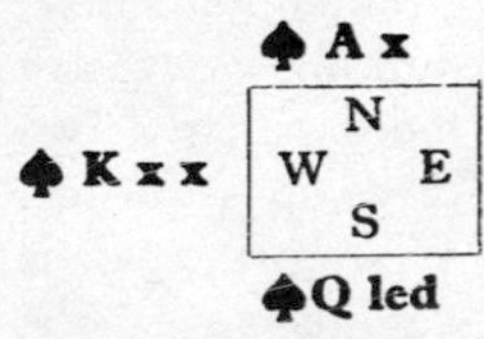

If South leads the ♠Q and you cover, his ♠J and even possibly his ♠10 will be made good. If you refuse to cover and South runs the ♠Q, the ♠A will be the only one left in dummy and it will have to be played on the second round. Your King will not have been caught and, if declarer is not able to trump it in dummy, you will win a trick with it. At any rate you won't have helped him towards any free tricks. Remember that South is virtually certain to hold at least the Knave if not the 10, or he would have been leading *towards* his unsupported ♠Q in the hope that East held the ♠K.

The second "don't" is don't cover when you can see a sequence of two or more cards *unless* your own holding is a doubleton-honour. If you don't cover in this case dummy's

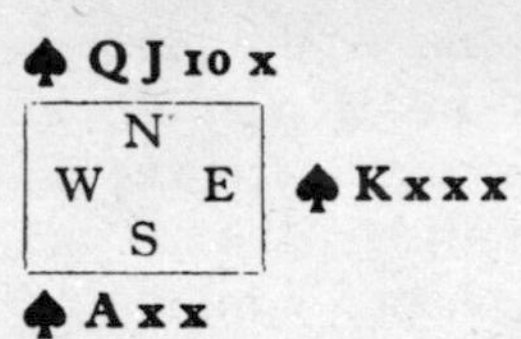

"little x" can be played the second time and your ♠K caught without effort. Here, however, you should refuse to cover either the ♠Q or ♠J. Hold up until the last of the touching honours is led, and even then only cover the third if you can see it is expedient. If you cover when the ♠Q is led, South will win with his ♠A and dummy's remaining cards will be good. If you refuse to cover he will probably continue with the Knave. Again you refuse and then, on the third round, South can't avoid playing his ♠A, which leaves your ♠K the master.

Often, of course, dummy won't have more than two cards in sequence. Your principle is not to cover the first but to cover the second. Follow the cards in this lay-out carefully. North's ♠Q is led. Don't cover, but cover if the ♠J is next led, which will promote your ♠10. Give that ♠10 to West, though, and see what waste you can cause by covering the first time.

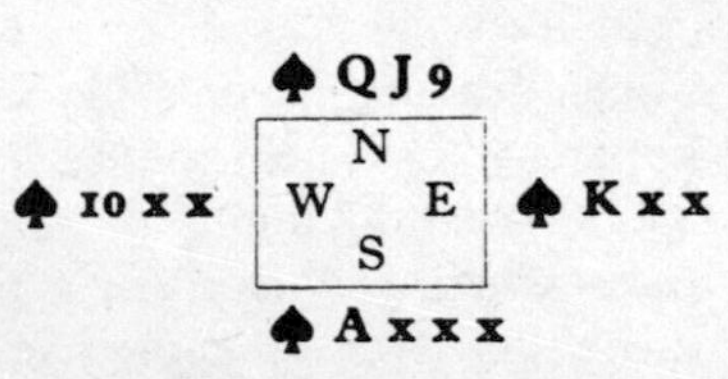

If you cover the lead of the ♠Q with your ♠K South will win with the ♠A and is now in a position to finesse North's ♠9 against West's ♠10, for four tricks in the suit. If you don't cover the ♠Q you kill the finesse position.

The third "don't" is never to cover if you know that it cannot help either your partner or yourself, in other words, if you know there is no promotion possible for either of you. This situation generally arises on occasions when you know that your opponents are long in a suit and that your partner is short. These are the cards which appeared in our example where, in normal

♠Q x x

N
W E ♠K x x
S

circumstances, you would certainly cover if the ♠Q were led. Suppose, however, that South had opened the bidding with 1♠ and after a 2♢ response from North he had rebid 3♠. This, you will remember, shows at least a six-card suit. If South has six spades and you can actually see six others, how many has West got? Obviously not more than one so there cannot be any possible hope of a promotion for him. Covering, therefore, may only help declarer who may be wondering whether to finesse or play his ♠A in the hope of dropping the King-singleton from West. Your play of the ♠K covering the ♠Q would eliminate his guess.

Here, of course, even in the same bidding circumstances, you *would* cover, forcing declarer to use his ♠A, two top cards for one, knowing that it will promote your ♠10 for one trick in the suit.

Now here are two final pieces of advice. Firstly, never cover just from force of habit. Try to work out whether there may be something in it—a promotion—for you or your partner. If there can't be, don't cover. Don't assist declarer from the realms of guesswork to the realms of certainty—the best of declarers guess wrongly at times. Lastly, never hesitate. If declarer leads an honour card, either from his own hand or from dummy and you have to decide whether or not to cover, if you sit back and wriggle and scratch your head and think, you might as well say out loud "Yes, I've got it, but I don't know whether to play it." This, from the viewpoint of a declarer who may be guessing what to do for the best, is tantamount to telling him. So try to make up your mind at Trick 1, when dummy goes down and such possible positions are revealed to you, what you will do if they arise during the course of play.

Forcing Declarer:

Another valuable line of defence is forcing declarer either to lose a trick or to use up some of his trumps for ruffing when he doesn't want to.

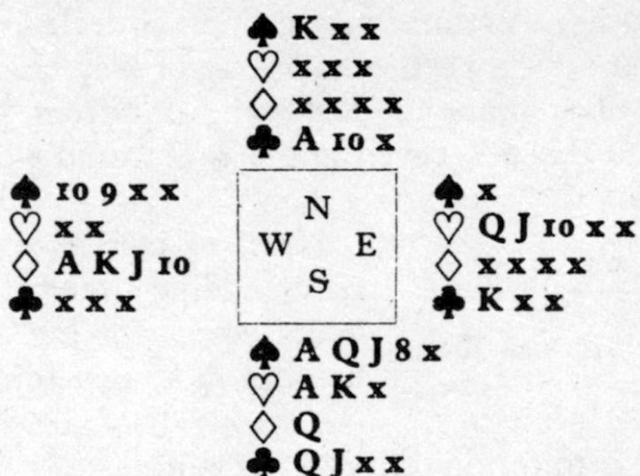

South is playing in 4♠ against which you, West, lead the ♢A. South drops the ♢Q so you realise that he almost certainly has a singleton. If, knowing that he will ruff it, you let this put you off leading another diamond, South will make his contract. On any other second lead he will have the "tempo". He will be able to draw trumps with one to spare in his own hand and, thereafter, lose only to the ♣K and a heart. Note the difference if you force him to trump. On your second diamond he must part with his fifth spade, which means that you now have as many trumps as he has. If he now attempts to draw trumps, all his teeth will be gone and, when he unavoidably loses to East's ♣K, East will return your diamond lead and you will win two more tricks in the suit. If, seeing this danger, when East discards a heart on his second round of trumps, declarer tries to get out of trouble by switching to the club finesse, East will win and will support your line of defence by leading another diamond. This will reduce South's trumps still further and you, West, will have a trump winner. Whatever he tries, declarer will be unable to make his contract.

One note of warning must be sounded here. Beware of this line of defence if it gives declarer what is known as a ruff-discard. This means that the lead allows him to ruff in one hand and discard in the other as would happen if North as well as South were short of diamonds. This can prove a fruitful source of extra tricks for him.

On p. 170 it was mentioned briefly that the various techniques of suit establishment were available to the defence as well as to declarer. We have already seen a defensive finesse and now we will examine "holding up" from the defence point of view.

Holding Up:

If you think back to declarer's play you will remember that he is frequently relying for his contract on establishing a long suit. Turn back to p. 177 and look at the hand there, which is an excellent example. It was essential to South to establish dummy's heart suit, but notice the wording, which was used deliberately—"so your only chance is to get one opponent to play the ♡A while you still have a small heart to lead to dummy". Suppose declarer *can't* get one opponent to play the ♡A while he himself still has one left to use as an entry card to dummy. Declarer wins West's ♣Q with his ♣K and leads the ♡Q, so it shouldn't be unduly difficult to guess what he has in mind. If West holds the singleton ♡A or the ♡A-x he will be unable to put a spoke in South's wheel, but if he can refuse to win either the first or second heart lead, South will never be able to get into dummy again, and will make only two instead of four tricks in the suit.

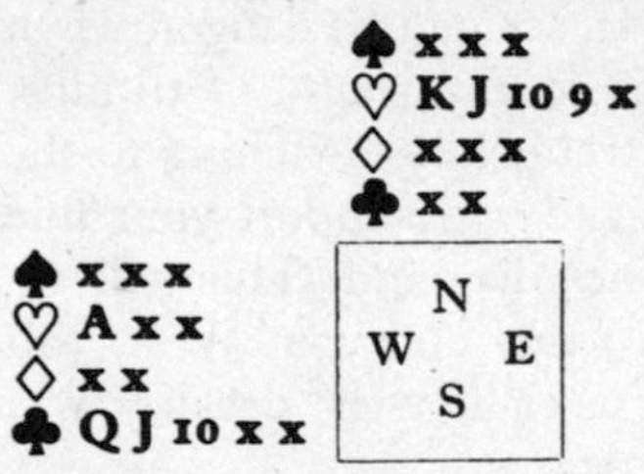

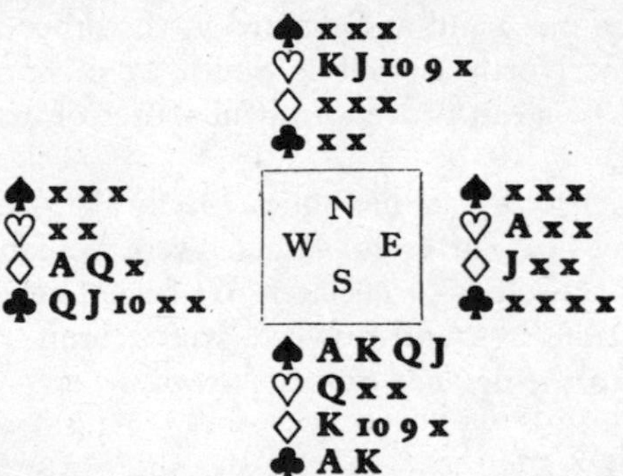

Here are the same North-South hands again but with the East-West hands altered. This time East has the ♡A and West the ◇A-Q. Look at it carefully. Against the same ♣Q lead from West, if East makes the mistake of winning either the first or second heart trick, it's all over. A club return will allow South to make four spades, four hearts and two clubs for certain. Even if East switches to a diamond, declarer has the suit guarded and can only lose two tricks in it. If East *holds up* his heart Ace twice, South's own hearts will be exhausted before the suit is established. East can win the third heart and lead a club, and the defence's club suit will become established while they still have the ♢A for an entry. They will make three clubs, two diamonds and the ♡A, breaking the contract.

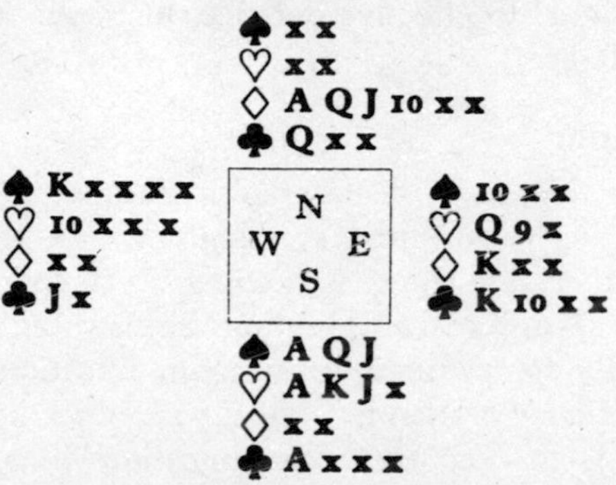

Here is quite a different but equally important example of a hold-up by the defence. South is in 3 N.T. after the bidding 1 ♡—2 ♢—3 N.T. West leads his fourth best spade on which East plays the ♠10 and South wins with the ♠J. You can see that unless declarer can establish North's long diamonds he has no chance of making his contract, and for this he will hope that West has the ♢K and that he can catch it by finessing. So having won the first trick he plays one of his two little diamonds and finesses dummy's ♢10. If East wins this with his ♢K declarer will win any return lead, and still has a diamond left to lead to dummy, to make his five established tricks in the suit. If East *holds up* his ♢K, allowing dummy's ♢10 to win, how different the picture becomes! South might decide to play off the ♢A, hoping to drop the ♢K if it started life as a doubleton with West, or he could return to his own hand by way of the winning heart finesse and lead his second diamond, finessing again. Now East's ♢K would spring into action and the dummy hand would be dead. Its only other possible entry card, the ♣Q, would be killed by East's ♣K.

You see, therefore, that holding up in the right place can be vital to effective defence, just as it can be vital to declarer.

Ducking:

This, just as in declarer play, means playing a low card when you could play a high one. In practice it is much the same thing as holding up though there is a technical difference. Holding up is used tactically, generally to try to destroy communications between the opponents' hands, while with ducking the emphasis is to keep the communications intact so as to win more tricks later.

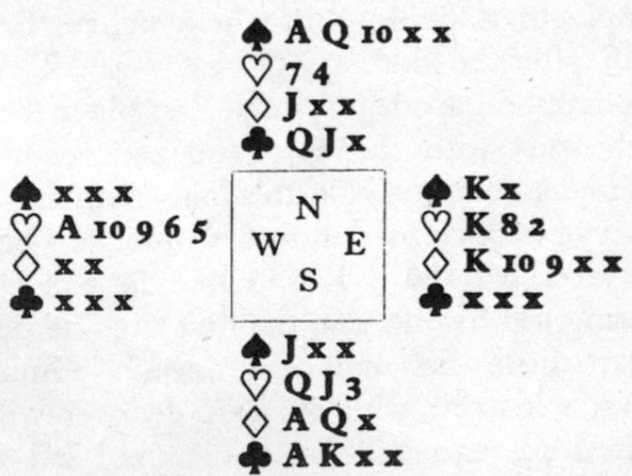

South opened 1♣, North bid 1♠ and South rebid 2 N.T. which North raised to 3 N.T. Against this you, West, lead the fourth best of your longest suit, the ♡6.

You have only a forlorn hope of doing any damage with it but when your partner, East, produces the ♡K —which, of course, wins—your hopes rise. You can see your own hand and dummy but your knowledge of bidding tells you that South's rebid shows 16–18 points but that if he had good spade support he would have shown this instead of bidding No Trumps. It follows, therefore, that East has at least a chance of holding a spade trick. You yourself have no possible entry card to your hearts unless this hope comes off. Can you see how it helps you? Winning with the ♡K, East returns the ♡8, declarer playing the ♡J. *This you must duck.* If you don't South will make his contract, because South will be able to win your third heart lead and, when the spade finesse loses to East, he will have no heart left to lead to you. Nor will he be able to find any other entry to your hand, although you have two priceless established hearts left. If you boldly duck the second heart, though, you will find that South cannot come to his nine tricks without two in spades, to establish which he will have to lose the lead to East and East will have a heart left to lead to you. South will have to play his ♡Q which you will take with the Ace and play out your two good hearts.

The clue to this line of defence is when you see no chance of defeating a contract unless you can establish a suit like this, and you have no outside entry to it.

This is not the only aspect of ducking for which you must be on the look-out. Suppose the spade suit happens to be divided like this and your partner, East, on lead part of the way through the hand, plays a spade.

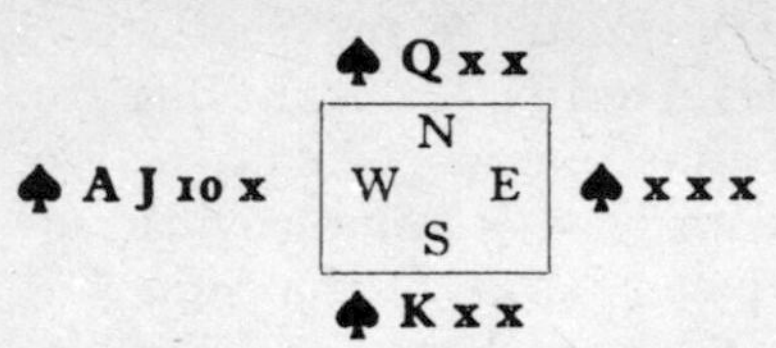

This may be because a clever declarer has deliberately contrived that East has no other suit left to lead, or perhaps because any other alternative looks even less promising. You can't, of course, see South's hand, but he plays low. If you, West, play the ♠A dummy will play low, and later dummy's ♠Q and South's ♠K will be good for two tricks. If instead you duck, playing your ♠10 which forces the ♠Q in dummy will win, your remaining ♠A-J will have become a tenace over South's ♠K-x, and he will only win the one trick in the suit. This is only really a variation of second hand playing low as he did in the first example of this chapter, except that now you are third hand and not second.

This matter of ducking in defence can be a bit difficult. You can't see the East or South hands and if it happens that East has the ♠K instead of South when you duck you'll be allowing dummy's ♠Q to win for nothing, giving declarer one trick in spades instead of none. You will, therefore, have to try to judge, both from the bidding and from the cards played so far, who has the ♠K. Furthermore, it is also possible that declarer only needs one spade trick to make his contract, or that you only need one to defeat him. These intricacies baffle many experienced players, so don't be too worried if they baffle you too!

Unblocking:

Occasions will arise in defence when you fear, or can even see, that a card you hold will get in your partner's way so, just as declarer did, you seek for a way to get rid of it, to unblock for your partner. Most such situations are technically highly advanced and have no place in a beginner's book but it is worth sparing a moment to look at a simple example.

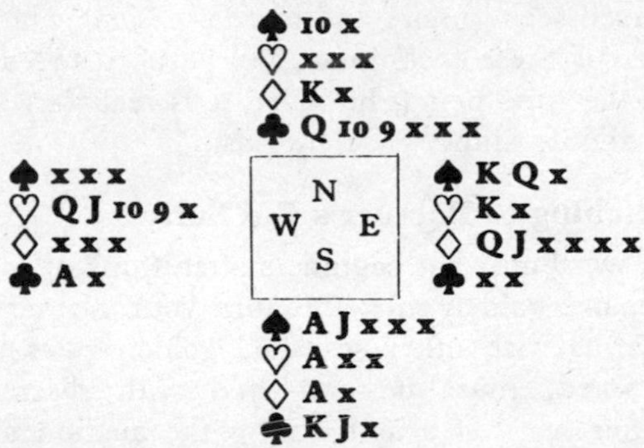

South is playing in 3 N.T. against which your partner, West, leads the ♡Q. If you, East, play correctly South hasn't got a hope, but if you fail to produce the ♡K on your partner's ♡Q at this first trick he will canter home. Let's have a look at why. The lead will, of course, be from the top of a sequence, which as East you recognise at once. This means that South, for his No Trump bid, almost certainly has the ♡A which he will hold up until he is sure you are unable to return a heart. If West's ♡Q is allowed to win, South holding up, and West then leads a second heart *you will have to play the* ♡K. South will hold up again and you will be unable to lead a heart back. Whatever else you choose South will win and lead a club, knocking out West's one and only entry card before his hearts are cleared. If, however, you have the foresight to *unblock* by playing your ♡K on your partner's ♡Q, it doesn't matter what South does. Doubtless he will hold up his

Ace again in the hope that you, not West, have the ♣A, but West will win the second heart and lead a third, clearing the suit, which he will get in and make when poor South tackles his clubs.

As your skill increases with practice you will find yourself seeing more and more occasions when one or other of these techniques can be used to advantage. For the time being, however, it is really enough that you should know that they exist.

Switching to Partner's Bid Suit:

A word on what beginners often think of as another defensive golden rule—"Return your partner's lead". This, as with other so-called golden rules we have examined, must be employed with discretion. If partner has bid a suit during the auction and then becomes the opening leader, and if his own suit is headed by a tenace such as A-Q or K-J, or even by an unsupported honour, he will avoid leading it. He will probably have made a temporising lead hoping to get you in *so that you can lead it to him*. If a strong tenace in his suit goes down on the table in dummy you will be able to see that the lead is useless, but if dummy has weakness in it, any missing strength will be with declarer. Unless, therefore, you have reason to believe that something else would be better, you should switch to your partner's bid suit at the first opportunity you get. Here are two typical examples for you to compare:—

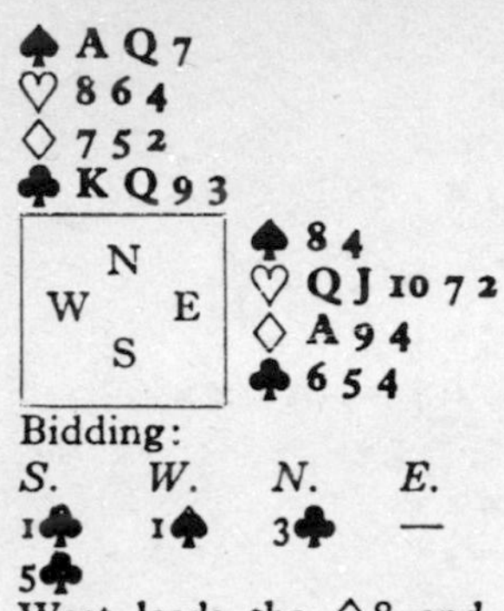

Bidding:

S.	*W.*	*N.*	*E.*
1♣	1♠	3♣	—
5♣			

West leads the ◇8 and East wins. It is pointless to return the obviously "top of nothing" lead and equally pointless to play a spade to West's bid. East should lead his ♡Q, both through declarer and up to weakness in dummy.

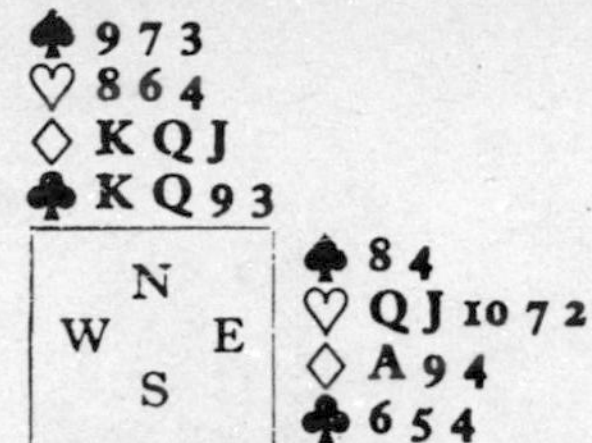

Against exactly the same bidding and the same lead from West, East has exactly the same hand. It would be pointless to return the diamond lead which is just as clearly "top of nothing". East must lead his ♠8 through to West's bid. If West happens to have the ♠A-Q x x x over South's ♠K J x, East will be able to ruff the third round.

Returning a Trump:

We've already seen the damage an opening trump lead can do to a declarer who is anxious to use one or more of dummy's trumps for ruffing. Similarly, from the East seat, a trump return can often do untold damage to an otherwise certain contract. It can also, of course, get East out of trouble if he has a difficult return to choose—he too can use the process of elimination, and find that this means he must lead a trump! Here, to end this chapter, are two final examples:—

By way of a 2♣ opening bid South has got into 4♠—perhaps a trifle ambitious but without active opposition he will make it. West, with no very good lead available, chooses a "top of nothing" heart. South wins East's ♡J with his ♡A and immediately leads a second heart, clearly hoping to get in one or more ruffs. East wins and, if he returns

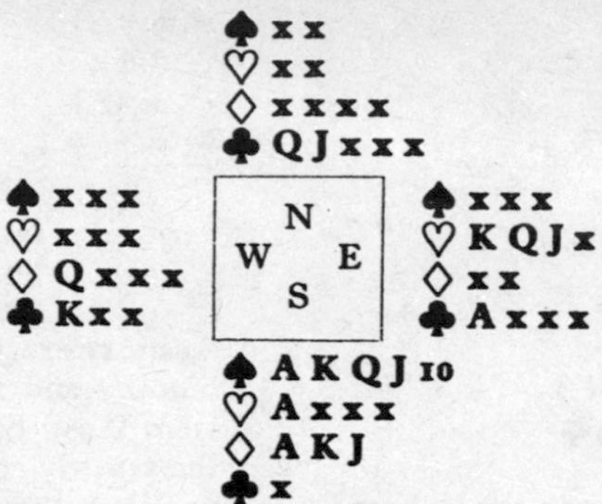

anything *except* a trump, South will be able to get in his two ruffs, losing only one heart, one club and one diamond. A trump return means that he will only be able to ruff one heart instead of two, and so will go one down. It is interesting to note, by the way, that had West chosen a trump lead originally, as he well might have done, the contract would have gone two down. As declarer must lose the lead to a heart before he can get his ruff in the suit, East would have backed his partner's line of defence by returning a second trump.

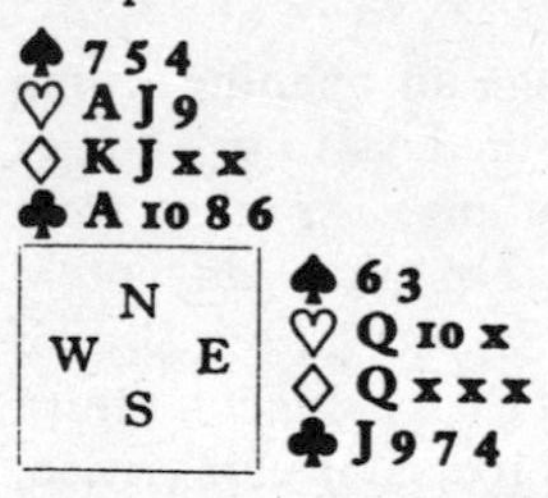

West leads an apparent "top of nothing" club against South's 4♠ contract, dummy's ♣6 is played and East sees that it is only necessary to play the ♣7, which South wins with the ♣Q. He then leads a heart, finessing the ♡J which East wins with his ♡Q. This is a clear moment of no lead being attractive. East does not want to lead *into* any of dummy's honour positions as any of his own may turn into tricks if conserved. He, therefore, by a process of elimination, arrives at a trump return.

QUIZ ON CHAPTER 17

1.

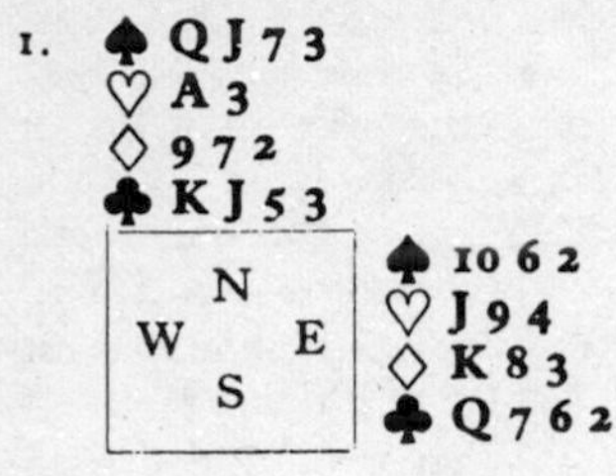

West leads the ◇6 against South's 3 N.T. contract.

(a) If the ◇6 is a fourth best what diamonds, if any, higher than the ◇6 does South hold?

(b) Declarer plays dummy's ◇7 on the ◇6. What should East play?

(c) If East's card wins, what should he lead at Trick 2?

2.

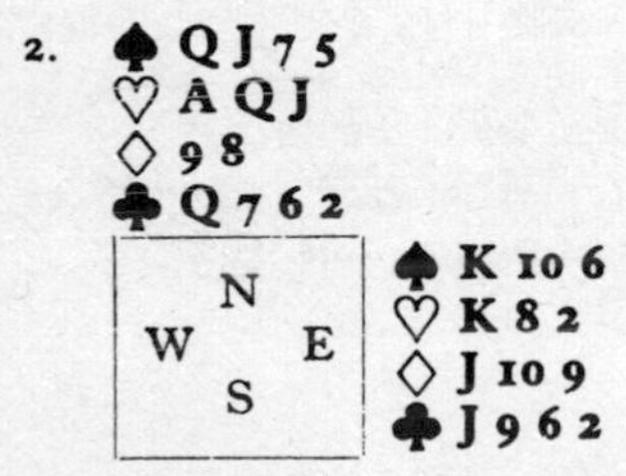

West leads the ♡9 against South's 3 N.T. contract. Dummy's ♡J is played and East wins with the ♡K.

(a) What does East know about West's heart holding?

(c) What should East lead at Trick 2?

3.

North:
♠ K 7 6
♡ 8 6 4
◇ A Q 3
♣ K 10 6 4

East:
♠ A Q J 10
♡ 9 3
◇ 8 7 6 4
♣ 9 8 4

West leads the ♠9 against South's club contract. Dummy's ♠6 is played.

(a) What card should East play to this trick?

(b) What can East assume about West's lead?

(c) What should East lead at Trick 2?

4.

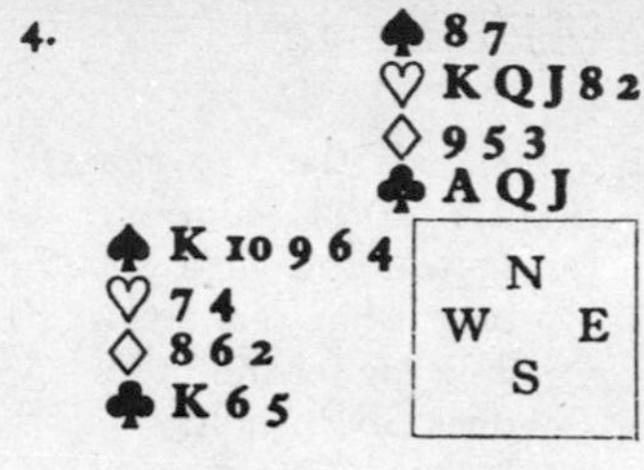

West leads the ♠6 against South's 3 N.T. contract. East plays the ♠A and South a low spade. East leads the ♠5 and South plays the ♠J.

(a) What is the only hope of defeating 3 N.T.?

(b) What card should West play at Trick 2?

(c) What should this card indicate to East about West's spade suit?

5.

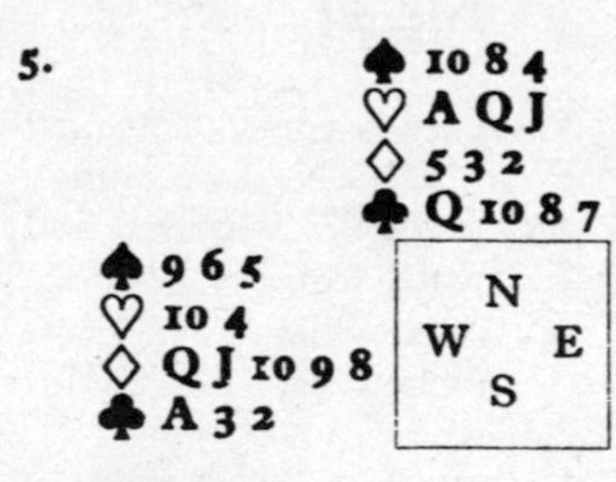

West leads the ♢Q against South's 3 N.T. contract. South wins with the ♢K and leads the ♣4.

(a) What card should West play to this trick?

(b) Why?

6.

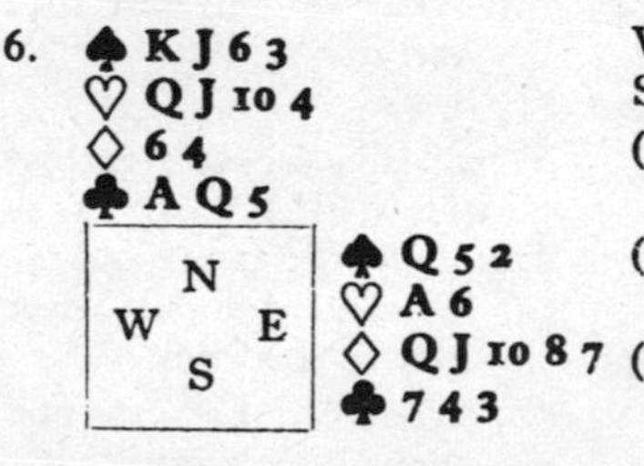

West leads the ♡2 against South's 3 N.T. contract.

(a) How many hearts does West hold?

(b) What card should East play to this first trick?

(c) What should East play at Trick 2?

7. 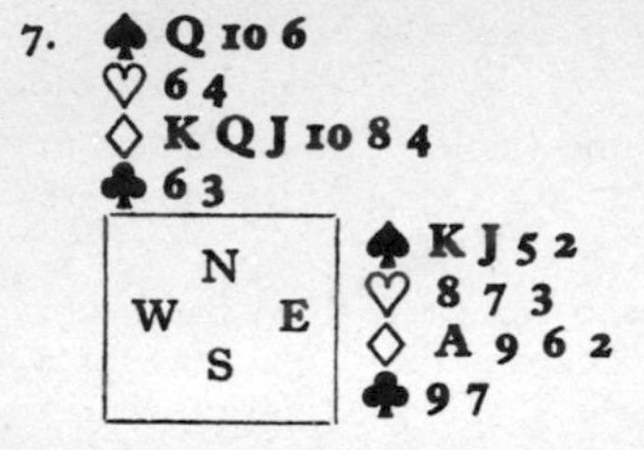

West leads the ♡K against South's 3 N.T. contract. South wins this with the ♡A and leads the ◇5 to dummy's ◇10. West follows with the ◇3.

(a) What should East play to this trick?

(b) What knowledge, if any, has East about West's heart holding?

(c) Having held up the ◇A on the first round, if a second diamond honour is now led from dummy, what should East play this time?

(d) What should East play when he gains the lead?

8. 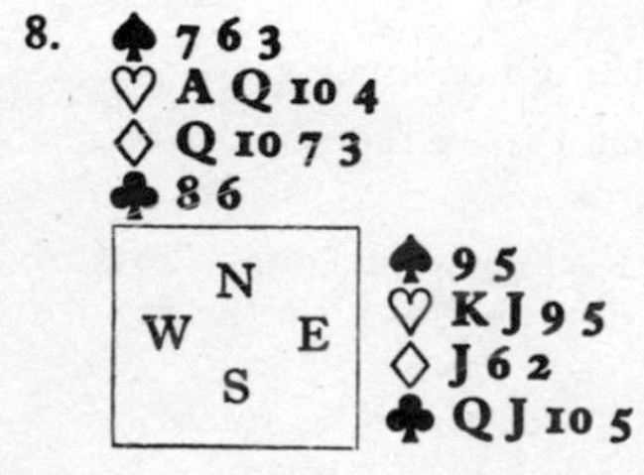

South opens 1◇ and West intervenes with 1♠. The final contract is 3◇, the opening having been raised by North. West leads the ♡8, dummy's ♡10 is played and East wins with the ♡J.

(a) For what reason do you think West led a heart?

(b) What should East lead at Trick 2?

9. (a) 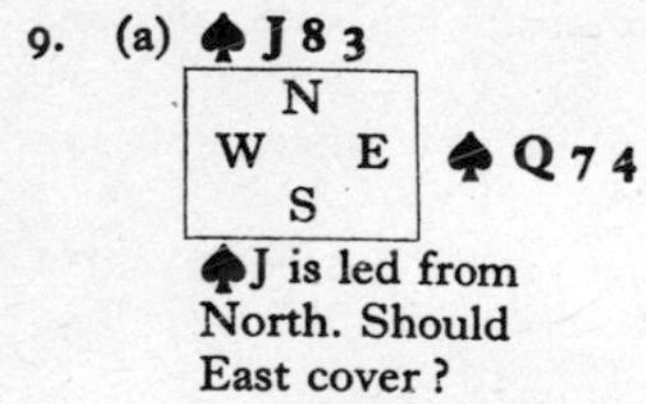

♠J is led from North. Should East cover?

(b) 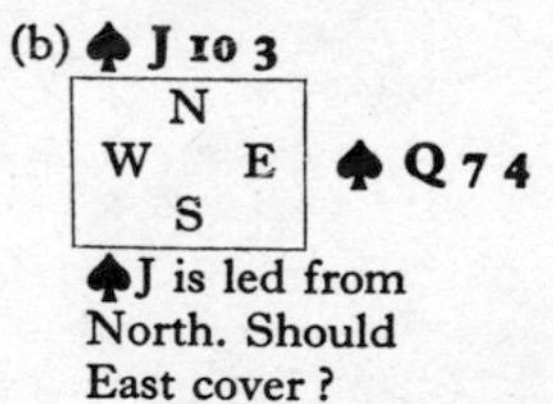

♠J is led from North. Should East cover?

QUIZ ON CHAPTER 17—ANSWERS

1. (a) South can have only one (Rule of Eleven), and it might be *either* the ♢A, ♢Q, ♢J or ♢10, which are not in sight.

   (b) ♢K. There is no reason for East, third hand, not to play high. If South's card is the ♢A it may force it. If it is one of the others, the ♢K will prevent it from winning a trick.

   (c) ♢8, returning his partner's lead *through* South's holding.

2. (a) East's knowledge is negative rather than positive. The lead is clearly "top of nothing" which may be from three or a doublton. It cannot be a fourth best as this would leave only two to be located while four can be seen already!

   (b) ♢J, which has two advantages—it is towards weakness in dummy and is the top of a sequence.

3. (a) ♠10, the lowest of touching honours.

   (b) East can only assume that it is the top of a doubleton or of three worthless cards.

   (c) ♡9, towards dummy's weakness and hoping to find strength with West. If East should have the luck to find West with the ♡A-Q over declarer's King, he might get in a ruff. At any rate he wants West first to lead the spade *through* to him again.

4. (a) The only hope is that East has three spades and that he will be able to gain the lead before these are exhausted and before declarer can cash his nine tricks.

   (b) ♠4, *ducking*, as he has no possible entry to his suit if East is unable to lead it to him.

   (c) It should indicate to East that West started with a five-card suit. If the ♠6 is the fourth best and he now plays a lower one, it is a fifth best.

5. (a) ♣2.

(b) The ♣A is West's only entry card to his diamonds, which are not yet established. South may be intending to finesse the ♣10 and East may hold either the ♣J or ♣K to win and lead a diamond. If not, nothing is lost except the hope of defeating 3 N.T. and South will make the ♣A later anyway.

6. (a) Four—if the ♡2 is West's fourth best he can't have a lower one.

(b) ♡A. It is pointless to hold up with North's cards in view.

(c) ◇Q. Similarly it is pointless to return a heart so East should explore the possibilities of his own suit.

7. (a) ◇2.

(b) West certainly holds the ♡Q and probably the ♡J too. If not he has the ♡10. Lacking three honours he would lead fourth best, not the ♡K, against a No Trump contract.

(c) ◇A. Four diamonds appeared on the first trick of the suit and East rightly held up his ◇A to prevent declarer from establishing his long cards. There is only one other diamond unaccounted for, and whether South or West has it, South certainly won't have a third to use as an entry to dummy.

(c) ♡8, his highest remaining card in his partner's led suit.

8. (a) Almost certainly West has a tenace or an unsupported honour in his spades.

(b) ♠9, which is likely to be through declarer's honour holding to West's strength. There is also a chance that East, with a doubleton spade, will be able to get in a ruff on the third round.

9. (a) Yes, East should cover the ♠J when led, in the hope of a promotion for West.

(b) No, East should not cover the first time, but should cover if the ♠10 is led next.

CHAPTER 18

Signals & Discards

♠♡♣◇♠♡♣◇♠♡♣◇♠♡♣◇♠♡♣◇♠♡♣◇♠♡♣◇

FINALLY we come to signals and discards, which are important enough to merit a chapter on their own and are, indeed, the main backbone of the defence.

We know already that declarer has the advantage of being able to see both his own hand and dummy's and of being able to plan them as one unit. He can actually see his long suits, his short suits, where he may be able to get in a helpful ruff or establish a suit for discards. The defenders can see none of this. They have the inferences of the bidding and, after the opening lead, a view of dummy. The opening lead may have given a positive message or it may have revealed virtually nothing, which is not enough to make the defence into an intelligent combined operation. The added defensive weapon is a system of signals and discards.

This system is based on the play of a high card to encourage your partner to continue, or to lead, a specific suit, and a low card to discourage him, and can be used both when following suit or when discarding on a suit of which you have none. This will be easier to understand when you see examples, which we are coming to in a moment but as a beginner you cannot possibly be expected to notice and remember every card your partner plays. Nor, of course, will your partner see and remember every card you play, but if you get into the right habits from the very start of your career, and your partner does the same, gradually you will find yourself noticing more and more and getting valuable information out of what would otherwise be meaningless cards. Remember the basis of this information which is that a high card says "Yes, I like it", and a low one says "No, I don't". A high card says "Yes, please, lead—or continue leading—this suit" and a low one says "Lay off—this will do us no good at all".

	♡ **Q 7 3**	
♡**A** led	N W E S	♡ **9 5 4**

We'll examine first how to play your cards when you are following suit, that is, playing to a card led. Here West, your partner, leads the ♡A. As you can see the ♡Q in dummy you know he also has the ♡K, but have you any personal interest at all in a heart continuation by West? None, so you play your lowest heart, the ♡4.

	7 5 3	
♡**A** led	N W E S	♡ **Q 9 4**

Now the ♡Q is in your hand so again you know West holds the ♡K. Defending a suit contract, and if you don't specifically want West to change to another suit, it is safe to encourage him to go on with his hearts. If it does nothing else it may force declarer to ruff with sad consequences such as you saw on p. 244, so you play your ♡9 and, if he gets the message and continues with the ♡K, you play the ♡4.

This play of a high card followed by a lower one is called a "peter". We shall be going into its full value to the defence in a moment, but first let us look at a few more examples of when to play a high encouraging card.

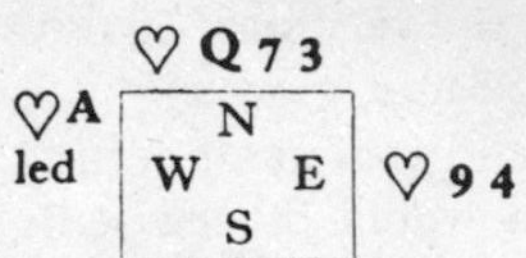

Defending a suit contract your partner leads the ♡A and now you want him to continue the suit for quite another reason—you yourself can ruff the third round with a little trump before declarer draws them. So you encourage West to continue hearts by playing the ♡9 on his first lead.

Compare these next two hands, in both of which West is leading a heart because you bid the suit during the course of the auction. When he plays the ♡A you *want him* to continue the suit because his next lead of it will be through dummy's ♡Q to your ♡K-J, so you play your ♡9. Note that you play the highest card you can conveniently spare. The ♡8 would probably carry the message, but the ♡9 will be even clearer. In this example, though, defending, say, a diamond contract, you bid your hearts without any top honour worth the name. When partner leads your ♡A there's nothing you could want less than a heart continuation, so you play your ♡3, and hope that your partner will be able to guess that, while you don't want a heart led again, you would very much like a switch to spades.

	North: ♡ Q 7 3	
♡A led	N / W E / S	♡ K J 9 8 4

	North: ♠ K J x, ♡ Q 7 2	
♡A led	N / W E / S	♠ A Q 10, ♡ 10 9 8 4 3

We'll take the principle and apply it to a full hand with rather interesting results. West leads your ♡K and you, East, hoping for a spade switch, discourage as

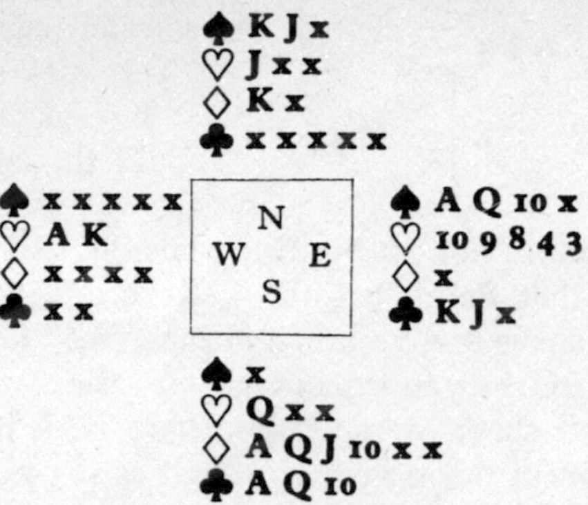

hard as you can with the ♡3. But West refuses to be discouraged. He knows you are asking for a switch and can guess that this very likely means you would like a spade. He has, however, plans of his own. Diamonds are trumps and in spite of the discouraging ♡3 he goes on to cash his ♡A. *Then* he switches to a spade which you win and return a third heart for West to ruff. West will try another spade but South is able to ruff this. He plays low to his ◇K and takes the club finesse which wins, but this is his only entry to dummy and, though he can draw trumps and make his ♣A, he cannot avoid losing one more club trick, losing in all three hearts, a spade and a club.

You can see, therefore, that whether you have bid a suit or not, you must be sure to tell your partner whether or not you want him to continue it if and when he gets the chance. In this example, leading to your

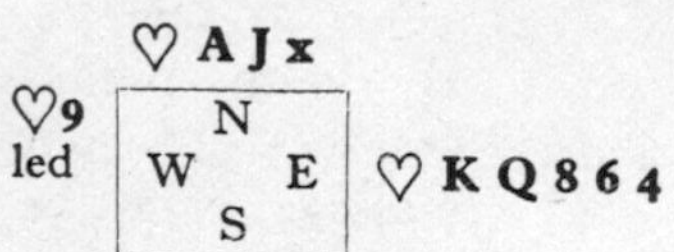

heart bid, West plays the ♡9 and declarer plays dummy's ♡A. You *do* want West to lead the suit again if he gets in,

so you encourage—say "Yes, please", with the ♡8. Take away your ♡K, though and when the ♡9 is led you know that South, not your partner, has the ♡K. In fact you know that South has the ♡K-10 and the last thing you want is to give him a cheap "free" finesse against your ♡Q, so you discourage with the ♡3.

In all these examples you have been in the happy position of having either a high card you could spare with which to encourage, or a low one if you wanted to discourage. Often the cards will not be so kind and you will find yourself with nothing but high ones when you want to discourage and vice versa, with nothing but low ones when you want to encourage. When this happens you simply do the best you can, and you'll be surprised at how frequently your partner will be able to get the message anyway. West leads the ♡A to your

♡ Q 5 3

N

♡ A 4 2 W E ♡ 10 9 8 7 6

S

bid, and you are unable to be really discouraging because your lowest card is the ♡6. West, however, if he looks around, can see the ♡2-4 in his own hand and the ♡3-5 in dummy. The ♡6 must, therefore, be the lowest you have, so West will read it clearly as discouragement. Conversely, this time though you want to encourage, you have only the ♡-4 3-2. Play the ♡4.

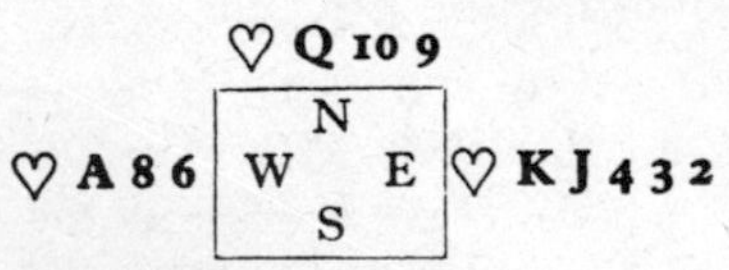

If South produces the ♡5 your message will be perfectly clear because, although the ♡4 is only a low one, why didn't South play either the ♡2 or ♡3 if he had them? You, therefore, have them, so are at least playing as high as you can.

Whether or not to encourage a lead can often depend on your interpretation of the card led. For instance, if West leads the ♡K when you haven't bid the suit you will know that he has the ♡Q. You are, therefore, happy with the lead and, unless you particularly want him to switch to something else, should encourage with the ♡9. Give yourself the ♡9 4 2, though, without the ♡J, and you have no interest in the suit. You make a mental note, of course, that your partner has the ♡Q and may also have the ♡J, but as far as you yourself are concerned, you have no interest, so discourage with the ♡2.

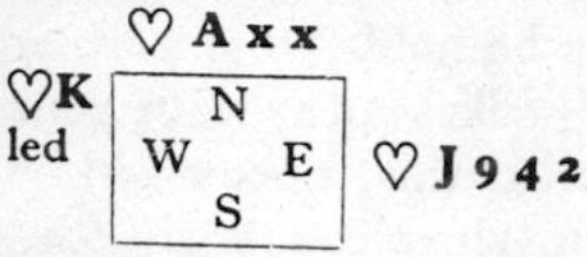

	♡ **A x x**	
♡**K** led	N W E S	♡ **J 9 4 2**

Sometimes the one card, particularly if it is a lowish one and all you can spare, may not be enough to convey your message, and this is where the "peter" comes in. Petering, or playing a card followed as soon as possible by a lower one, makes the position absolutely clear, and even if the two cards are only the three followed by the two, this is a peter and, therefore, encouraging. Suppose we take an example similar to the last but change your cards. Your partner leads the ♡K and, reading the position as before, you encourage as best you can with the ♡4. West, however, can't see enough helpful cards to be certain of the message,

	♡ **A x x**	
♡**K** led	N W E S	♡ **J 4 3 2**

so he switches to another suit. Next time hearts are played, or if you have to discard on a suit you are short of, when you play your ♡2 you complete the message.

Defending No Trump contracts the various situations will be slightly different. Remember you will be hoping to set up, or establish, a long suit of your own or your partner's. Very particularly if, in order to protect whatever honour cards he holds, your partner leads a "top of nothing" and strikes lucky with your long suit, in a distribution such as this, a peter will be

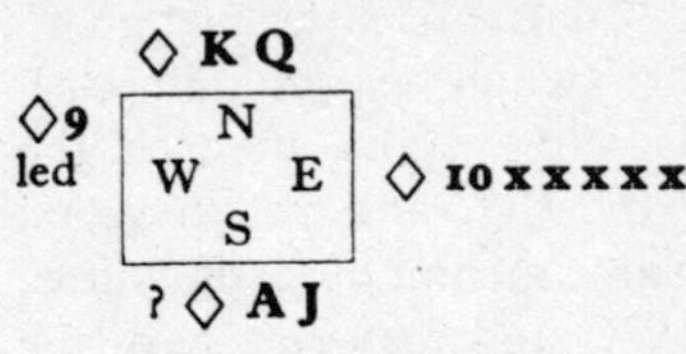

invaluable. Clearly, declarer will be able to win two tricks in diamonds but, if West has led from the top of three and can get in in time, he will be able to lead you a diamond for four tricks in the suit. The principle, of course, is the same—play high if you want to encourage, whether for your partner's sake or your own, but you would not, at No Trumps, want to encourage partner to continue if you held a doubleton whereas, against a trump contract, you wanted him to go on so that you could get a ruff.

So far all our examples have been of positions where you were deciding whether or not to encourage when following suit to an opening lead, but either defender can, of course, use the signals at any time they are available during the play of the hand. They can also be used with potent effect when discarding, that is, when throwing a card away when you are unable to follow suit. The most likely occasions for this are when declarer is drawing trumps, of which you are short while your partner still has some, or when declarer is trying to establish a suit, or running established cards in it, and you are short of it. A high discard will tell your partner that if and when he gets in you would like this particular suit led. Please remember the converse, though, a low card will tell him you *don't* want it led.

Suppose you are defending a diamond contract, which you only need three tricks to defeat. You have only two possible winners in your own hand, but there is always a chance that your partner will come up with a third. Hearts haven't been touched yet, and declarer is drawing trumps. You follow suit twice but, when he plays a third round you have your chance. Discard the highest heart you can spare, the ♡8. Now if your partner wins even one trick, he will know what to lead to you. Change your hand, however, substituting the ♡2 for the ♡8.

♠ 5 3 2
♡ A K 8 3
◇ 8 6
♣ 7 6 4 2

This time, unless you are pretty sure you will get the chance of a second discard to complete the message, it is better not to risk discarding anything as discouraging as the ♡3. Discard the ♠2 and if you do then get a second discard, throw the ♣2. When you have clearly warned your partner off leading either black suit it is only logical for him to realise that the only chance is for you to have something in hearts which, for some reason, you were unable to signal to him.

♠ 5 3 2
♡ A K 3 2
◇ 8 6
♣ 7 6 4 2

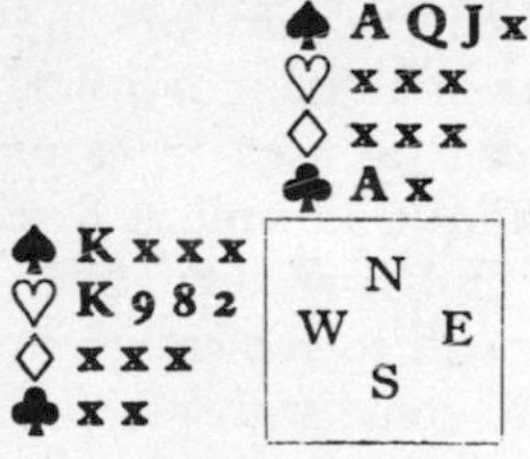

You can also signal the possession of lesser cards than Aces. As West defending a club contract you lead, for want of anything better, a trump. Declarer goes up with dummy's Ace and leads a second round and then a third, on which you have to discard. Here's your chance to show East which red suit to lead if he gets in. Either, from his point of view, will be *towards* weakness in dummy, but if you can make him choose hearts, not diamonds, this may well be through declarer's strength in the suit. If he finesses your ♡K will win and if he plays the Ace, your ♡K will be good if either you or your partner can get into the lead again later.

Still with these same two hands visible, let's imagine a different situation. Playing in 5♣ against your trump lead, declarer plays low from North and, to your pleasure, your partner East wins with the ♣K. looking for two more tricks to defeat the contract, East cashes the ♡A. If you thoughtlessly play the ♡2 on this he will assume that you have no interest in the suit and will probably try a switch to diamonds. You must, therefore, play the ♡9 to say "Yes, please, this is what I want". If, instead of cashing the ♡A, he cashes the ◇A, you must play your smallest diamond, saying "No, thank you, I have no interest in this suit", and, although a small diamond is not an active encouragement for him to lead hearts, it is his only logical attempt to find a trick in your hand.

Signalling, showing a wish for a particular suit to be continued, or to be led at the first opportunity, is based on the fact that the normal way to play any suit, either following or discarding, is to shed the smallest and most worthless first. To play them in a different order, therefore, higher before lower, can be used to carry this special significance. If you find it difficult at first don't worry. In fact you won't find it as difficult to make the signals yourself as you will to remember to look for your partner's, but it will come with practice and if, right from the start, you have learned to give your signals, you won't suddenly find you have something new to learn about the play of your cards because you will already be playing them that way.

QUIZ ON CHAPTER 18

1.

West leads the ◇2 against South's 3 N.T. contract.

(a) How many diamonds has West?

(b) How many diamonds has South and how many of them are higher than the ◇2?

(c) What should East play to this lead if dummy's ◇4 is played?

2.

North: ♠ 7 6 4 ♡ K J 6 ◇ A 3 ♣ A Q J 7 4

West: ♠ A K J 8 5 ♡ A 7 ◇ 9 7 2 ♣ 8 6 3

N
W E
S

Against South's 4♡ contract West leads the ♠A.

(a) If East plays the ♠9 on this, what should West lead at Trick 2, and why?

(b) If East plays the ♠2 instead of the ♠9, what should West lead at Trick 2, and why?

3.

North: ♠ Q 8 2 ♡ Q J 10 4 ◇ A Q 6 ♣ 7 5 3

N
W E
S

East: ♠ K J 7 4 ♡ 7 3 2 ◇ 7 5 2 ♣ A 8 4

Against South's 4♡ contract West leads the ♠A.

(a) What card should East play and why?

(b) If West next leads a small spade, and dummy's second small one is played, what should East play?

(c) If East's card wins, what should he lead next?

4.

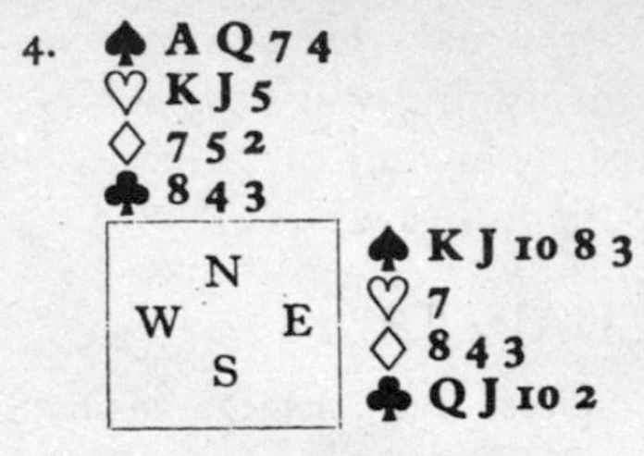

Against South's 4♡ contract West leads the ♢K, South winning with the ♢A and then playing off three rounds of top trumps.

(a) What card should East play on West's ♢K lead ?

(b) What knowledge has he, if any, of West's diamond holding ?

(c) What two discards should East make on the second and third rounds of trumps ?

5.

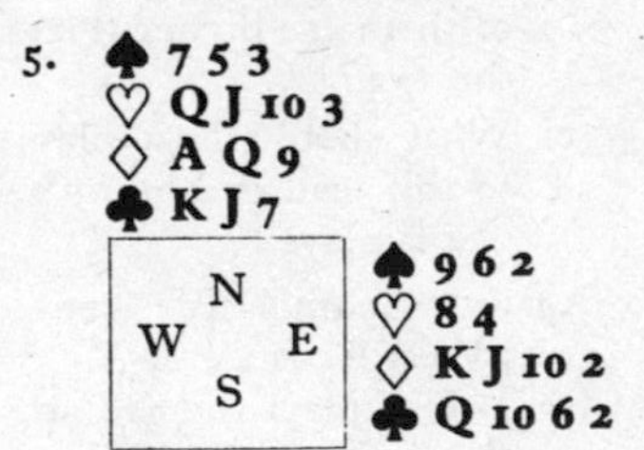

Against South's 4♡ contract West leads the ♠A.

(a) What knowledge, if any, has East about his partner's spade holding ?

(b) What card should he play on this trick and why ?

6. ♠ 7 5 6 4
♡ Q J 10 4
♢ A Q 9
♣ 9 7

N
W E
S

♠ 8 3
♡ 9 8
♢ 8 7 6 3
♣ J 10 8 6 2

Against South's 4♡ contract West leads the ♠A.

(a) What chances have East-West of defeating the contract ?

(b) What card should East play at Trick 1 ?

7. ♠ A Q 5
♡ J 9 7 4
♢ 8 5 3
♣ A Q 7

N
W E
S

♠ K J 10
♡ 8 2
♢ Q 9 2
♣ K J 8 5 4

Against South's 4♡ contract West leads the ♢K.

(a) What knowledge, if any, has East about West's diamond holding ?

(b) What card should East play on the ♢A and why ?

QUIZ ON CHAPTER 18—ANSWERS

1. (a) West has four diamonds—this is surely a fourth best and, being the ♢2, cannot have a fifth best below it.
   (b) South can only have one diamond, and it is bound to be higher than the ♢2!
   (c) ♢7. If South's singleton is the Ace or King it is bound to make. If it is the ♢6, the ♢7 will prevent it from making. If it is the ♢10, this will win, but North's ♢J will not become a subsequent winner.

2. (a) ♠K. East is clearly starting a peter. If he has ♠9-x, South will have ♠Q x x and East will be able to win the third round with a ruff. If East has ♠Q x x South will have a doubleton, but will be forced, perhaps unhappily, to ruff the third round himself.
   (b) ♠K. Perhaps a difficult one. East is certainly not starting a peter and he has, therefore, got *either* a singleton or three worthless spades. In the first case he will be able to ruff the third round, and in the second, South's ♠Q cannot be better than a doubleton and he will be forced to ruff.

3. (a) ♠7, the highest he can spare to encourage West to continue the suit.
   (b) ♠J, which is good enough with the ♠Q on the table.
   (c) ♠K, which may well win a third trick if West started with ♠A x or ♠A x x as, in either case, South will have another and be unable to ruff.

4. (a) ♢3. He has no interest in a diamond continuation if West gets in again.
   (b) West certainly has the ♢Q and very possibly the ♢J as well.
   (c) First the ♠8 and then, completing the peter, the ♠3, telling his partner to lead this suit if he regains the lead.

5. (a) At this point he only knows that West will probably hold the ♠K too.

(b) ♠2, discouraging a continuation. Unless West has a particular reason now to continue spades, he will find a switch to one or other of the minor suits, either of which would be quite good for East.

6. (a) They have one chance, that is that West has the ♠A and ♠K to only four, in which case declarer will have three. Whether these include the ♠Q or not, the defence can take three spades (either the ♠A-K-Q or the ♠A-K and a ruff), and may possibly come to one more trick in either trumps or clubs.

(b) ♠8, starting a peter to encourage West to continue. If he is to get in a ruff it must be quickly.

7. (a) East knows that West has the ♢K and probably some lower diamonds.
have the ♢J.

(b) ♢2. If you think that East should encourage at this point, consider what happens if West plays the ♢A and then a small one. If East's ♢Q wins he will have a most unpleasant return lead and the defence will also have lost a "tempo". If East plays the ♢2, discouraging, West is likely to try a switch to either spades or clubs, either of which would be ideal for East, and his ♢Q can make later if it is going to.

Epilogue

YOU have come now to the end of this book and no one will be unduly surprised, least of all your teachers, if you feel over-awed at the amount there is to learn. If, however, you have assimilated what you have read, your bidding will be on a sound and adequate basis and your card play, both as declarer and defender, will be developing along the right lines. You will be able to go out into the big wide world of Contract Bridge and hold your own.

Don't let nagging relatives or know-it-all friends alarm you with tales of all you don't yet know. Contract Bridge is a difficult game to play and only time and practice can carry you on from being a beginner to a learner-player, and thence to even higher things. Indeed if it were not a difficult game it would not have gained world-wide popularity in the brief span of fifty years since its introduction—a popularity which is increasing every day. No two hands are exactly alike, each deal brings its problems both in bidding and in play, intriguing and different, and in this lies its fascination and charm.

Contract Bridge has become more than the social asset it used to be, and is now virtually a necessity. Other games may come and go, but no attempts to surplant it have shown the slightest signs of success. If you are learning because you want to be able to join in a friendly and interesting pastime with family or friends, or whether you aspire to the heights of the tournament world, you will be amply rewarded for your efforts.

TABLE OF STANDARD LEADS

Holding	*Against Trump Contracts*	*Against No Trump Contracts*	*Holding*	*Against Trump Contracts*	*Against No Trump Contracts*
A K Q J or more	**A**	**A**	**J 10 9 x x**	**J**	**J**
			J 10 x x x	**x**	**x**
A K Q x x x	**A**	**A**			
A K Q x x	**A**	**K**	**10 9 8**	**10**	**10**
A K Q x	**A**	**K**	**10 9 x x**	**10**	**10**
A K x	**A**	**K**	**A Q J x x**	****A**	**Q**
***A K**	**K**	**K**	**A Q 10 9 x**	****A**	**10**
A K J 10	**A**	**A**	**A Q x x x x**	****A**	**x**
A K J x	**A**	**K**	**A J 10 x x**	****A**	**J**
A K J x x	**A**	**x**	**A 10 9 x x**	****A**	**10**
A K J x x x x	**A**	**A**	**K J 10 x x**	****J**	**J**
A K x x x x	**A**	**x**	**K 10 9 x x**	****10**	**10**
A K 10 9 x	**A**	**10**	**Q 10 9 x x**	****10**	**10**
A K x x x	**A**	**x**	**A x x**	****A**	**x**
K Q J x x	**K**	**K**	**K J x**	****x**	**x**
K Q 10 x x	**K**	**K**	**K x x**	****x**	**x**
K Q x x x	**K**	**x**	**Q 10 x**	****x**	**x**
Q J 10 x x	**Q**	**Q**	**J x x**	****x**	**x**
Q J 9 x x	**Q**	**Q**	**K x x x**	****x**	**x**
Q J x x x	**x**	**x**	**x x x**	Top card followed by middle.	
			x x	Top card first.	

*Note the difference here. With the Ace and King and some other cards, either honours or small, you should lead the Ace. With the Ace-King alone, or bare, lead the King and then the Ace, which indicates to your partner that you can ruff the third round.

**Leading from these combinations and others like them is to be avoided against suit contracts unless nothing less dangerous or more promising can be found. Occasionally, however, they are impossible to avoid, for which reason they are included here.

SCORING TABLE

Points scored below the line by declarer and his partner, if the contract is made:—

For each trick over six, bid and made if trumps are	♣	◇	♡	♠
Undoubled	20	20	30	30
Doubled	40	40	60	60
Redoubled	80	80	120	120

	Not dbld.	*Dbld.*	*Re-dbld.*
For the first trick bid and made over six at No Trumps ..	40	80	160
For the second and each additional trick bid and made at No Trumps	30	60	120

The first pair to score 100 points below the line, in one or more hands, wins a **game**, a line is drawn across the card, and both pairs start with no trick score towards the next game. The first pair to win two games wins the Rubber.

Bonus Scores:

(Scored above the line to declarer and his partner)

	Not vul.	*Vul.*
Slams:		
Little Slam (12 tricks) bid and made..	500	750
Grand Slam (13 tricks) bid and made..	1,000	1,500
Overtricks: (Tricks won in excess of those required to fulfil the contract)		
Undoubled	Trick value	Trick value
Doubled	100	200
Redoubled	200	400
If doubled or redoubled and made, add "Insult" bonus	50	50

Rubber, Game, or Part-Score:

For winning Rubber if opponents have won no game	700
For winning Rubber if opponents have won one game	500
For unfinished Rubber, for having won one game	300
For unfinished Rubber, for having the only part-score	50

Honours: (Scored above the line by either side)

For holding all five trump honours (A, K, Q, J, 10) in one hand	150
For holding any four of the five trump honours in one hand	100
For holding all four Aces in one hand at No Trumps	150

Penalties:

(Scored above the line by declarer's opponents if the contract is not made)

Undertricks: (Tricks by which declarer fails)

	Not vul.			*Vul.*		
	Un-dbld.	*Dbld.*	*Re-dbld.*	*Un-dbld.*	*Dbld.*	*Re-dbld.*
For the first undertrick	50	100	200	100	200	400
For each subsequent undertrick ..	50	200	400	100	300	600

GLOSSARY OF BRIDGE TERMS

Above the Line The part of the score card reserved for penalty and bonus points.

Arranging Arranging the cards in acceptable order. If declarer wishes to arrange the cards in dummy he must say "Arranging", or the first card touched counts as played—which can be disastrous.

Artificial Bid A call not carrying its obvious natural meaning such, for instance, as the Acol Two Club opening bid.

Auction The first period of the game, during which players may bid in rotation, competing for the final contract.

Average Hand A hand containing one quarter of the high cards in terms of points. (See "Point Count".)

Balanced Hand A hand with no singleton or void. The "pattern" of suit length would be 4-3-3-3, 4-4-3-2, or occasionally 5-3-3-2.

Below the Line The part of the score card reserved for scoring trick points towards game.

Bid During the Auction to call in a suit or No Trumps, to double or redouble if doubled. A pass (No Bid) does not rank as a bid, but either a bid or a pass ranks as a call.

Bidding The action of making a bid. Another name for the Auction.

Biddable Suit A suit long and strong enough to justify suggesting it as a possible trump suit.

Blackwood An artificial, or conventional bid, designed to assist in slam bidding.

Bluff Any bid or play designed to deceive your opponents.

Bonus Additional awards of points scored above the line for making a doubled or redoubled contract, for holding honours or for winning the Rubber, etc.

Book — The first six tricks which declarer is required to win before tricks won count towards the contract.

Break — The distribution of the outstanding cards in any suit in opponents' hands, i.e., six outstanding cards can break 6—0, 5—1, 4—2 or 3—3.

Break the Contract — As defenders, to win enough tricks to prevent declarer from making his contract.

Business Double — See "Penalty Double".

Call — Any bid in the Auction, including a pass.

Cash — To lead out a winning card and take a trick with it.

Contract — The final bid in the Auction which decides the denomination, etc. in which the hand is to be played.

Control — The commanding position or card in a suit, enabling the holder to win a trick whenever the suit is led.

Convention — An artificial bid or sequence of bids carrying a meaning other than the apparent natural one. Conventions must always be announced to the opponents.

Coup — A special advanced type of end-play designed to win extra tricks.

Cover — To play a higher card than the one previously played to a trick.

Cross-ruff — To trump first in one hand and then in the other, which may be done either between dummy and declarer or the defenders.

Cue Bid — An artificial bid used by advanced players to show a control card, generally exploring slam possibilities.

Cut — To separate the pack into two parts, placing the lower part on the upper.

Deal — To distribute the cards to the four players.

Dealer — The player who so distributes the cards.

Declarer — The player who gains the right to play both his own hand and dummy's.

Deep Finesse — See "Finesse".

Defeat — Same as "Break the Contract".

Delayed Game Raise — A second round responder's bid, made after responder has heard opener's rebid.

Denial — A bid showing lack of support for partner's bid. Also a "Negative Response" in various conventional sequences.

Discard — To play a card not of the suit led and not a trump, making no attempt to win the trick, or to get rid of an unwanted card.

Distribution — The manner in which the cards are divided between the four players in any one deal.

Double — A bid increasing the value of tricks won, and also increasing the penalties if the contract is not made.

Double Finesse — See "Finesse".

Double Jump / *Double Raise* — A raise of partner's bid suit increasing the level one more than was necessary to make a supporting bid.

Doubleton — An original holding of only two cards in any particular suit.

Down — Used to indicate that declarer has failed in his contract.

Draw — The procedure for determining partners, dealer, etc.

Draw Trumps — Continuously to lead trumps until the opponents have none.

Drive Out — To force the play of a particular high card from an opponent's hand.

Drop — A play which endeavours to capture an adverse high card without loss to one's side ("Play for the drop").

Duck — To play a low card when able to play a high one which might or could win the trick.

Dummy — Declarer's partner—his hand exposed on the table.

Duplicate — A form of Contract Bridge used for Tournaments and Matches, in which the hands are preserved and replayed by other players.

Echo — See "Peter".

End-Play — An advanced play, generally contrived by declarer, designed to gain extra tricks.

Enemy — Your opponents.

Entry — An established winning card which enables a player (or dummy) to gain the lead.

Establish — To make good a particular card or cards, by driving out the adverse high cards.

Exposed Cards — Cards possibly accidentally dropped or played in error, contrary to the Laws of the game.

False Card — To play a card out of the natural order for the purpose of deceiving opponents.

Finesse — An attempt to win a trick with a card lower than another still held by the opponents.
Deep Finesse: An attempt to win a trick with a card lower than two or more still held by opponents.
Double Finesse: To finesse twice against two equal high cards.
Two-way Finesse: A card combination in which the finesse may be taken against either opponent.

Fit — Good mutual support in the combined partnership hands, length and/or high cards in partner's suit, etc.

Follow Suit — To play a card of the suit led. It is compulsory to follow suit if possible.

Forcing Bid — Any bid which conventionally *demands* a reply from partner if no intervening bid is made which will relieve him of his obligation.

Freak — A hand of highly abnormal and unbalanced distribution.

Free Bid	A bid made voluntarily, usually over an intervening bid which has removed any obligation to bid.
Game	A score of at least 100 points below the line.
Go Down	As declarer, to fail in the contract.
Grand Slam	A contract to make all thirteen tricks.
Guard	A card which protects another higher card from dropping on an opponent's winning card.
Guarded Honour	An honour card protected by another card or cards against immediate capture by an opponent's higher card.
Hand	The thirteen cards dealt to one player. Also the four hands making up one deal.
High-Low	See "Peter".
Hold Up	To refuse to play a high or winning card in order to try to retain control of the suit led.
Honours	The Ace, King, Queen, Knave and Ten of the trump suit. The four Aces at No Trumps.
Honour Trick	An Ace or King-Queen combination. See "Quick Tricks".
Idle Card	Any card not a potential winner or a guard to same.
Inferential Force	A bid which, though not unconditionally forcing, partner will accept as requiring an answer.
Intermediates	Tens, nines and eights which, though not "tops", add to the general strength of the hand.
Intervening Bid	A bid made by an opponent after one player has bid and before his partner has responded.
Jump Bid	Any bid higher than the one necessary to beat the previous bid or at a higher level than necessary to show support.
Knock Out	See "Drive out".

Lead — The first card played to a trick; the card so led. A player leads *away* from his own hand, *through* second hand, *towards* his partner, and *up to* fourth hand.

Lead-directing Bid — A bid made specifically with the intention of indicating a lead to partner if subsequently the defenders.

Limit Bid — A bid stating the upper as well as the lower limit of the strength held; never forcing but may be highly encouraging.

Little Slam — A contract to make twelve of the thirteen tricks. Also know as Small Slam.

Long Suit — A suit of five or more cards in one hand.

Loser — A card which cannot win a trick.

Major Suits — Spades (♠) and hearts (♡).

Master Card — A card that can be beaten only if it is trumped.

Minor Suits — Diamonds (◇) and Clubs (♣).

Negative Response — A bid denying possession of more strength than already shown: a bid in response to a conventional or artificial bid, denying certain specific values.

No Trump — When declarer contracts to play without a trump suit.

Odd Trick — The seventh trick won by a side (after the "book" of six).

Off Lead — Not being the leader; or, being leader, to play a card in an attempt to put another player *on* lead.

On Lead — Having the right to lead, either as declarer's left-hand opponent or just having won a trick.

Opener — The player whose right it is to make the opening bid.

Opening Bid — The first bid made in the Auction.

Opening Lead — The first card played to any particular deal.

Overbid	To contract to win more tricks than you can make.
Over-call	To make a bid over an opponent's bid; to make a bid higher than the preceding one.
Over-ruff	To play a higher trump to a trick which has already been trumped, or ruffed.
Overtake	To play a higher card on one of partner's which has already won the trick.
Over-trick	Any trick won by declarer in excess of the number required to fulfil his contract.
Pack	A pack of cards, 52 in number. Sometimes known as "deck".
Part Score	Any score below the line insufficient to complete a game.
Pass	To call without making a bid. Correct form, "No Bid".
Penalty	Points scored above the line by defenders, as when declarer fails to fulfil his contract.
Penalty Double	A double made with the intention of adding to the penalty available, in anticipation of defeating the contract. Also "Business Double".
Penalty Pass	A pass made over partner's Take-out Double, with the anticipation of collecting penalties.
Peter	Also "Echo" and "High-low", the play of one card followed by a lower card, either when following suit or discarding, as a signal to partner of interest in the suit.
Point Count	A method of hand valuation in terms of high cards. The Acol system uses Milton Work's count, Ace = 4: King = 3: Queen = 2: Knave = 1.
Positive Response	A response in reply to a forcing bid from partner, showing certain values as opposed to negative ones.
Pre-emptive Bid	An opening or responding bid made at an unnecessarily high level, with the object of obstructing the opposition bidding.

Prepared Bid	A bid made out of the natural sequence with the idea of facilitating the rebid. To be avoided as far as possible.
Protective Bid	A bid, generally fourth-in-hand after two passes, with the object of "protecting" partner's pass.
Psychic Bid	A bid made primarily with the object of deceiving opponents and causing them trouble, though it may well have the same effect on partner!
Quantitative Bid	Bids showing the top limit of the strength of the hand in the light of the bidding thus far, generally inviting a slam if partner holds additional strength to that already shown.
Quick Tricks	Cards which can be expected to win an immediate or early trick. Ace = 1 Q.T., K-Q = 1 Q.T., A-Q = 1½ Q.T., K-x = ½ Q.T. and so on. Once widely used as a method of hand valuation.
Raise	To make a bid increasing your partner's contract, either in a suit or in No Trumps.
Rebiddable Suit	A suit long enough or strong enough to bid a second time without support from partner.
Redouble	A bid which again doubles the already augmented values of tricks or penalties incurred for a doubled contract.
Responder	The partner of a player who has made a bid.
Reverse Bid	Bidding a lower-ranking suit before a higher one in unusual circumstances (i.e., bidding the lower-ranking of adjacent suits first).
Revoke	Failure to follow suit to a card led if able to do so.
Rubber	Net points won or lost, including the bonus for being the first to win two games.
Ruff	To play a trump when another suit has been led.

Sacrifice Bid — An intentional overbid made in the hope of preventing an even worse score if opponents make their contract.

Safety Play — A play made to ensure the best available result in the event of an unfavourable distribution.

Sequence — Three or more touching cards of one suit: also a series of bids (bidding sequence) in the auction.

Set — To break or defeat the contract.

Set Up — See "Establish".

Shaded Bid — A bid made on rather less than the understood requirements for it.

Shape — Pattern of suit length in hand, as 6-5-1-1, meaning a 6-card suit, a 5-card suit and two singletons.

Show Out — A player who fails to follow suit to a card led is said to "show out" by revealing that he holds none of it.

Shuffle — Mixing the cards together before the next, and after the previous deal. Also known as "make".

Side — A partnership: the two partners or their hands.

Side Suit — At a trump contract, a long or strong suit other than the trump suit, generally one declarer will hope to establish.

Sign-off Bid — A rebid made to show that, though the hand was worth the previous bid made, it has no additional values to offer.

Singleton — An original holding of only one card in any particular suit.

Small Slam — See "Little Slam".

Squeeze — An advanced play which forces opponents to part with vital cards.

Stop or Stopper	Any card or holding of cards in a particular suit which will stop the run of that suit by opponents.
Suit Preference Signals	Special discard signals for advanced use only, indicating lead choice.
Support	To increase the level of the bidding in partner's bid suit: to hold sufficient cards in partner's bid suit.
Switch	Being on lead after winning a trick, make the next lead in a different suit.
Take-out Double	A conventional double requiring partner to bid his best suit or bid in No Trumps. Sometimes called Informatory Double.
Tempo	An important time-factor in the play of the hand.
Tenace	A combination of high cards with one or more missing, as A-Q-J, or A-J-10. The sort of holding subject to finesse.
Throw-in	A deal on which all four players pass. The deal is then thrown in and the deal passes to the next player in rotation.
Throw-in Play	Purposely losing a trick to get off lead so that the return lead will be to that player's advantage.
Top of Nothing	The highest card of a worthless suit, generally top of three.
Touching cards	Two adjacent cards in one suit, i.e., Q-J or 8–7.
Touching Suits	Adjacent suits in ranking order, i.e., ♠ and ♡,♡ and ◇, ◇ and ♣.
Trick	Four cards played in rotation by each of the four players.
Trump	Card of the suit designated as trumps, having a higher trick-taking power than the other suits. To trump—see "Ruff".
Trump Suit	The suit designated during the auction as trumps.

Unbalanced Hand	One containing a singleton or void or one predominantly long suit.
Unblock	To get rid of a high card or cards which may interrupt the run of, or entry to, a suit.
Underbid	A bid at a lower level than justified on the strength held: also a bid insufficient to beat the previous one made.
Underlead	To lead a low card from a combination headed by one or more honours.
Under-trick	Each trick by which declarer fails to fulfil his contract.
Void	An original holding of no card at all in a particular suit.
Vulnerable	Having won a game towards the Rubber, thus being liable to incur increased penalties or awards.
Winner	A holding which can be expected to win an immediate trick.
Yarborough	A hand containing not one card higher than a nine. Named in the early days of Whist after Lord Yarborough.